IMAGES of America

MILAN

Ann Basilone-Jones and Ashley Moran

ARCADIA PUBLISHING

ISBN 978-1-4671-1399-1

Published by Arcadia Publishing
Charleston, South Carolina

Printed in the United States of America

Library of Congress Control Number: 2015937577

For all general information, please contact Arcadia Publishing:
Telephone 843-853-2070
Fax 843-853-0044
E-mail sales@arcadiapublishing.com
For customer service and orders:
Toll-Free 1-888-313-2665

Visit us on the Internet at www.arcadiapublishing.com

This book is dedicated to the community of Milan—
ever loyal to the heritage and preservation of Milan.

Contents

Acknowledgments

Special thanks must be given to the many local historians who have come before us, making the job of researching the village of Milan's history a much simpler task. Wallace White, Charles Frohman, Lyle Latham, and Mary Falke's unyielding dedication to local history has been inspiring.

Thanks also go to the board of trustees of the Milan Historical Museum, both past and present, for their dedication to the mission and vision of the museum.

Thanks to the staff and volunteers of the Milan Historical Museum for their help in sharing the story of Milan with visitors.

The vast majority of images used are from the collections held at the Milan Historical Museum. Images from other sources are noted.

INTRODUCTION

By all modern accounts, Milan is a quaint and sleepy village located just close enough to the Lake Erie shore to warrant a visit by many passing tourists each year. But what many do not realize until after their visit is what a rich and unique history this little village possesses. From its Moravian missionary beginnings to the entrepreneurial spirit that forged its place in history, Milan has a story to tell. Being the birthplace of Thomas Alva Edison attracts tourists each year, but the beautiful village of Milan and the interesting history it possesses captures the imagination of all who come.

This book begins with the first settlers: the Moravian missionaries and their settlements. The first permanent settlers were the families displaced from Connecticut during the American Revolution. The burning of their homes resulted in legislation in 1792 that "released and quit-claimed to the Sufferers or their legal representatives or heirs" 500,000 Connecticut-owned acres in Ohio known as the Fire Lands. The village of Milan was platted by Ebenezer Merry in 1817, using the original Pettquoting streets as a guide. Merry also began the long history of commerce in Milan with the establishment of a gristmill and sawmill. Rapid population growth followed with new settlers venturing west for a piece of land and prosperity.

From there, the story weaves through the development of the Milan Canal and the rise of the shipbuilding industry. Milan was incorporated in 1833, in part to finance a three-mile ship canal linking the village of Milan with the Huron River. Prior to the advent of the railroad, farmers had to bring their harvest to the northern lake ports by wagon. The sandy, wet prairie roads above Milan were not easily crossed by harvest-laden wagons. The idea of the Port of Milan was born, and after six years of construction, the Milan Canal opened to lake vessel navigation on July 4, 1839. For the next 10 years, the village prospered. Business increased so dramatically that general stores were crowding all around the town square to keep up with business generated by the farmers on the one hand and the ship crews on the other. At one point, general stores lined the square, and most of the stores had a connection to the warehouses, so the farmers were given either cash or, more likely, credit in the stores in the form of chits or tickets that they could use to buy merchandise. A bustling inland port was created, although its fortunes did not last long.

The full circle comes with the transformation from bustling wheat port to the shady village that takes pride is preserving the architectural jewels its residents call home. The rapid development of the railroads spelled the demise of lake commerce, and Milan refused to allow the construction of a bridge over the navigable waters of the Huron River. Shipbuilding moved to natural ports capable of allowing the larger ships passage, and the last vessel passed down the canal for commercial trade in 1865. The wealth that had poured into Milan can still be seen in its architecture. Homes and businesses alike benefitted from the newly acquired wealth, but the fortune left quickly, leaving a peaceful and quaint town in its wake.

Milan is also the birthplace of inventor Thomas Alva Edison, and the small hillside brick home where he was born on February 11, 1847, remains an icon for locals and visitors to enjoy. His birth year also marked the peak of the Milan Canal. Edison spent his youth watching schooners load and unload cargo while hearing the sounds of a bustling port and shipbuilding industry at the base of his home. His love of Milan lasted throughout his life, inspiring this poem written by his sister Marian Edison Page and published in the *Milan Ledger*:

Beautiful hills of Milan,
I long to see you once more;
To tread on thy grassy carpet,
As I did in the days of yore.

Beautiful days of Milan,
Where I was so happy and free,
With my brothers and sisters far away,
In the land beyond life's sea.

Beautiful hills of Milan,
How oft in my dreams I see,
The father, the mother the loved ones,
That enjoyed thy beauties with me.

Beautiful hills of Milan,
Would I could see you again,
It would be sweeter to me than gold,
Or my name on the roll of fame.

The most famous citizen of Milan draws many visitors; however, the history and allure of Milan capture all who come. Many family histories are woven throughout the following pages, a journey into the past of a quiet village that has a remarkably interesting history. The village of Milan was a National Trust for Historical Preservation Distinctive Destination in 2002 and continues to attract visitors each year due to its peaceful tranquility.

One

Settlement and Founding

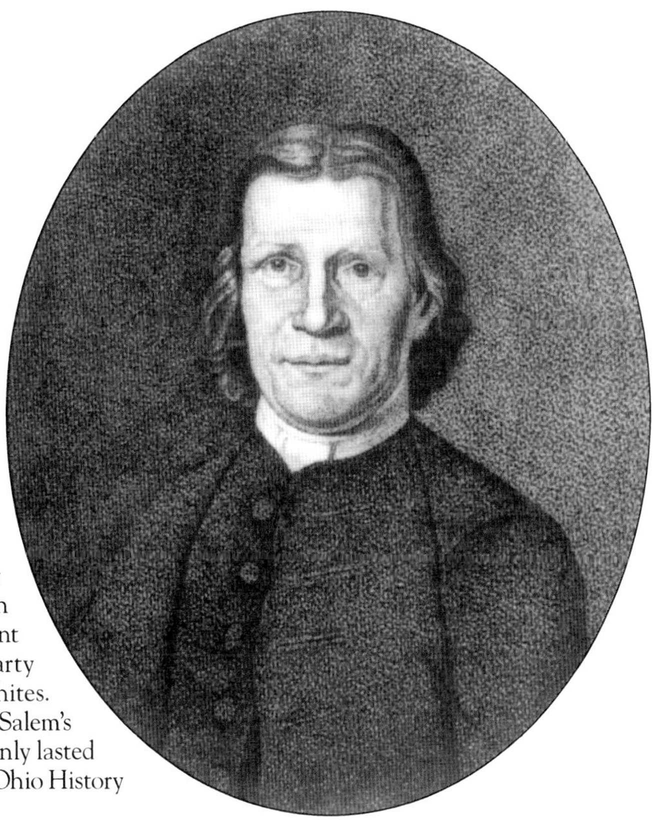

The first organized settlement in the Milan area was a Moravian mission. Following the massacre at Gnadenhütten, Ohio, Moravian missionary David Zeisberger fled to Ontario, founding Fairfield on the Thames River in 1785. On Tuesday, April 8, 1787, Zeisberger and his wife traveled on the Huron River on their way to a new settlement along the Sandusky River with a party of 100 converted Indians and six whites. Although a successful mission, New Salem's location was less than ideal, and it only lasted from 1787 to 1791. (Courtesy of the Ohio History Connection.)

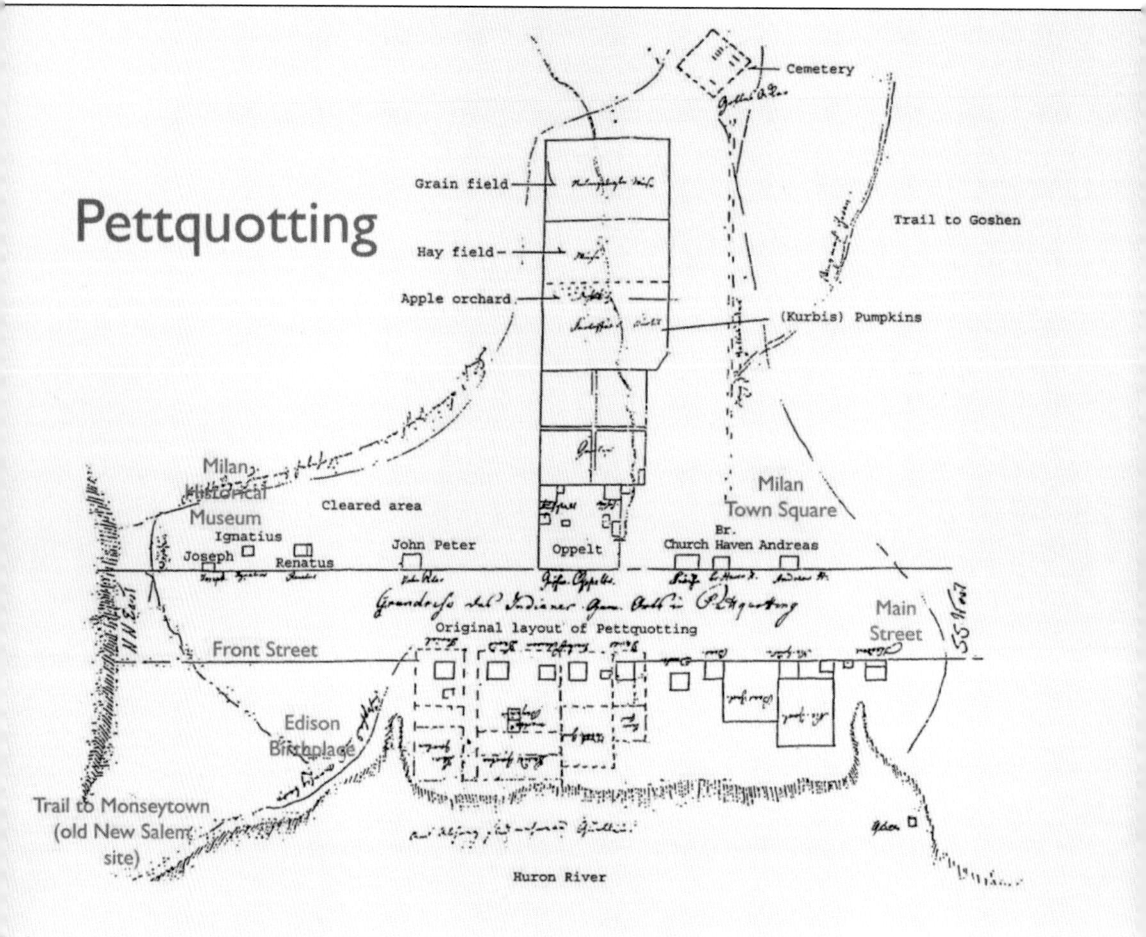

A new party left Fairfield, Ontario, led by Gottfried Sebastian Oppelt, for the 70-day journey to the location of Pettquoting, Ohio. They immediately began laying out the village and fields and building shelter. Eventually, the land was sold to the US government in the Treaty of Fort Industry and became part of the Western Reserve, which was sold to the Connecticut Fire Sufferers.

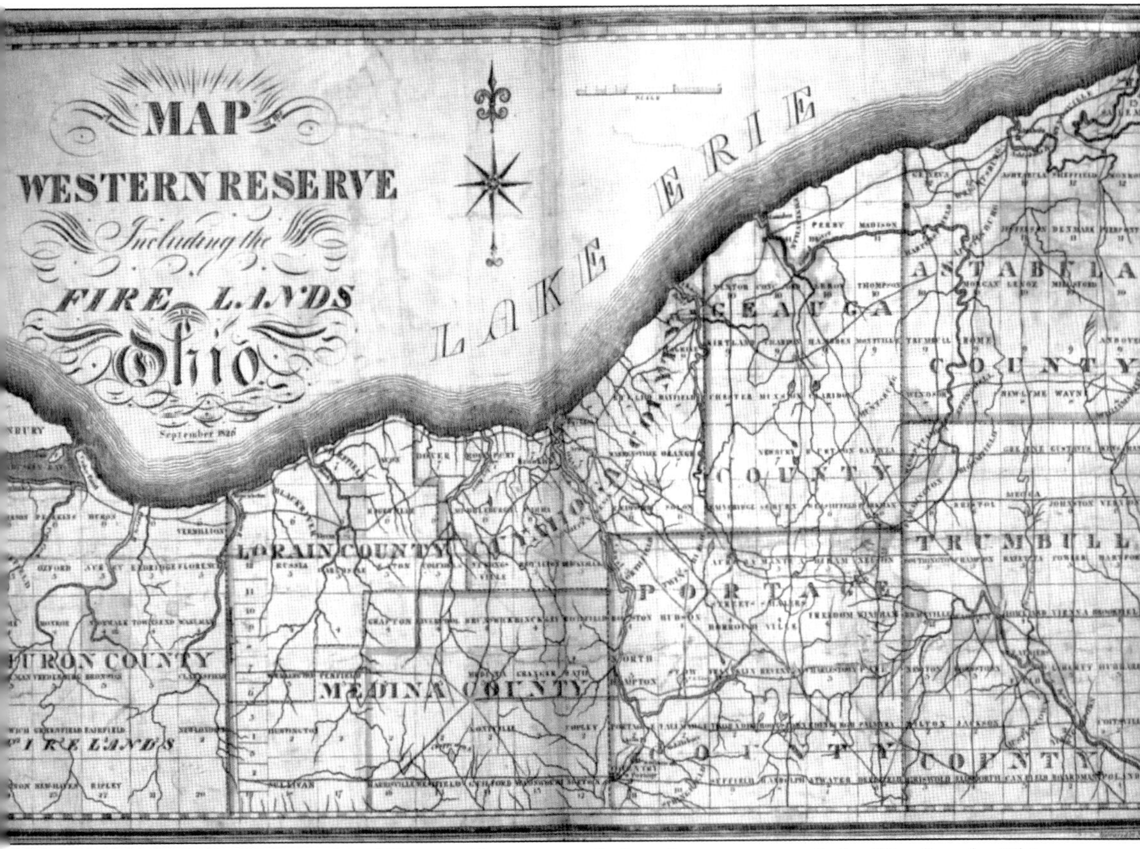

This map of the Connecticut Western Reserve includes the area named the Fire Lands. This land was given to those Connecticut residents whose homes had been burned by fires set by the British during the American Revolution. The Fire Lands were approximately half a million acres (25 square miles) made up of modern Huron and Erie Counties, plus Ruggles Township and the Marblehead peninsula.

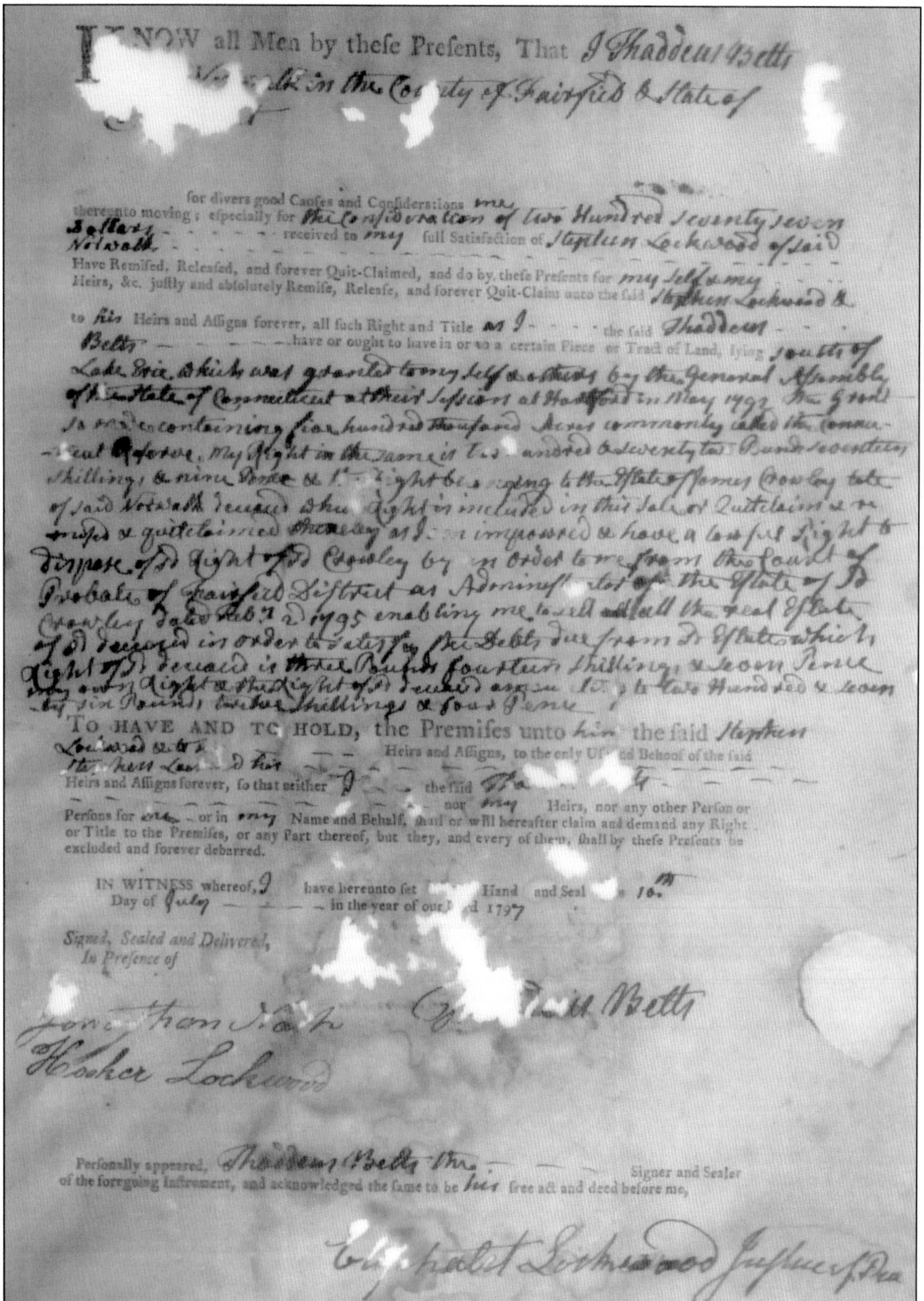

KNOW all Men by these Presents, That I Thaddeus Betts of Norwalk in the County of Fairfield & State of

for divers good Causes and Considerations me thereunto moving; especially for the Consideration of two Hundred seventy seven Dollars received to my full Satisfaction of Stephen Lockwood of said Norwalk

Have Remised, Released, and forever Quit-Claimed, and do by these Presents for my self & my Heirs, &c. justly and absolutely Remise, Release, and forever Quit-Claim unto the said Stephen Lockwood & to his Heirs and Assigns forever, all such Right and Title as I the said Thaddeus Betts have or ought to have in or to a certain Piece or Tract of Land, lying south of Lake Erie which was granted to my self & others by the General Assembly of the State of Connecticut at their Session at Hartford in May 1792 the Grant is made containing five hundred thousand Acres commonly called the Connecticut Reserve, my Right in the same is two hundred & seventy two Pounds seventeen shillings & nine Pence

TO HAVE AND TO HOLD, the Premises unto him the said Stephen Lockwood & to his Heirs and Assigns, to the only Use and Behoof of the said Stephen Lockwood & his Heirs and Assigns forever, so that neither I the said Thaddeus nor my Heirs, nor any other Person or Persons for me or in my Name and Behalf, shall or will hereafter claim and demand any Right or Title to the Premises, or any Part thereof, but they, and every of them, shall by these Presents be excluded and forever debarred.

IN WITNESS whereof, I have hereunto set my Hand and Seal this 10th Day of July in the year of our Lord 1797

Signed, Sealed and Delivered, In Presence of

Jonathan Nash

Hooker Lockwood

Thaddeus Betts

Personally appeared, Thaddeus Betts Junr. Signer and Sealer of the forgoing Instrument, and acknowledged the same to be his free act and deed before me,

Eliphalet Lockwood Justice of Pea[ce]

Thaddeus Betts, born May 3, 1724, in Norwalk, Connecticut, suffered losses when his house was burned during British general William Tryon's raid. He sold his Sufferers land deed to his son-in-law Stephen Lockwood on July 10, 1797. The quit-claim deed pictured here shows the sale of property in the Fire Lands for $277.

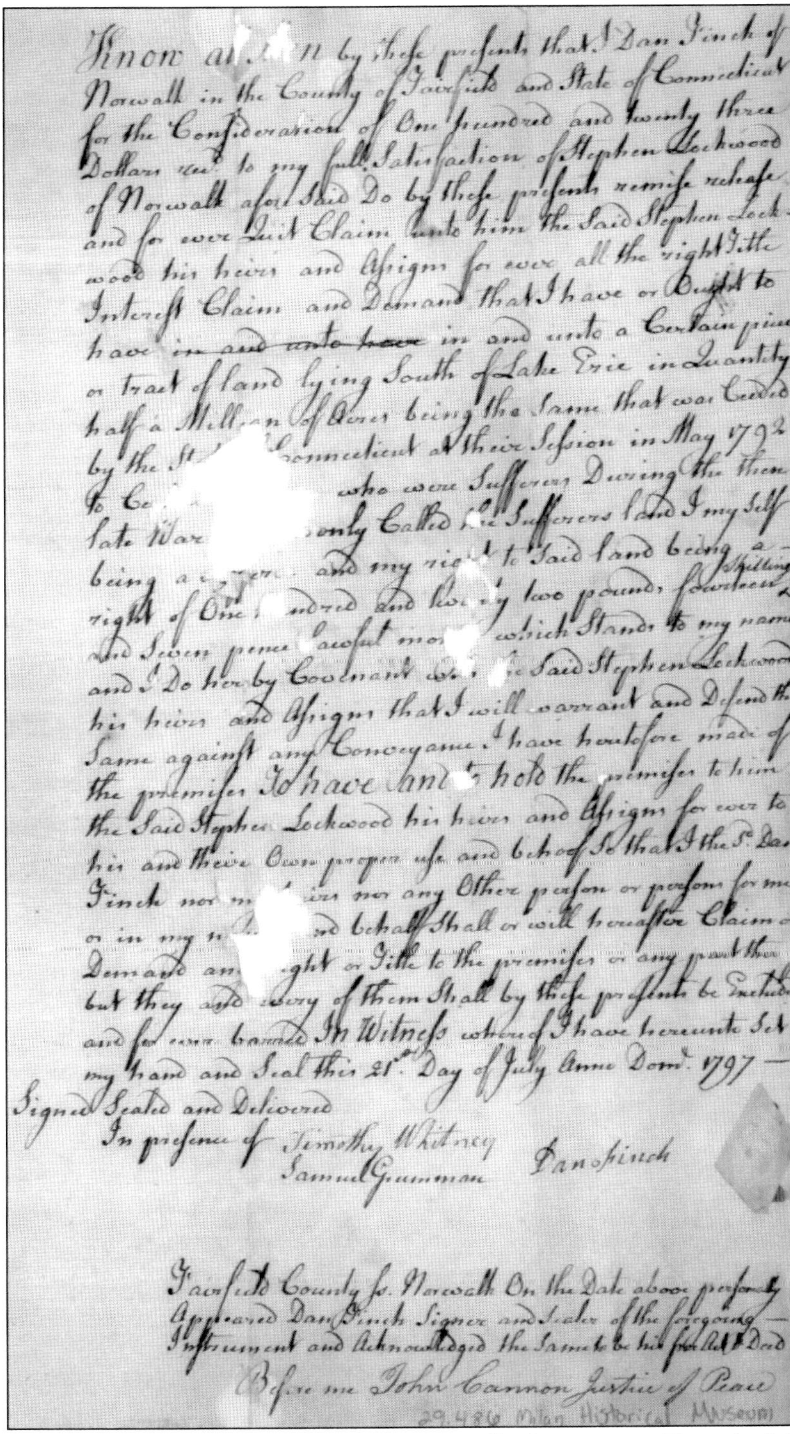

Know all Men by these presents that I Dan Finch of Norwalk in the County of Fairfield and State of Connecticut for the Consideration of One hundred and twenty three Dollars rec^d to my full Satisfaction of Stephen Lockwood of Norwalk aforesaid Do by these presents remise release and for ever Quit Claim unto him the said Stephen Lockwood his heirs and Assigns for ever all the right title Interest Claim and Demand that I have or Ought to have ~~in and unto have~~ in and unto a Certain piece or tract of land lying South of Lake Erie in Quantity half a Mill[illegible]n of Acres being the same that was Ceded by the St[illegible] Connecticut at their Session in May 1792 to Ce[illegible] who were Sufferers During the then late War [illegible]only Called the Sufferers land I my Self being a [illegible] and my ri[illegible]t to said land being a right of One [illegible]ndred and tw[illegible]y two pounds fourteen Shillings and Seven pence lawful mon[illegible] which Stands to my name and I Do here by Covenant w[illegible] the said Stephen Lockwood his heirs and Assigns that I will warrant and Defend the same against any Conveyance I have heretofore made of the premises To have and to hold the premises to him the said Stephen Lockwood his heirs and Assigns for ever to his and their Own proper use and behoof So that I the s^d Dan Finch nor m[illegible] [illegible]irs nor any Other person or persons for me or in my n[illegible] [illegible]d behalf Shall or will hereafter Claim or Demand an[illegible]ight or Title to the premises or any part thereof but they and every of them Shall by these presents be Excluded and for ever barred In Witness whereof I have hereunto Set my hand and Seal this 21st Day of July Anno Dom^i 1797 —

Signed Sealed and Delivered
In presence of Timothy Whitney
Samuel Grumman

Dan Finch

Fairfield County ss. Norwalk On the Date above personally Appeared Dan Finch Signer and Sealer of the foregoing — Instrument and Acknowledged the same to be his free Act & Deed
Before me John Cannon Justice of Peace

29.486 Milan Historical Museum

Stephen Lockwood was born August 16, 1754, in Norwalk, Connecticut. From the July 10, 1797, purchase of land from Thaddeus Betts, until November 1829, he bought and sold more than 5,700 acres in the Connecticut Western Reserve. This quit-claim deed is to Stephen Lockwood for lands in the Fire Lands from Dan Finch in 1797.

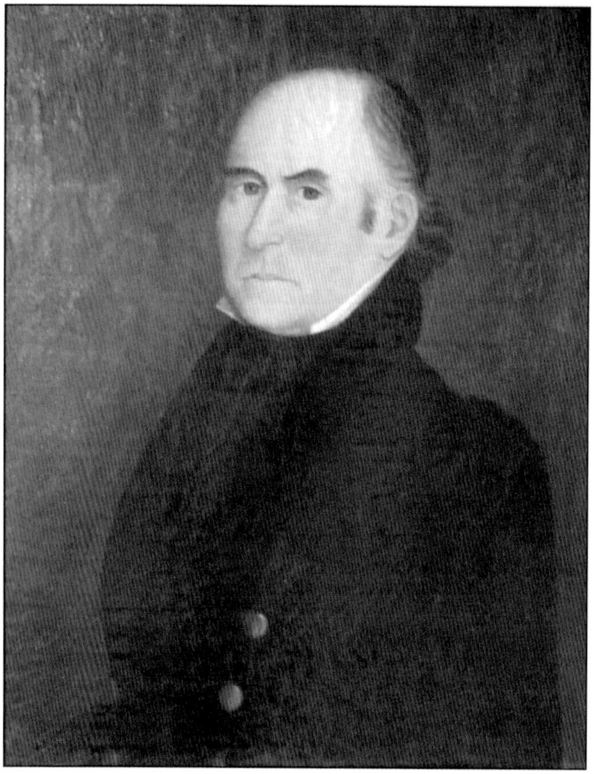

Jared Ward is thought to be the first Caucasian settler to come to Milan Township. He arrived in 1809, purchasing his farm on the west side of the Huron River from David Abbott. He also helped lay out the first roads in Milan Township.

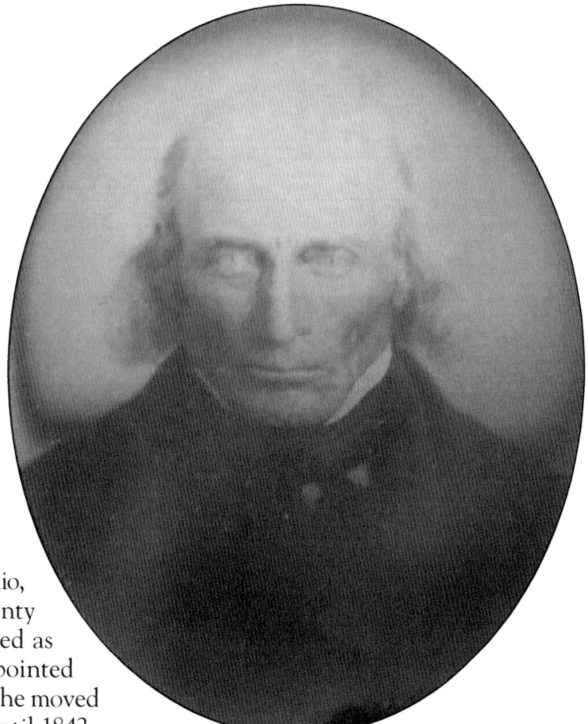

Frederick W. Fowler arrived in Huron, Ohio, on April 10, 1810. In 1811, the old county seat was established with Fowler elected as the first constable as well as being appointed deputy and jailer by the sheriff. In 1819, he moved to Milan, where he operated a tavern until 1842.

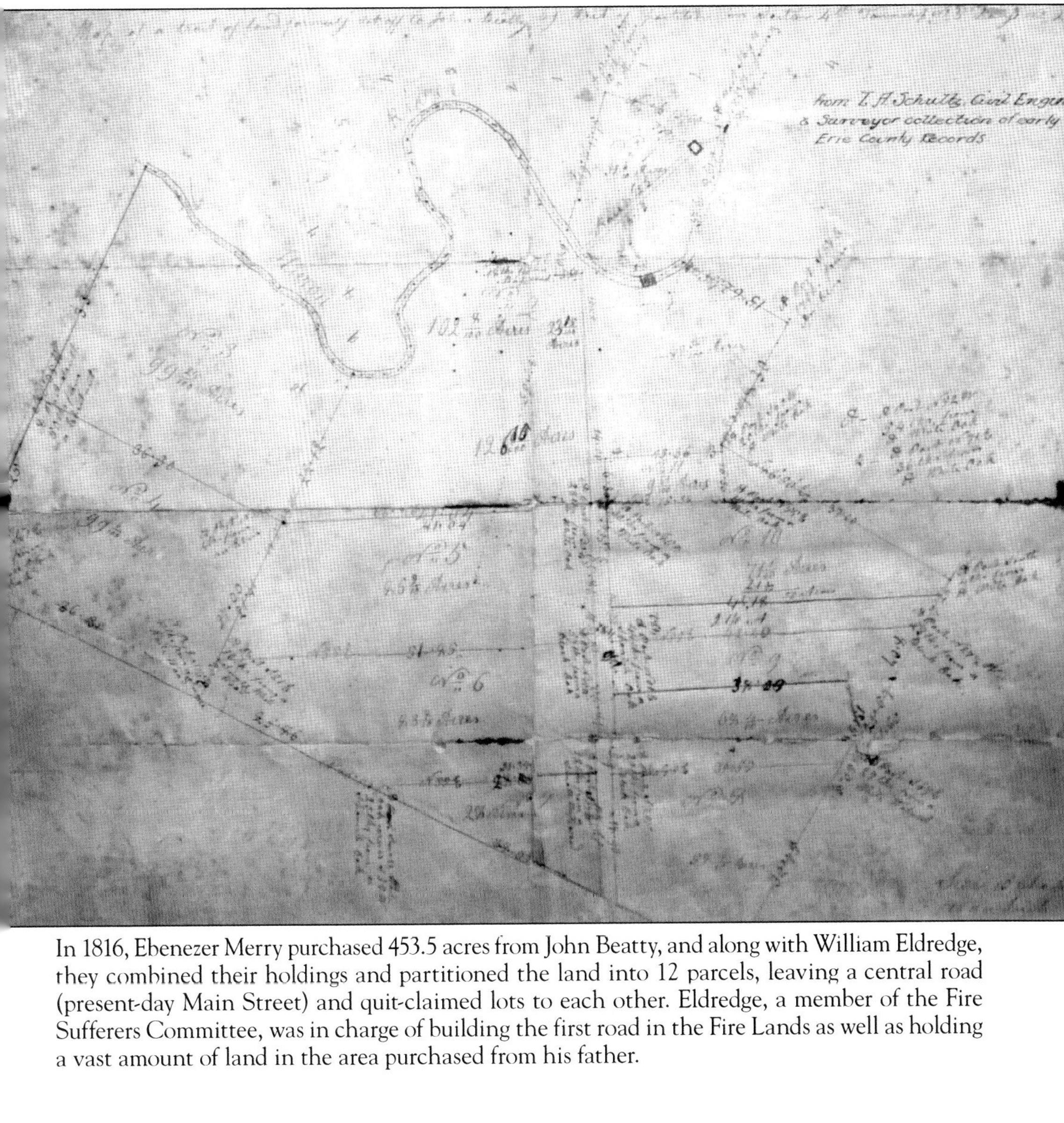

In 1816, Ebenezer Merry purchased 453.5 acres from John Beatty, and along with William Eldredge, they combined their holdings and partitioned the land into 12 parcels, leaving a central road (present-day Main Street) and quit-claimed lots to each other. Eldredge, a member of the Fire Sufferers Committee, was in charge of building the first road in the Fire Lands as well as holding a vast amount of land in the area purchased from his father.

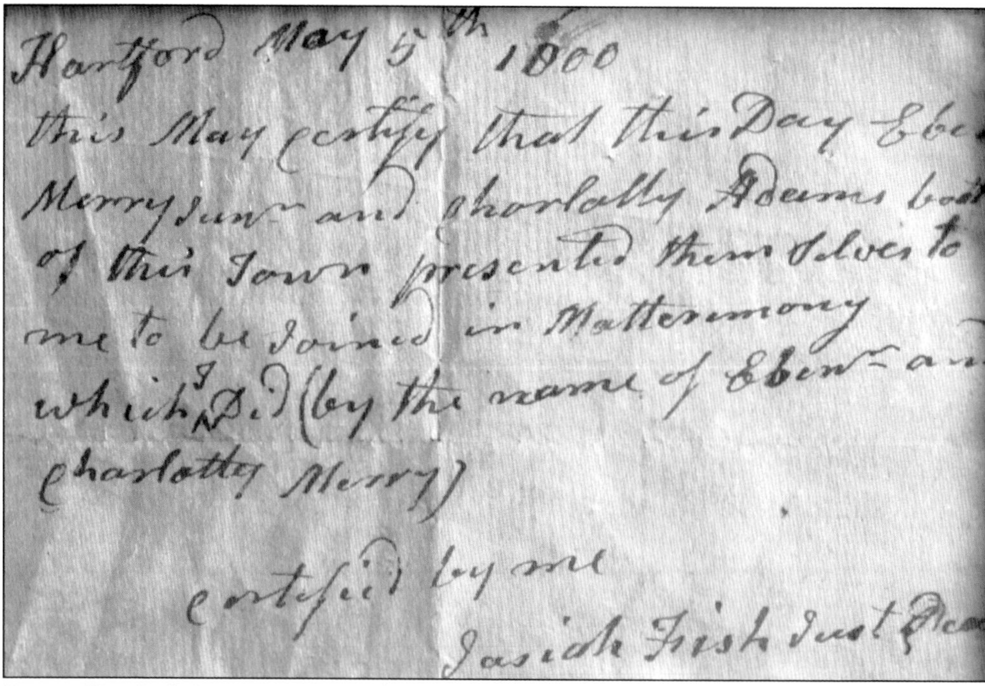

Hartford May 5th 1800
this May certify that this Day Eben
Merry Junr and Charlotty Adams both
of this Town presented them selves to
me to be Joined in Matterimony
which I Did (by the name of Ebenr and
Charlotty Merry)
certified by me
Josiah Fish Just Peace

Born in Hartford, Connecticut, on July 21, 1773, Ebenezer Merry married Charlotte Adams Merry on May 5, 1800. After their home in Mentor, Ohio, burned to the ground in 1809, they traveled to Avery (Abbott's Landing) with their four children.

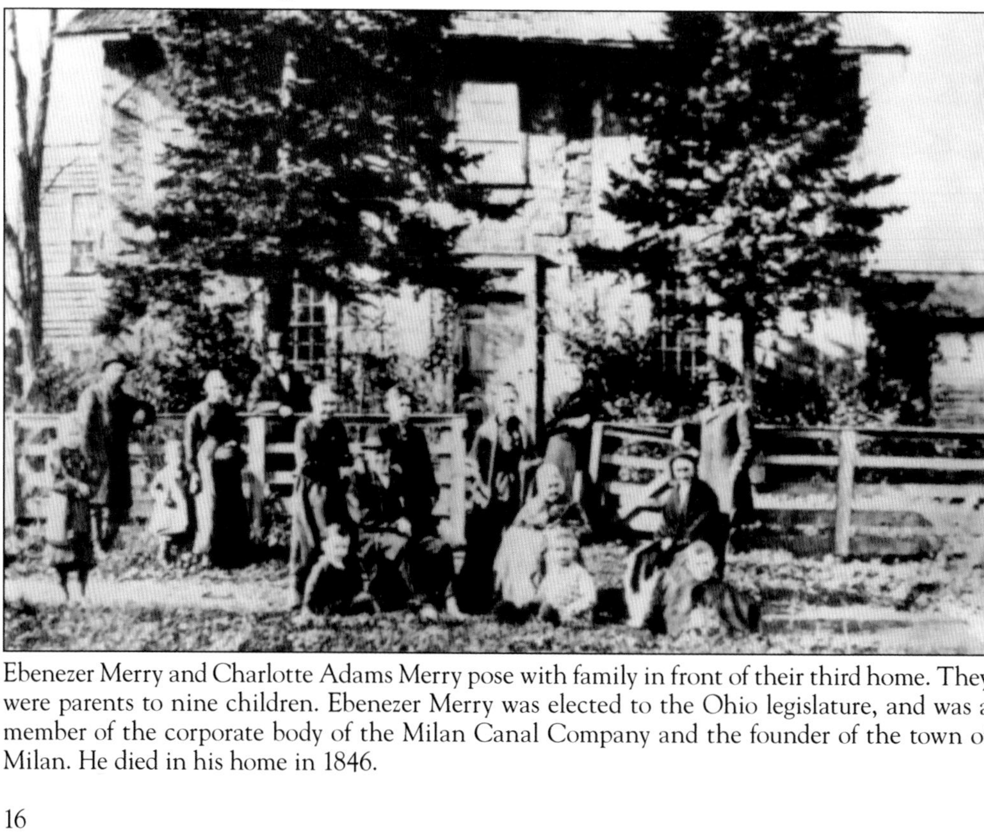

Ebenezer Merry and Charlotte Adams Merry pose with family in front of their third home. They were parents to nine children. Ebenezer Merry was elected to the Ohio legislature, and was a member of the corporate body of the Milan Canal Company and the founder of the town of Milan. He died in his home in 1846.

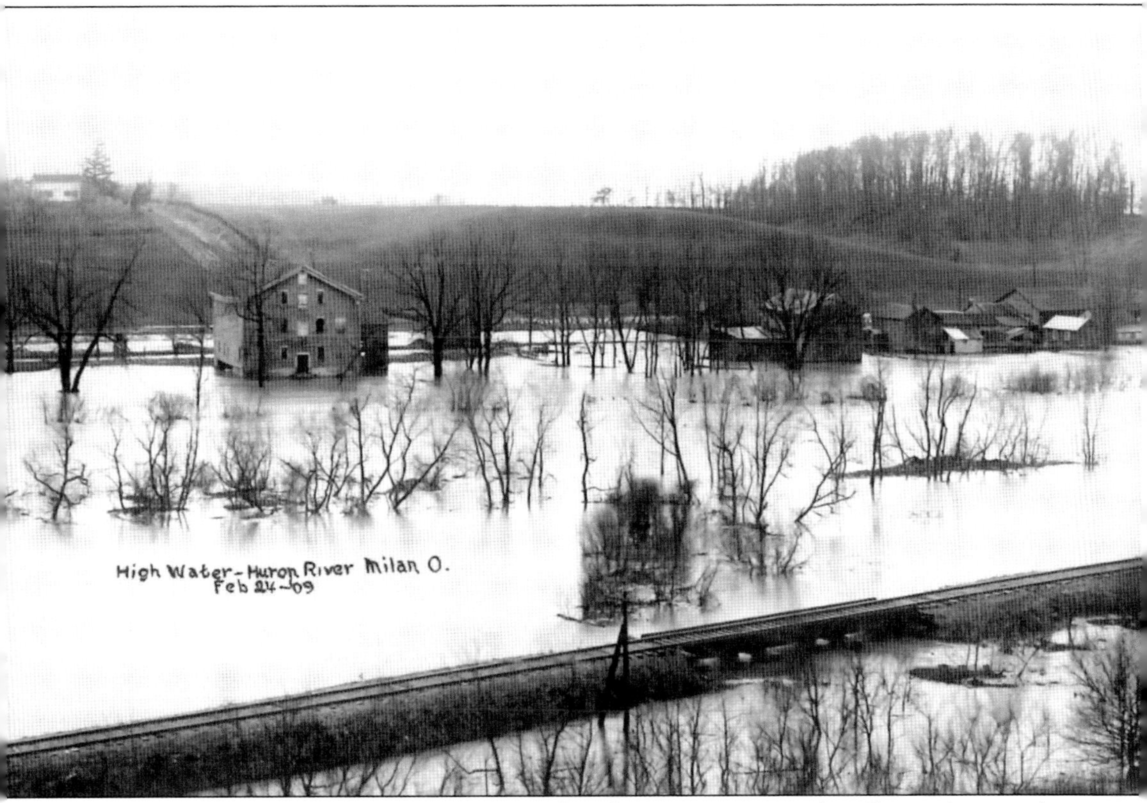

Ebenezer Merry built the first gristmill and sawmill in the area, prompting the village to be named Merry's Mill for a short period. Merry's first sawmill was moved during the construction of the Milan Canal when the course of the river was changed; his second mill can be seen to the right, with the carding mill to the left.

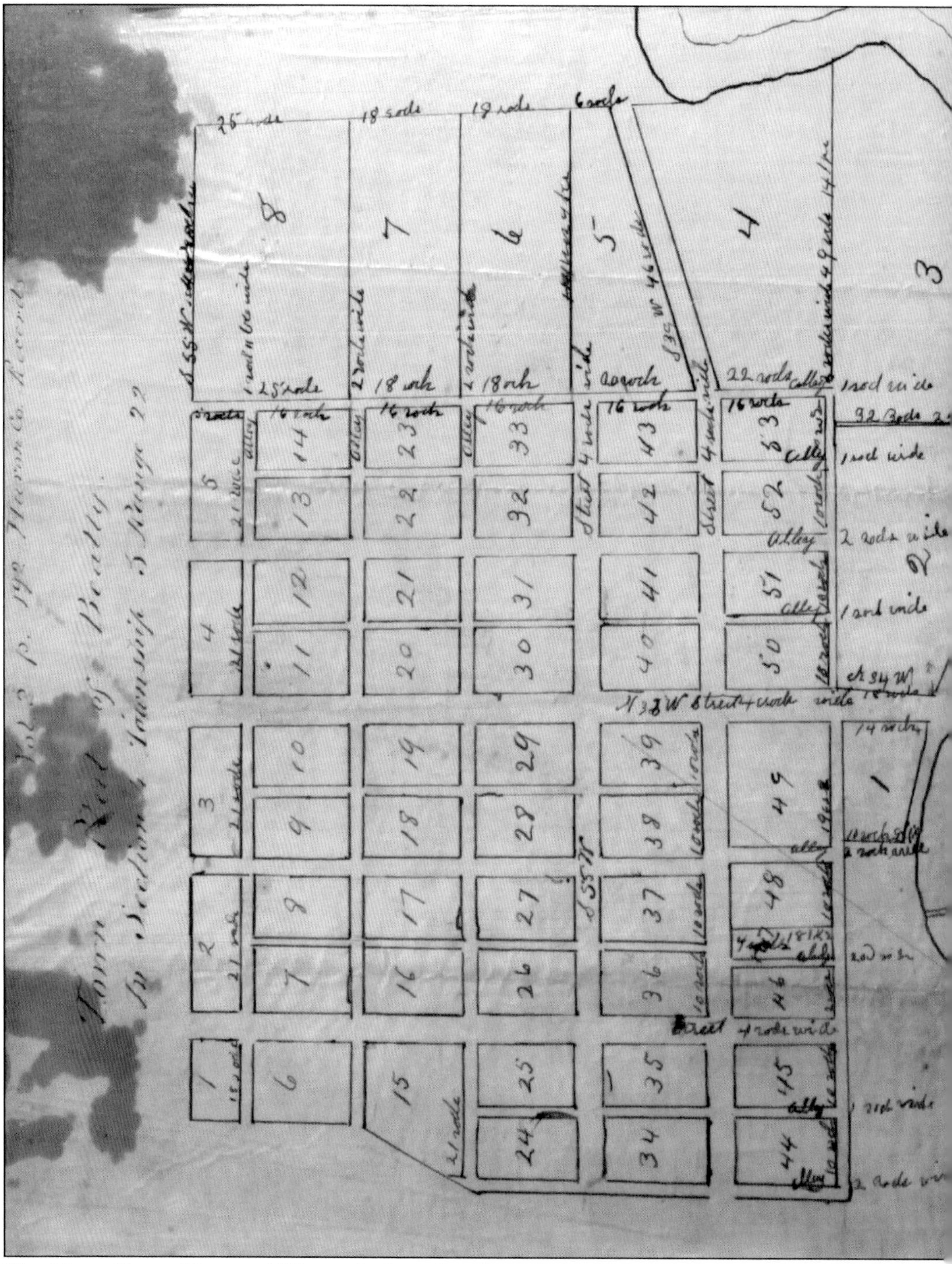

The Merry Platt of Beatty, 1817, was laid out by Ebenezer Merry as lots 2 and 12 of the earlier Merry-Eldredge Survey. Most of the 53 lots of the village were 10 by 16 rods or one acre (a rod being 16.5 feet). The streets were generally one chain wide, or 66 feet. Rods and chains were early

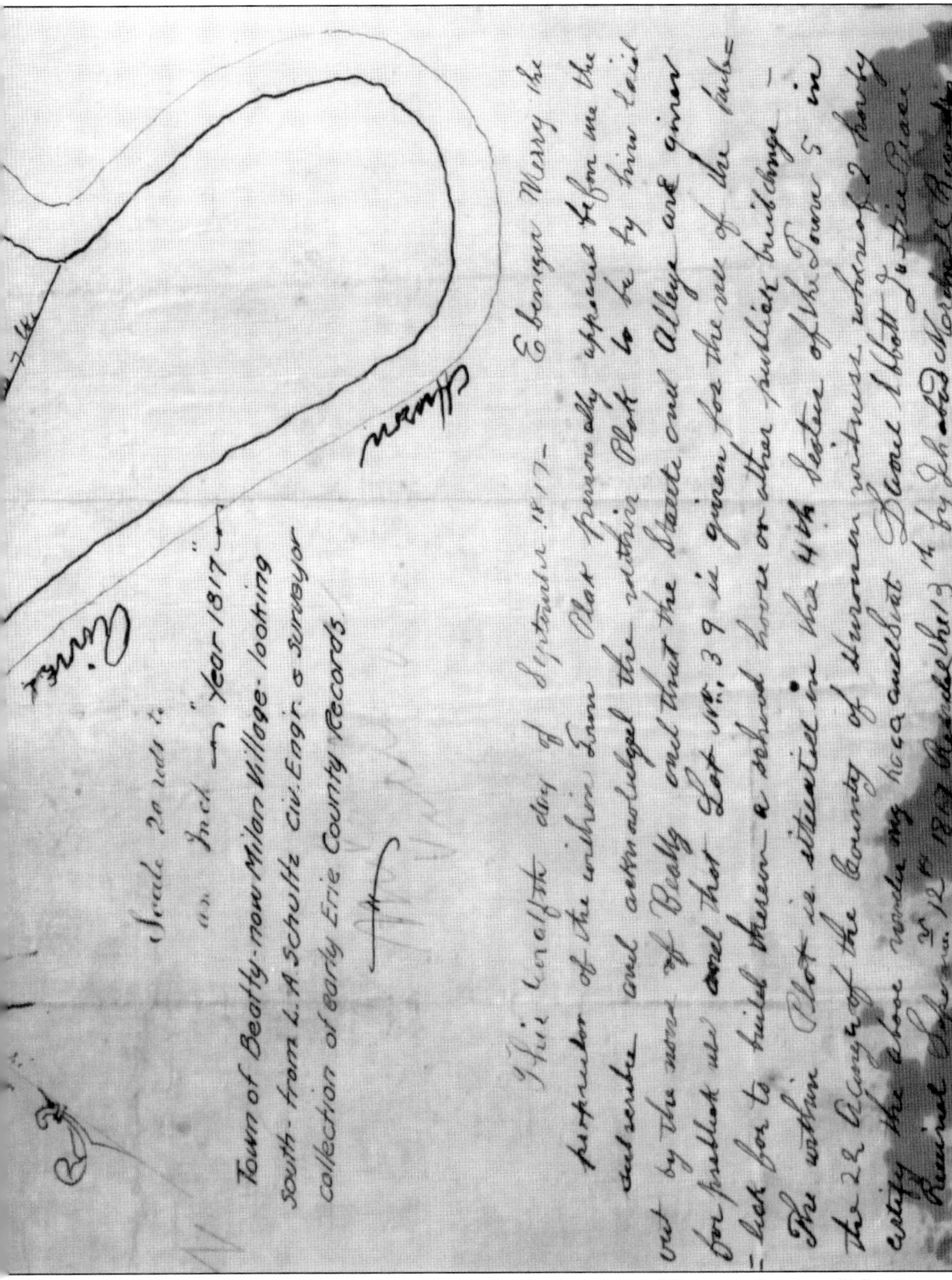

surveyor's units of measurement. The town was given the name of Beatty in honor of John Beatty, the original owner of the land, then became known as Merry's Mill Pond and finally, Milan.

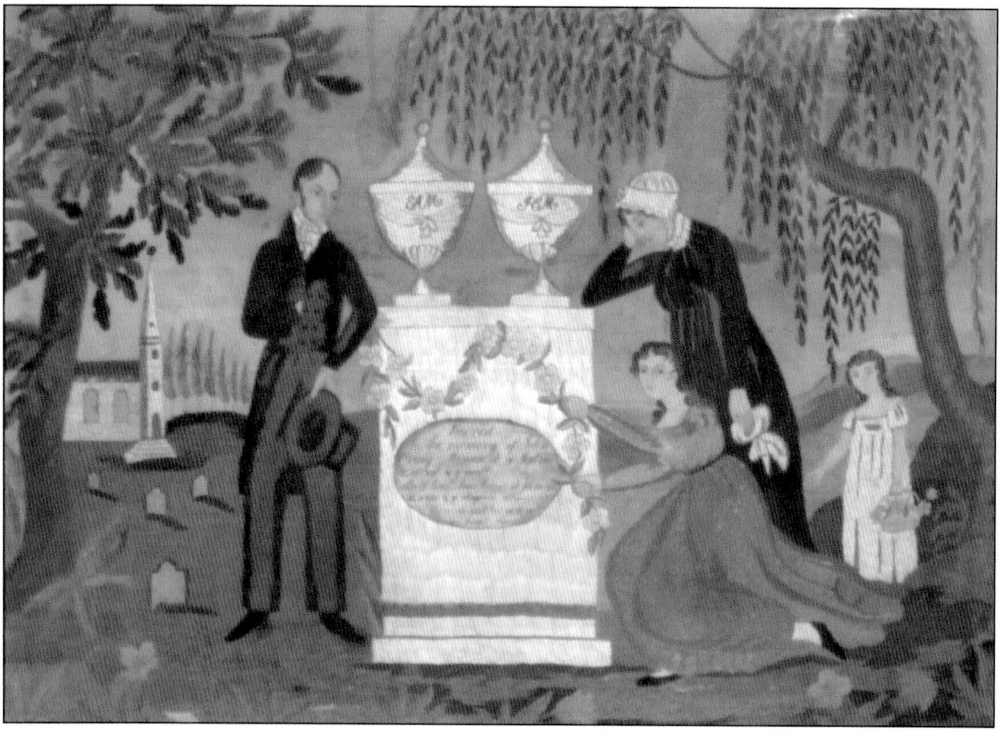

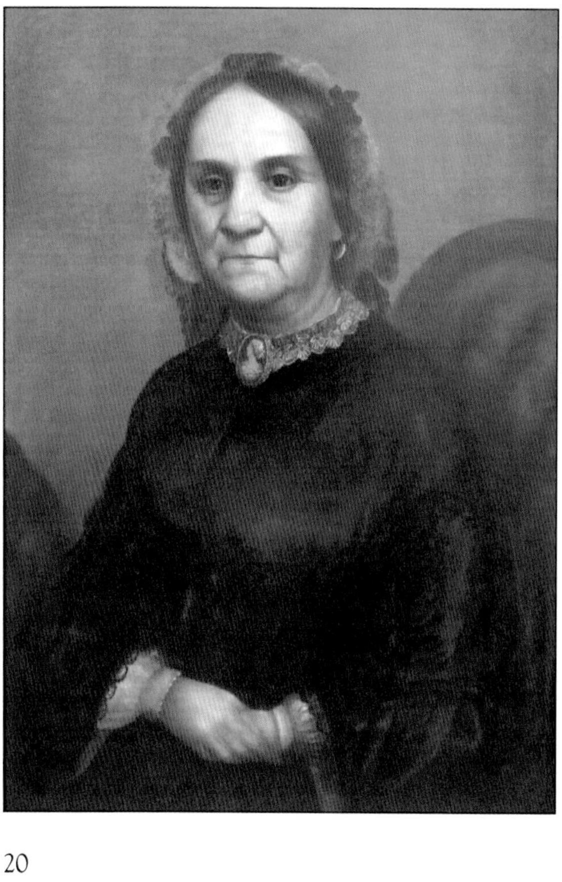

George and Mary (Craig) Minuse were married in New York City, eventually relocating their family to Milan Township, where they procured a farm. This Minuse family mourning portrait was embroidered by Mary (Craig) Minuse during the winter of 1816–1817 in memory of her children John Craig and Elizabeth Ann "Eliza Ann." The mourning portrait also shows a young Emmeline Minuse in the foreground, born March 3, 1802, and her sister Mary B., born January 8, 1810.

This painting shows Emmeline (Minuse) Marks in her later years. She married the Rev. Samuel Marks on March 28, 1842, in Milan. Samuel Marks was born in Marktown, Ireland, on November 19, 1797, and passed on February 28, 1882, in Huron, Ohio, where he served for more than 40 years at the Protestant Episcopal church.

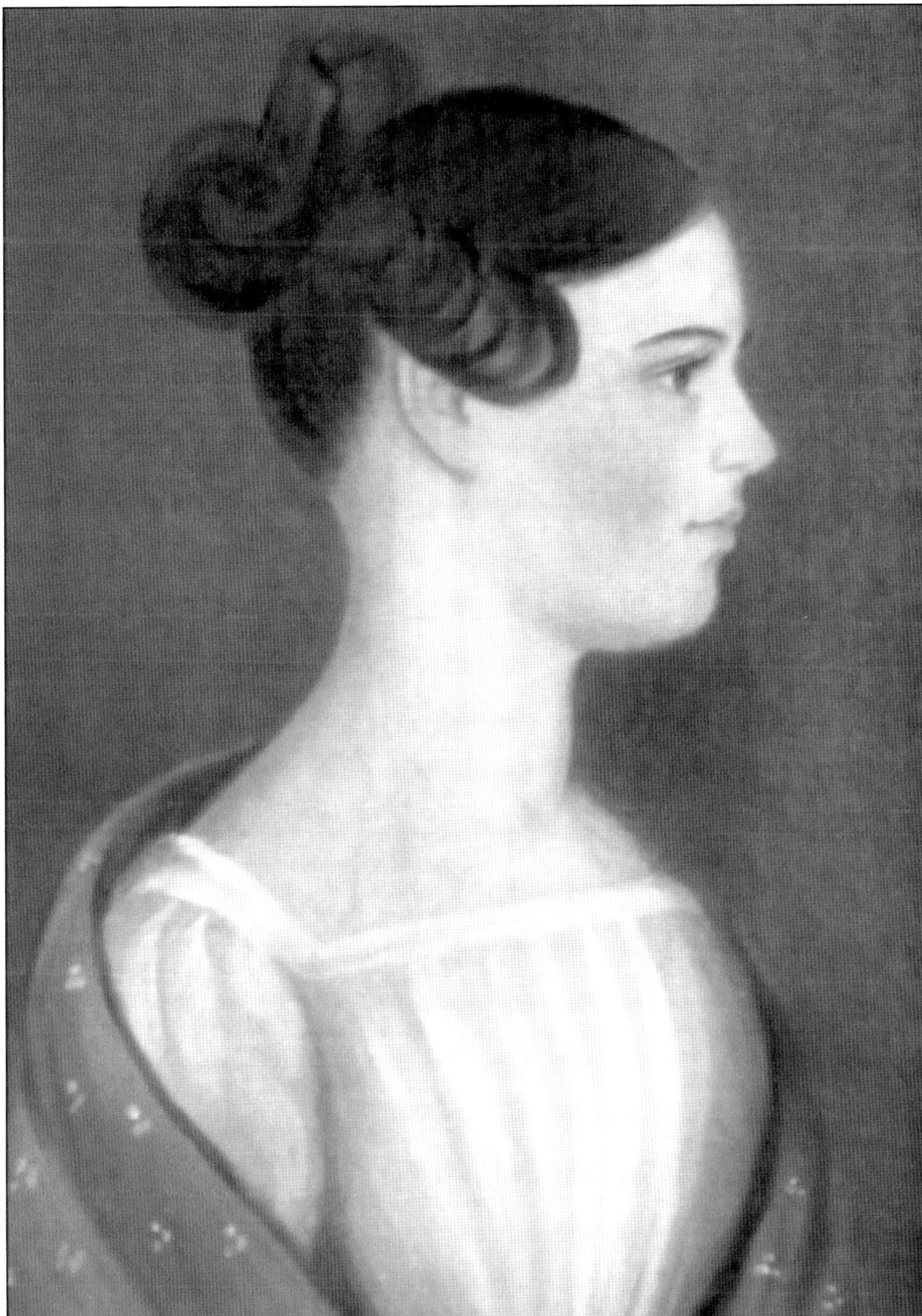

Jasper Miles was born in December 1782 at Brooklyn, Connecticut. He married Elizabeth Bailey in 1808 in Mehoomphany, Pennsylvania, and they moved to Milan in 1824. He used his artistic talents to help support his family for the next eight years. He painted homes, signs, and portraits of friends and neighbors. This is a portrait of Susan Miles, his daughter.

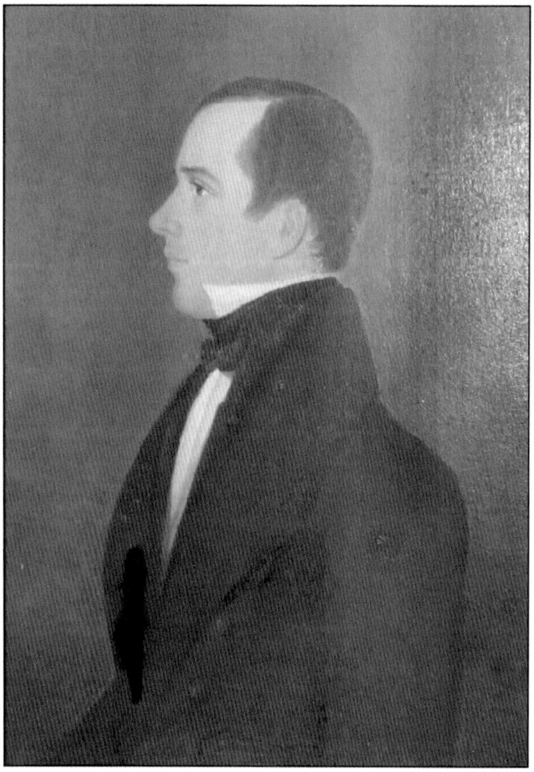

The Miles family moved to Berlin Heights, where they lived until Jasper's death in 1849. He was 67 years old. His wife, Elizabeth, lived with their son Henry until her death. This portrait is of Henry Bailey Miles.

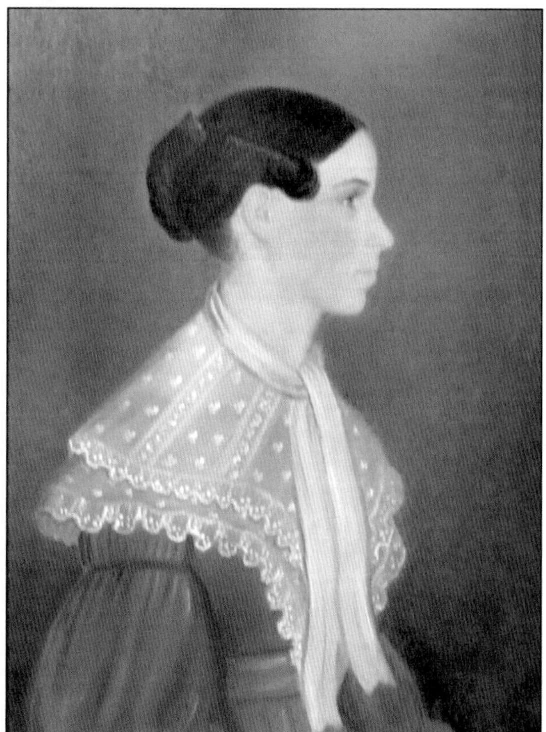

Pictured here is Laura Allen Miles, wife of Henry Bailey Miles. The Milan Museum also has portraits of Pearl Smith Allen and Rueben Allen.

Two

Schools, Churches, and the Town Square

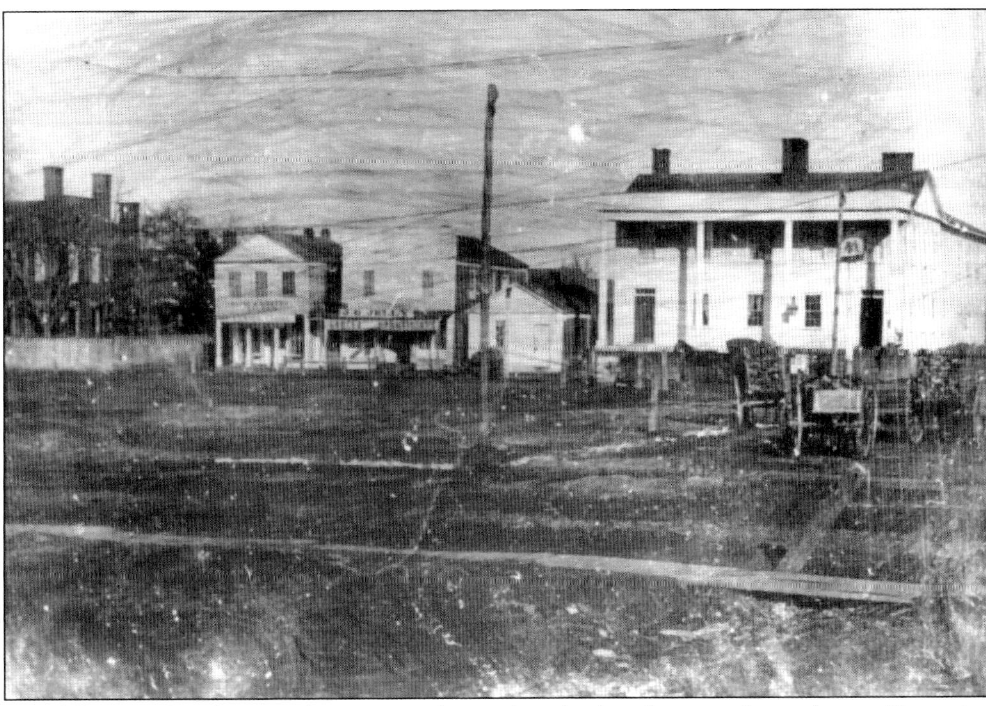

The following decades in Milan saw rapid growth in both industry and population. Tanneries, distilleries, a carding mill, coopers, doctors, and lawyers all opened for business. The square became the center of life in the village. The Old Eagle Tavern was built in 1827, and Seth Jennings was the first proprietor. It was known as the Milan Coffee House in 1828, and was the spot for celebration after the opening of the Milan Canal on July 4, 1839.

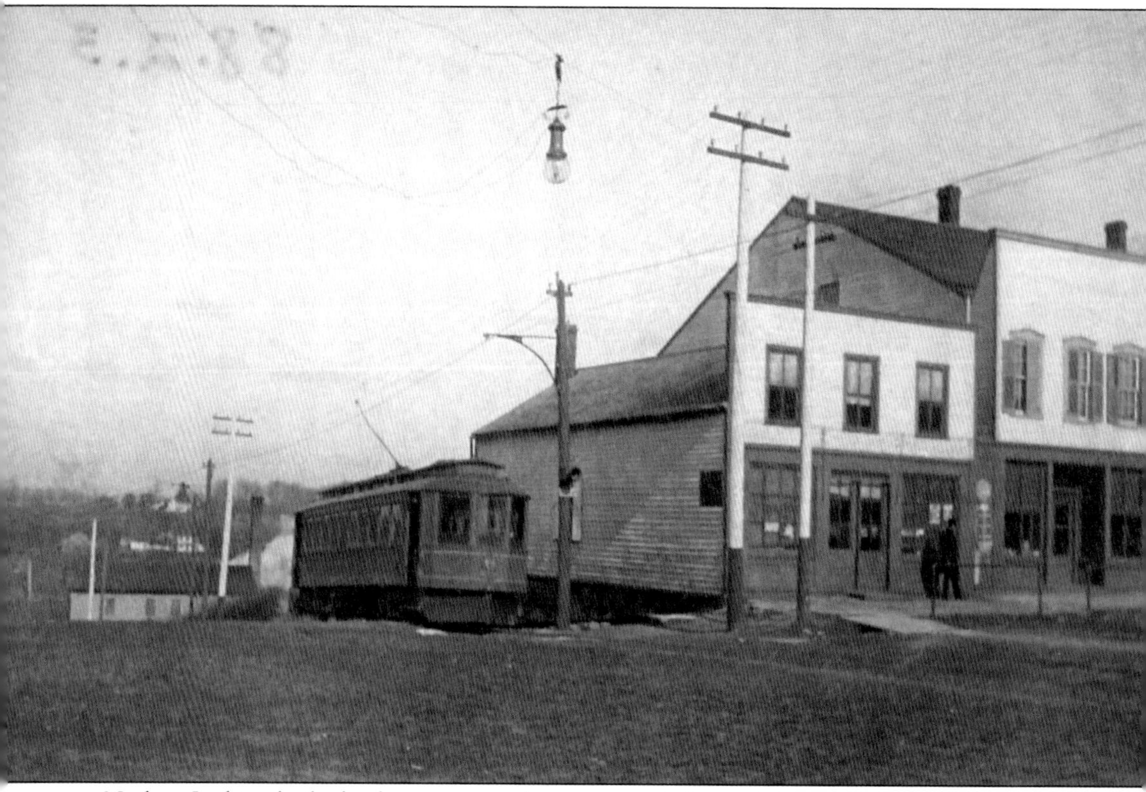

Nathan Jenkins built the first store on the square in 1821. In 1833, it was moved to the rear of the property, and the Mansion Tavern was constructed on the site. A fire burned the tavern to the ground, and the store was moved back to its original location.

In 1819, George Lockwood came to Milan with his brother Ralph. George was Milan's first postmaster, operating out of the store.

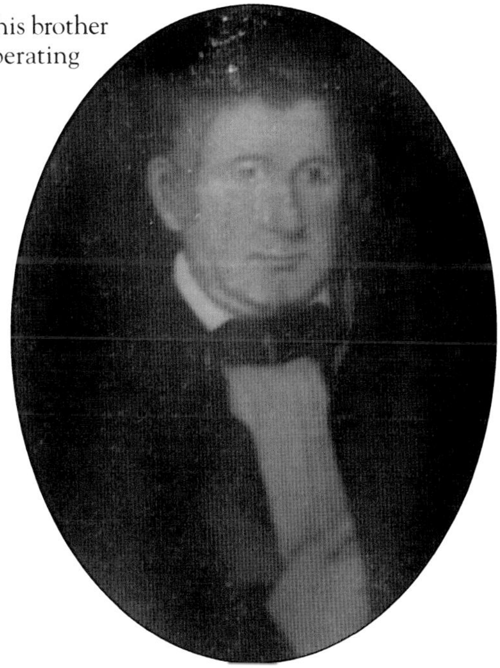

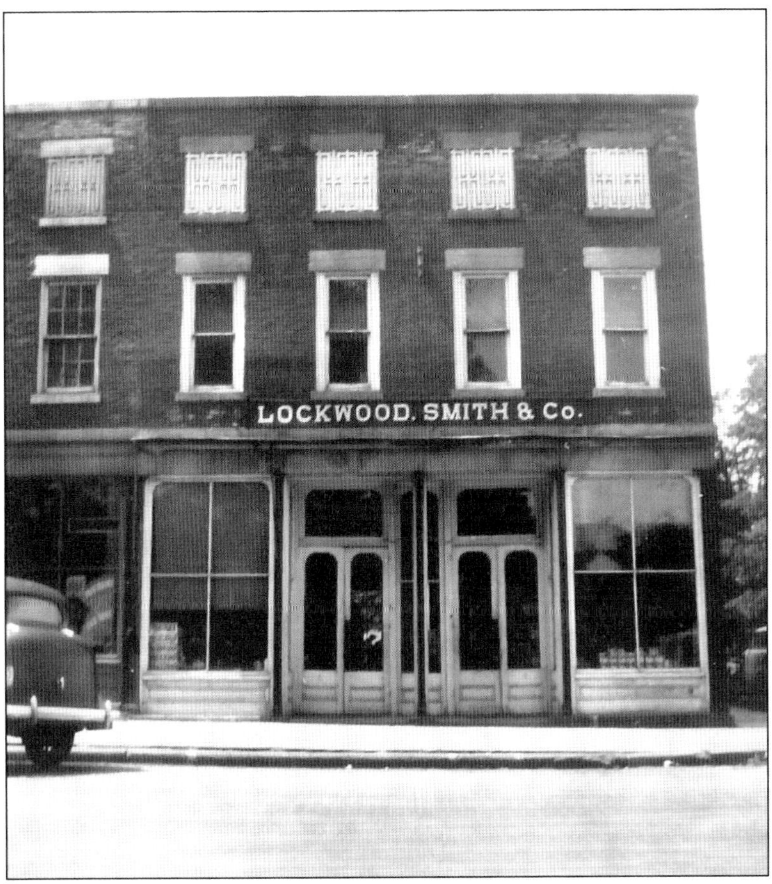

Shortly after the Lockwoods' arrival, they opened Lockwood, Smith & Co. on the west side of the square. Both George and Ralph Lockwood were instrumental in the development and financing of the Milan Canal Company.

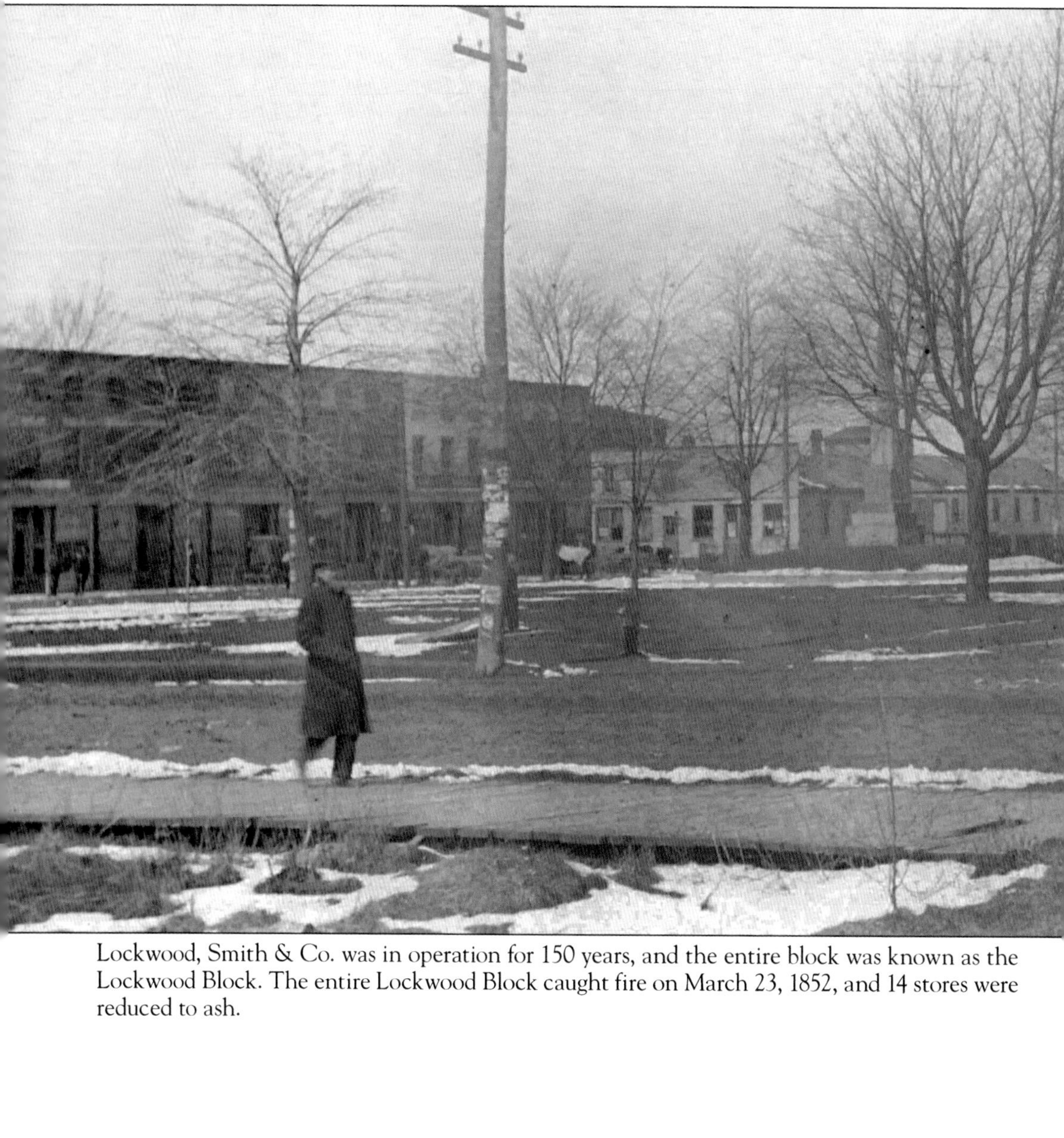

Lockwood, Smith & Co. was in operation for 150 years, and the entire block was known as the Lockwood Block. The entire Lockwood Block caught fire on March 23, 1852, and 14 stores were reduced to ash.

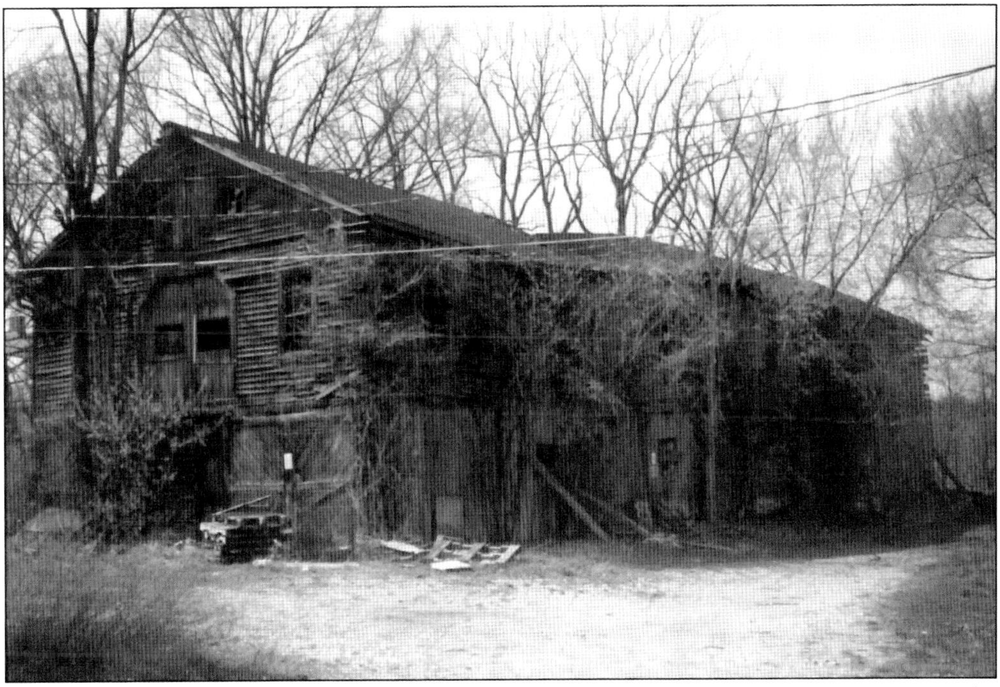

Milan's first tavern opened in 1820, owned and operated by Frederick W. Fowler. Known as the Exchange Place (Inn), it was a station for the stagecoach line operating between Sandusky and Columbus, Ohio. It burned to the ground in April 1852. This photograph shows the old stables shortly before they were torn down.

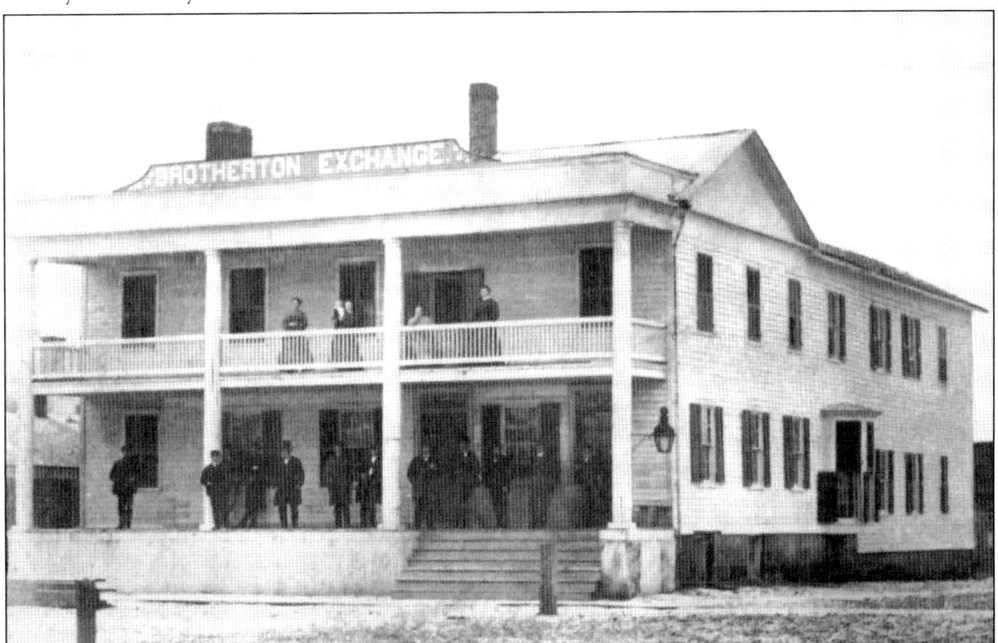

The Eagle Tavern was remodeled in 1870, a second story was added, and it was renamed the Brotherton Exchange. A fire destroyed the building on August 1, 1873, and it was later replaced by the township hall in 1876.

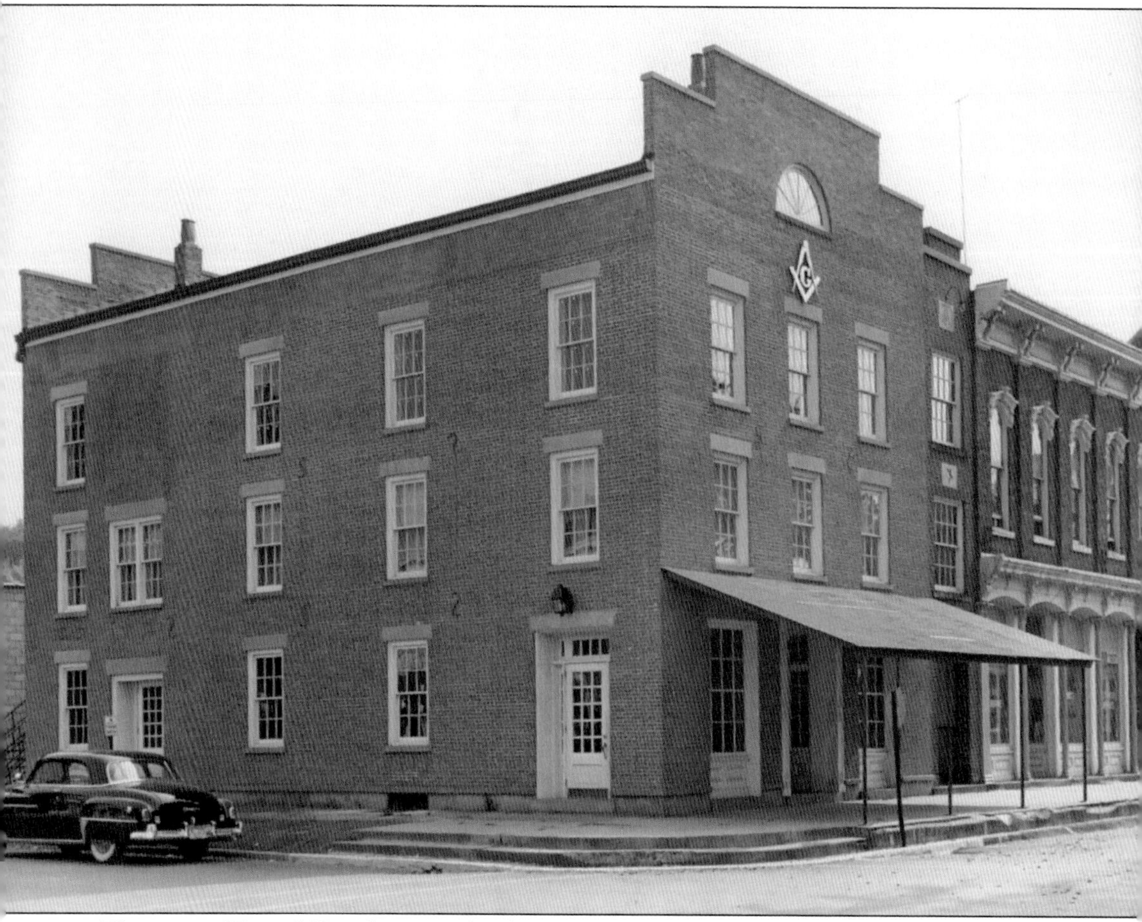

Thomas and Daniel Hamilton were brothers-in-law to Needham Standart, who married Margaret Hamiliton. They both became members of the firm Standart, Hamilton & Co. The building was built in 1826. Upon the removal of Standart, the Hamilton brothers were the most prominent contributors to the Milan Canal and other local projects. The economic crash of 1837 forced the brothers to suspend their businesses, which were heavily invested in real estate.

Needham Standart was born in Oneida County, New York, in 1791 and moved to Huron and then to Milan in 1818. He was one of the most prominent merchants, operating the firm of Standart, Hamilton & Co. In 1836, he moved to Cleveland to further his business opportunities and died in 1867.

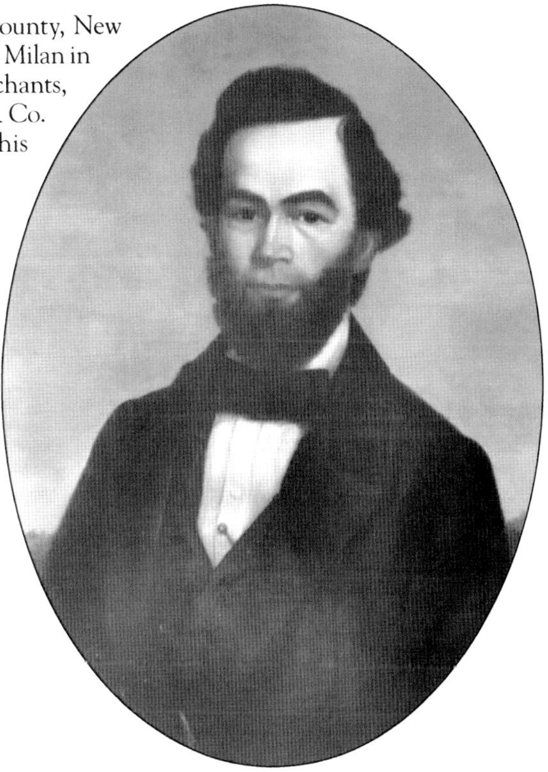

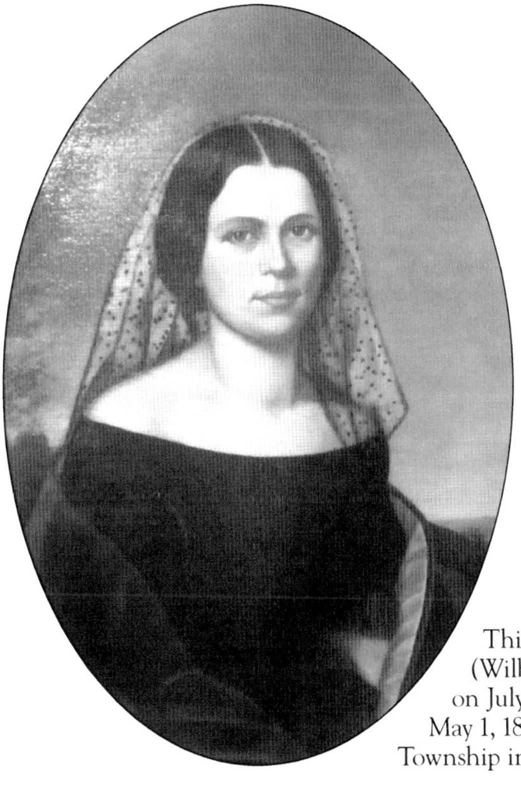

This painting shows Standart's second wife, Naomi (Wilbor) Standart. She was born in Leroy, New York, on July 7, 1798, and married Needham Standart on May 1, 1828. Standart shipped the first grain from Milan Township in 1825–1826.

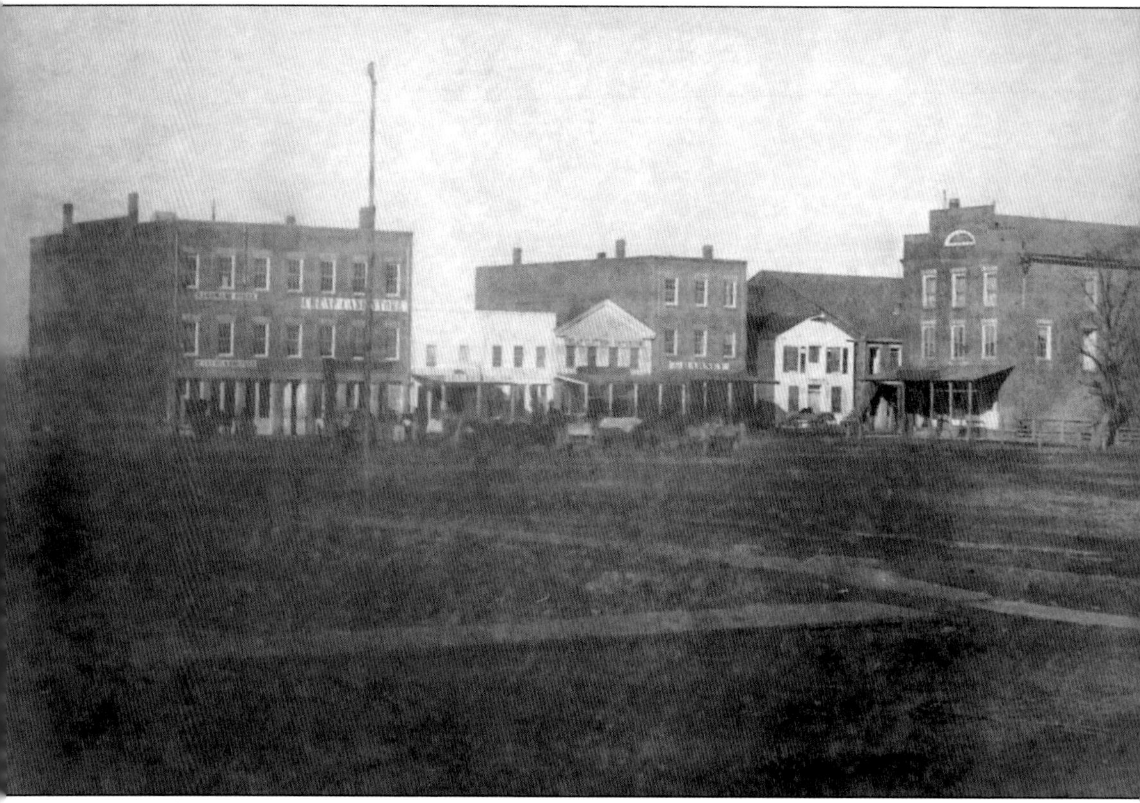

A graduate of Yale, Ebenezer Andrews began his law practice and mercantile business in the three-story brick building he built on the square in 1826–1827. Andrews was elected a director of the Milan Canal Company and also became a judge in the county probate court. This photograph shows the north side of the square with the original Andrews building as well as the eastern side of the square with the prominent Hamilton & Standart building.

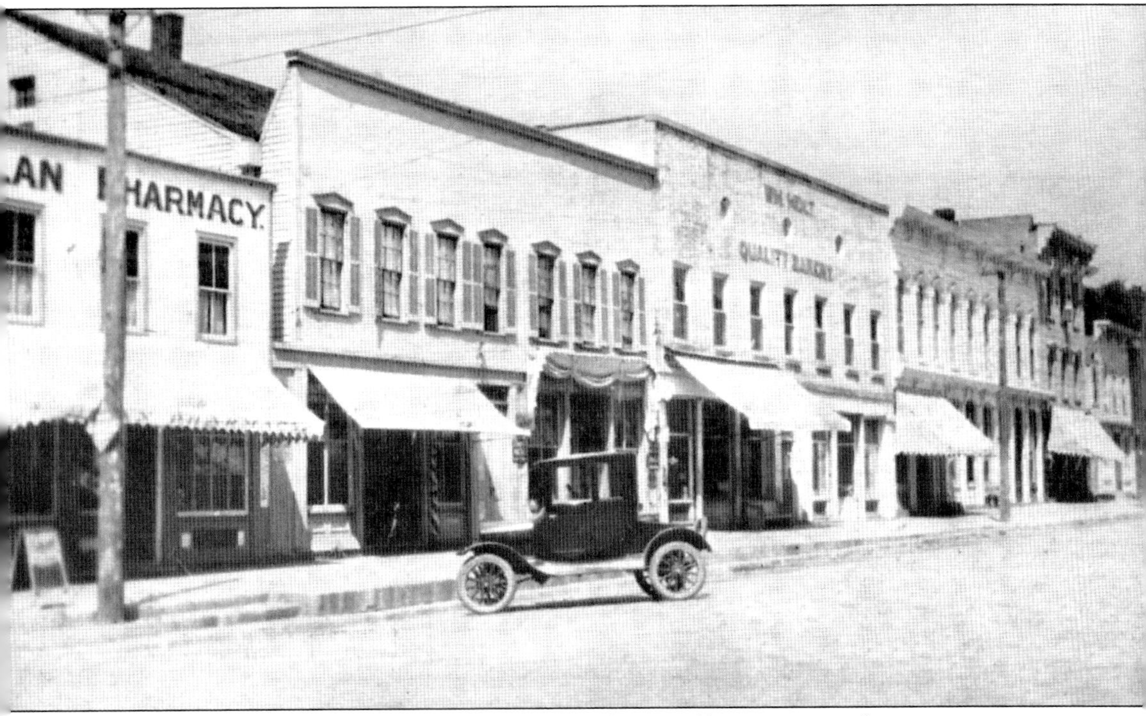

The third floor of the Andrews building, named Andrews Hall, was a center for town activities. William Molt, owner of the Andrews Building in 1909, removed the upper part of the building.

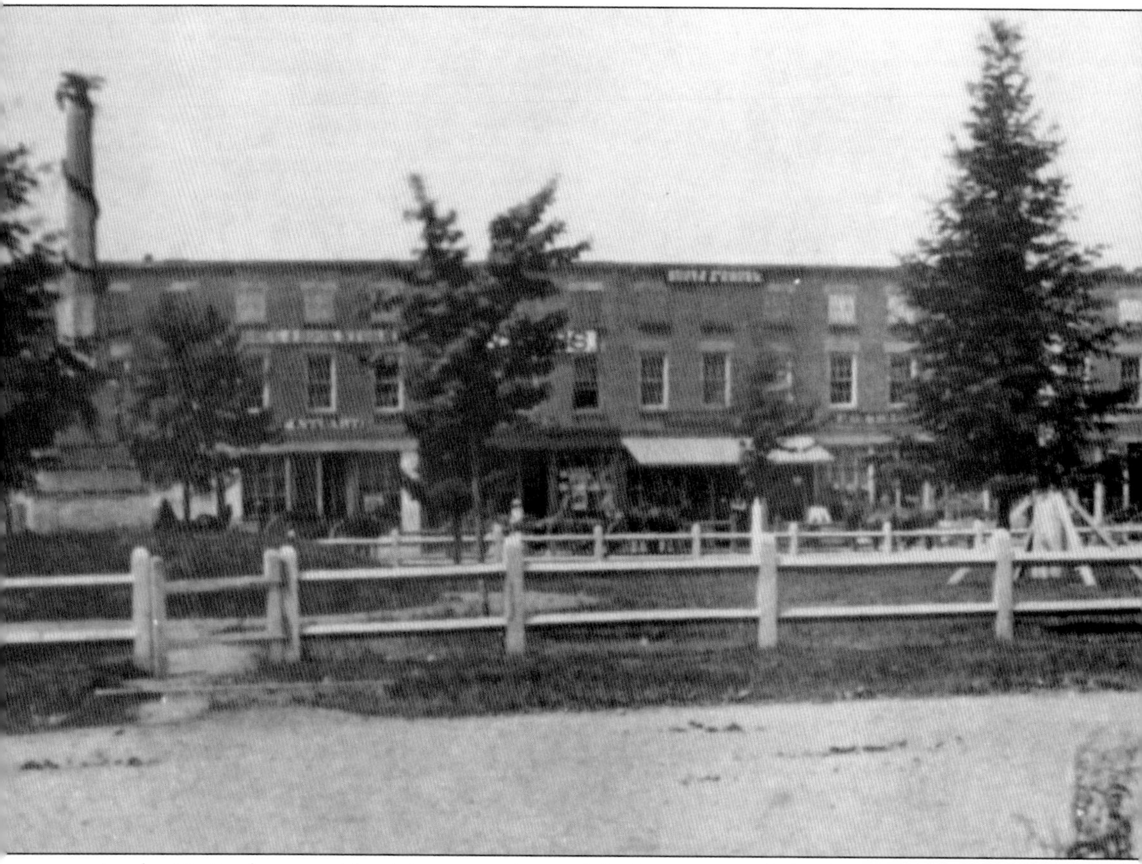

In the 1830s, the west side of the square housed the businesses of Mrs. Moyer's millinery, and Dr. Milo Stuart, the town druggist, opened shop in 1835. A fire on March 23, 1852, destroyed the entire block, which housed 14 stores.

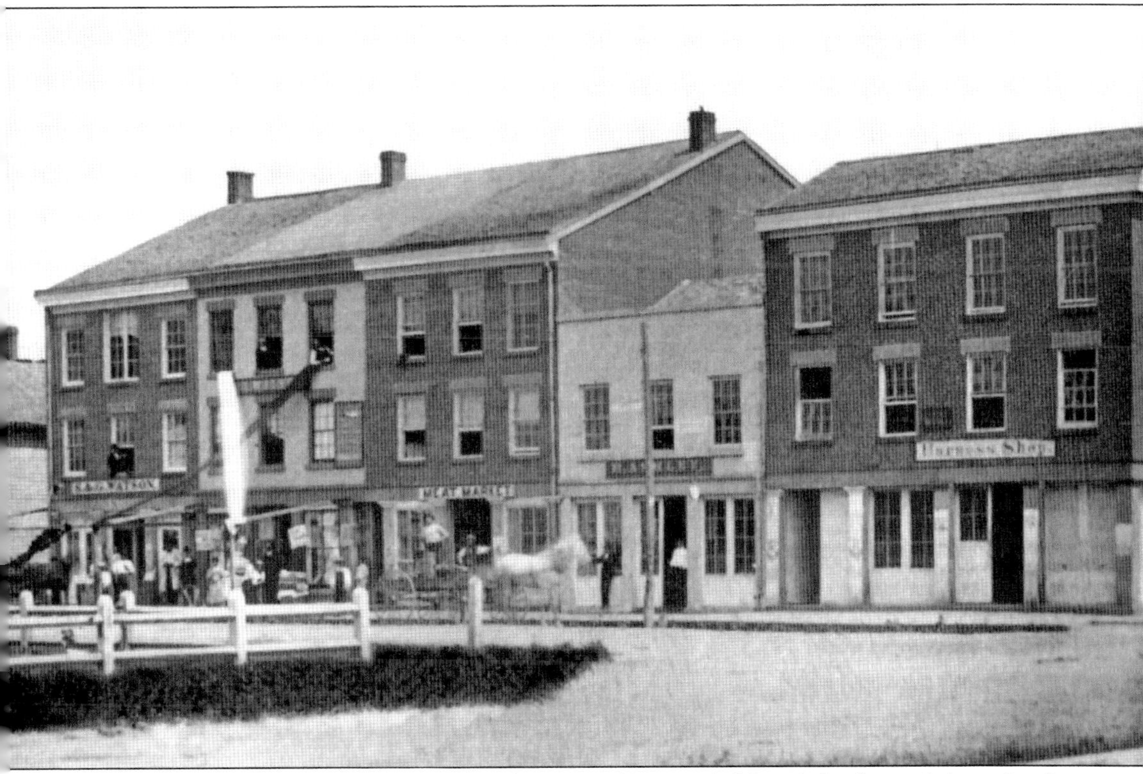

The south side of the square shows the jewelry store of Baxter Ashley. A fire burned this side of the square, including the township hall, in 1888. The upper story of the jewelry store was the telegraph office in later years.

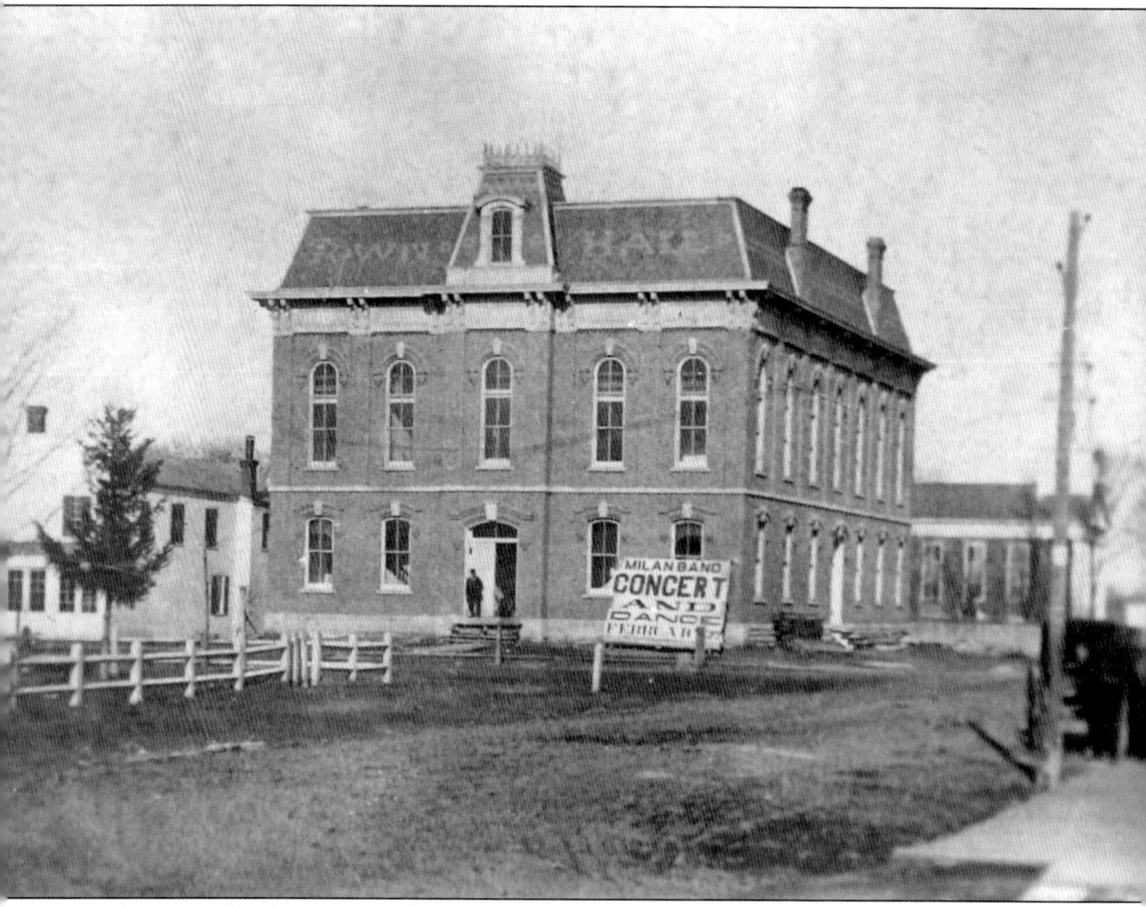

The original Milan Town Hall was built in 1876 on the site of the Brotherton Hotel, which had burned in 1873. The building was dedicated on July 4, 1876, serving as a center for township and village government.

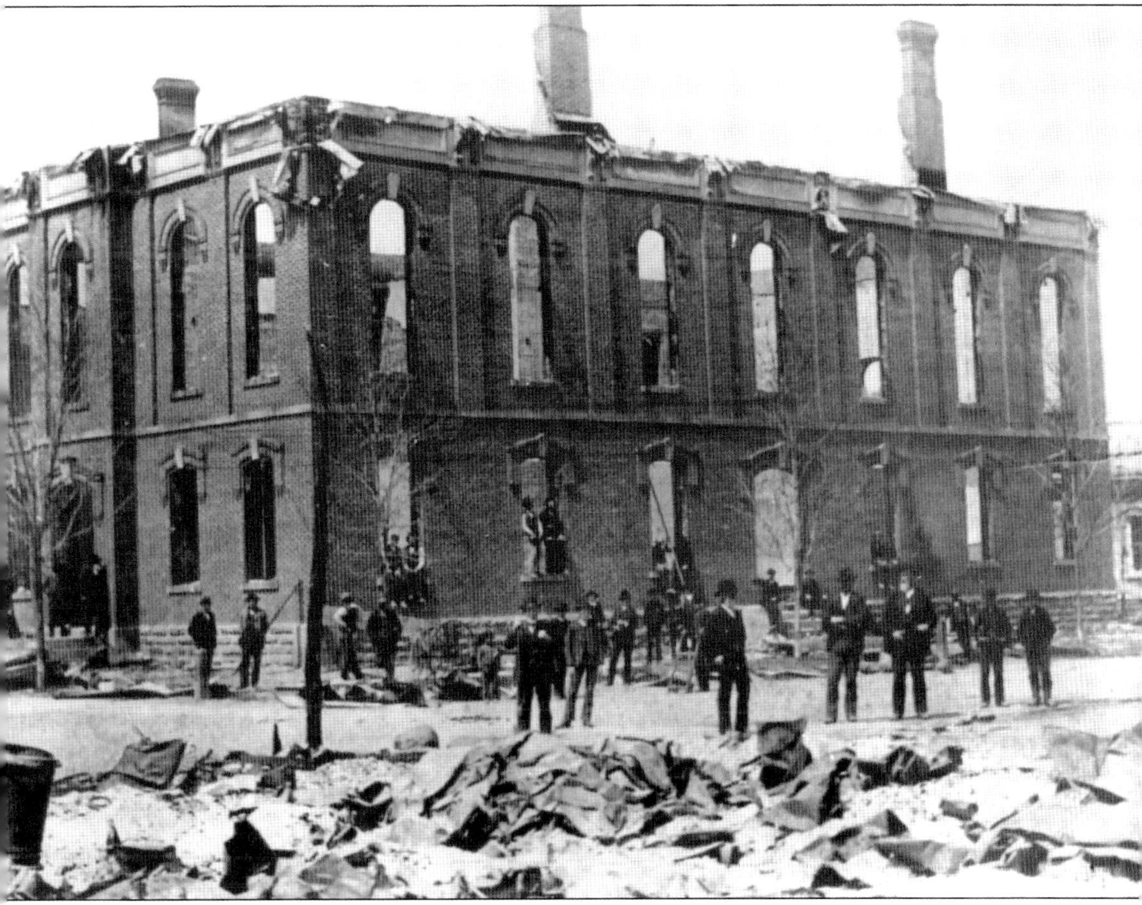

The Milan Town Hall caught fire on May 4, 1888. The entire south side of the square was destroyed, along with the town hall and the Presbyterian church. This photograph reveals that only the brick walls of the town hall remained.

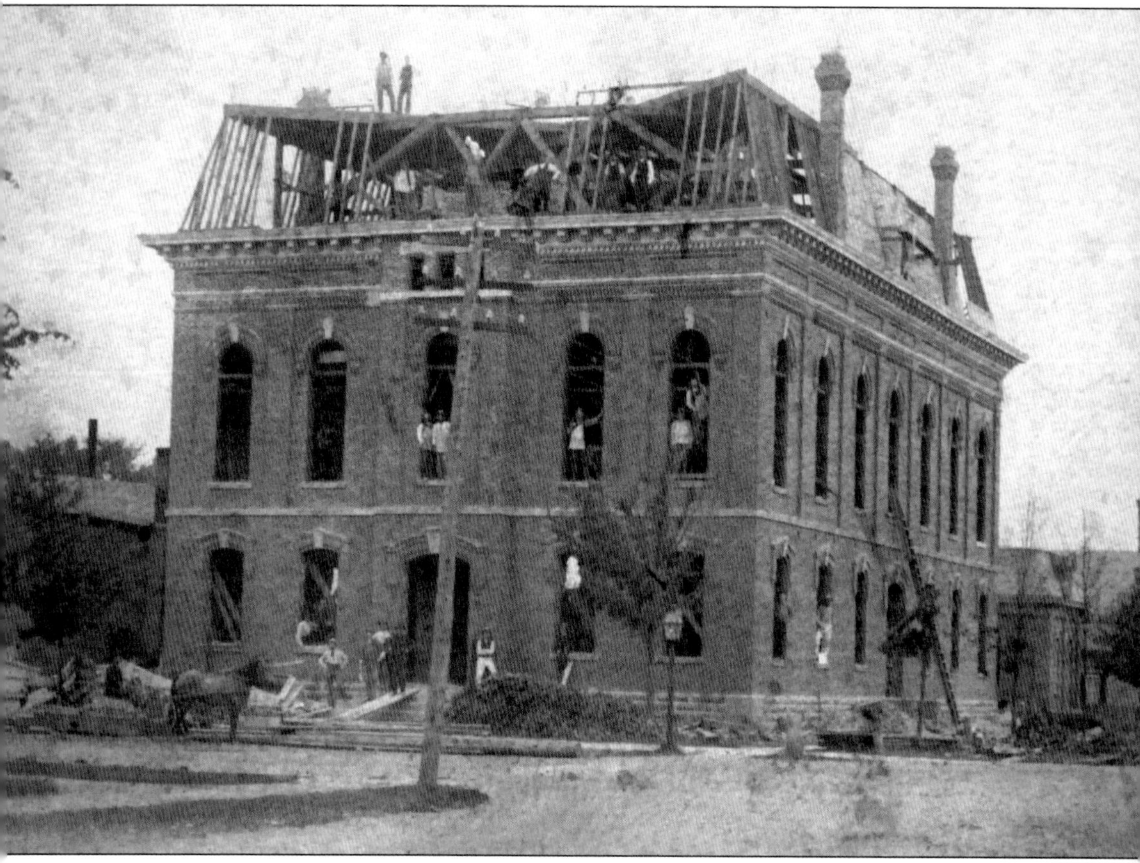

People came from miles to see the destruction the fire of 1888 caused. Milan Town Hall is shown here during its reconstruction the following year.

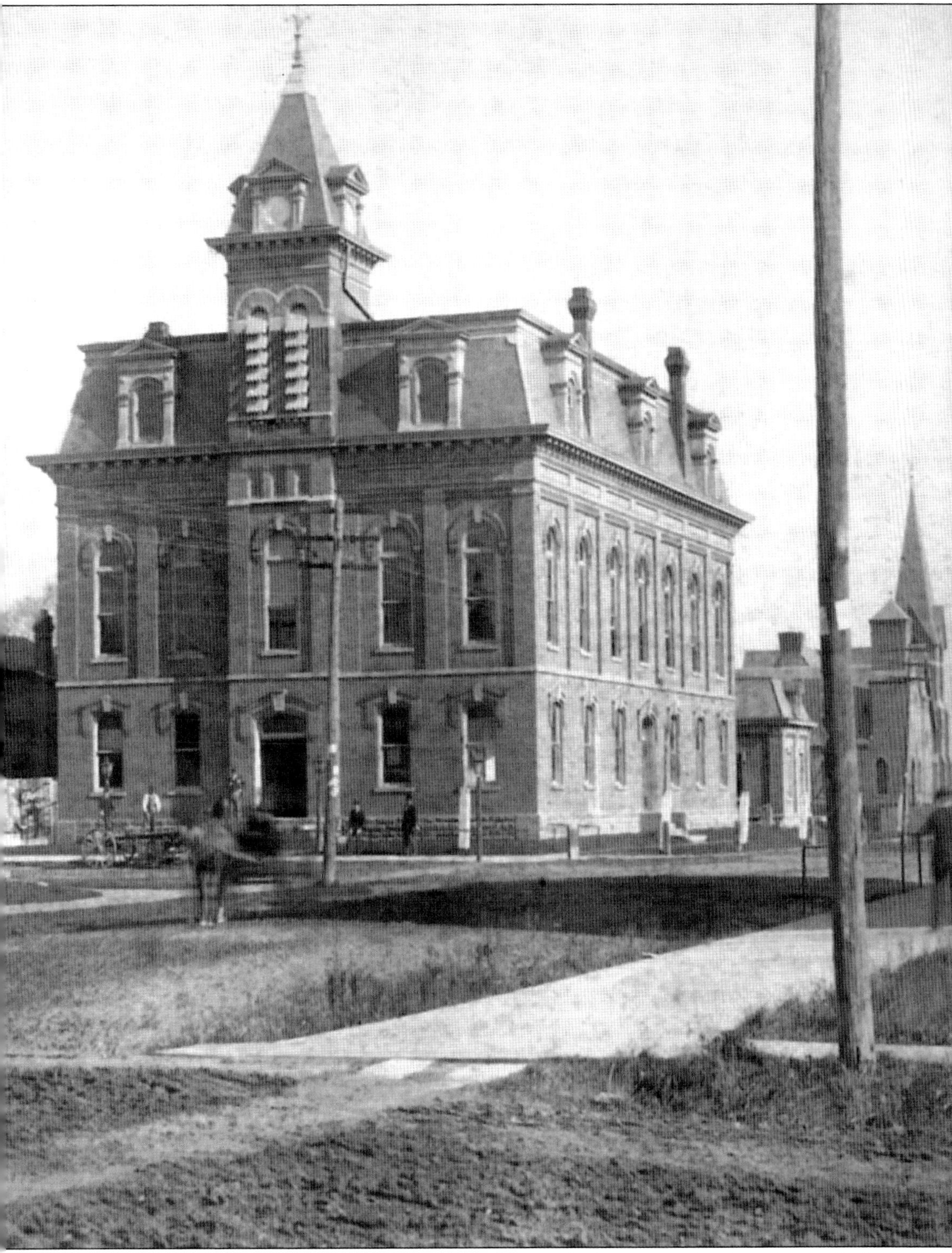

Capt. Henry Kelley donated the funds to add the full-story clock tower to the Milan Town Hall. The rebuilt town hall still stands and remains a center of community activity.

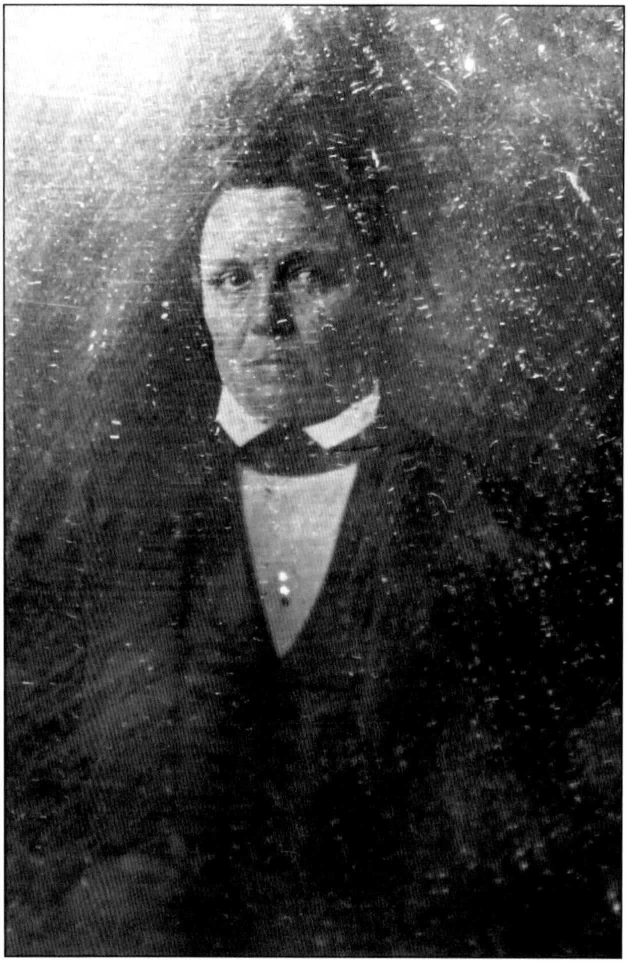

The Rev. Everton Judson came to Milan on October 4, 1829, as a traveler on his way to Marion, Ohio. The following Sunday, he performed a service in Milan and was convinced to stay. In 1835, he married Carrie B. Stuart, first assistant in the female department of the Huron Institute. Reverend Judson was pastor in Milan from 1829 to 1848.

In 1835, a meeting was called by Needham Standart and Reverend Judson for those interested in building a place of worship in Milan. Both members and nonmembers of the Presbyterian church financially supported the project. Construction of the building took two years and cost more than $8,000. Dedication of the structure took place on January 31, 1837.

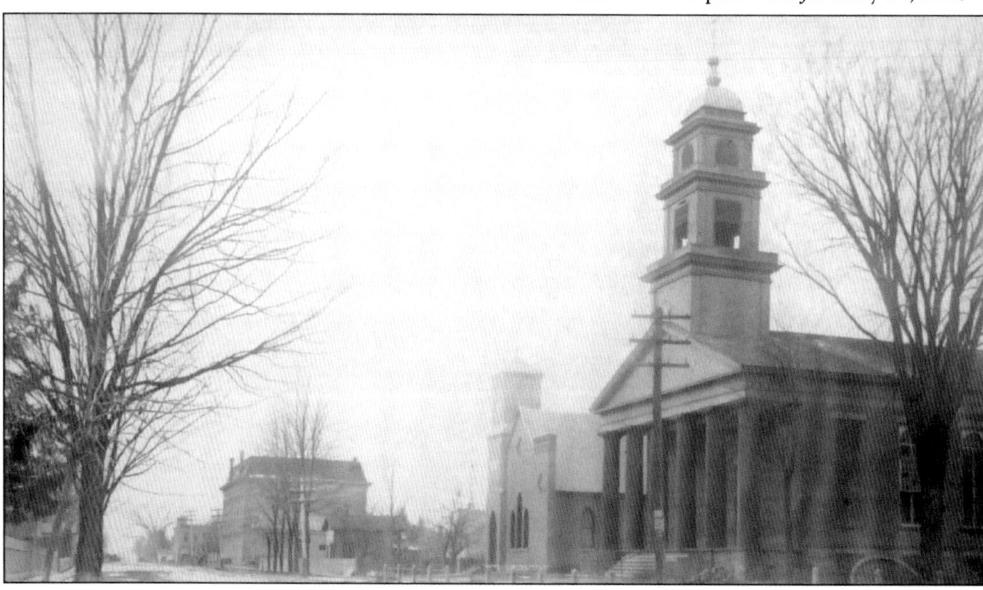

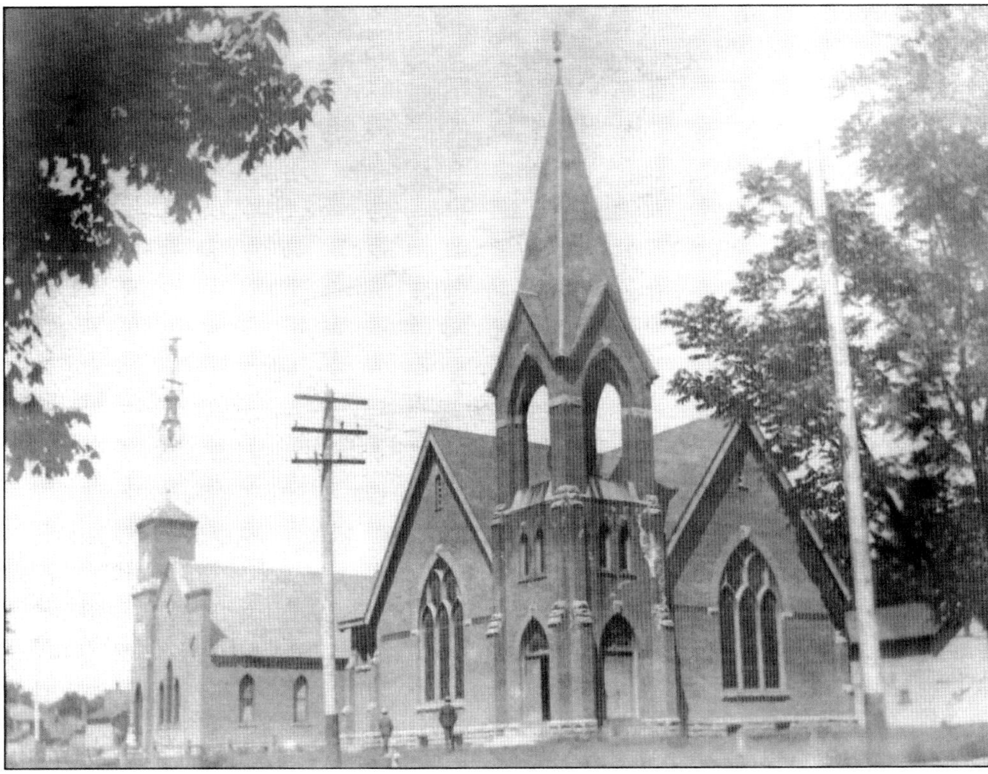

The Presbyterian church was rebuilt after the fire of 1888. A spark in the steeple set fire to the supporting wooden structure, allowing burning wood to fall into the church below. The new church was completed in May 1890.

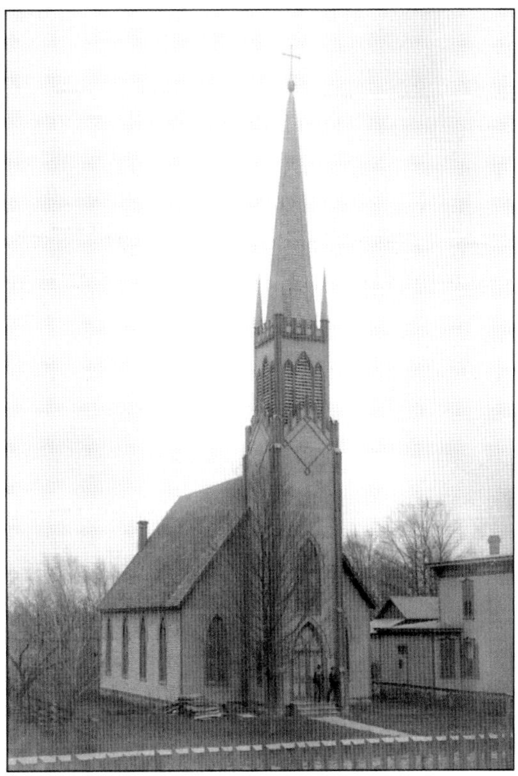

The Protestant Episcopal church was built in 1847 between Merry and Williams Streets. It was destroyed by a fire in 1867, and a new church was built. The church was razed in 1915 when the congregation disbanded.

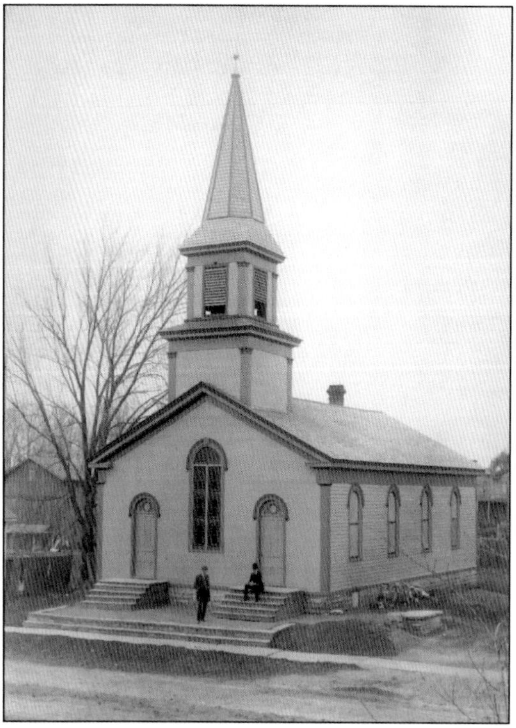

The old Methodist church was built in 1843; it later became the Steeple Mill when the congregation built a brick building at the southwest corner of Center and Church Streets in 1892. The steeple was not added until three years later.

The Methodist church, built in 1892, was destroyed by a fire on Christmas Sunday 1930. For several months, the congregation met in the Presbyterian church chapel and then moved to a space in the Kelly Block while planning the construction of a new church.

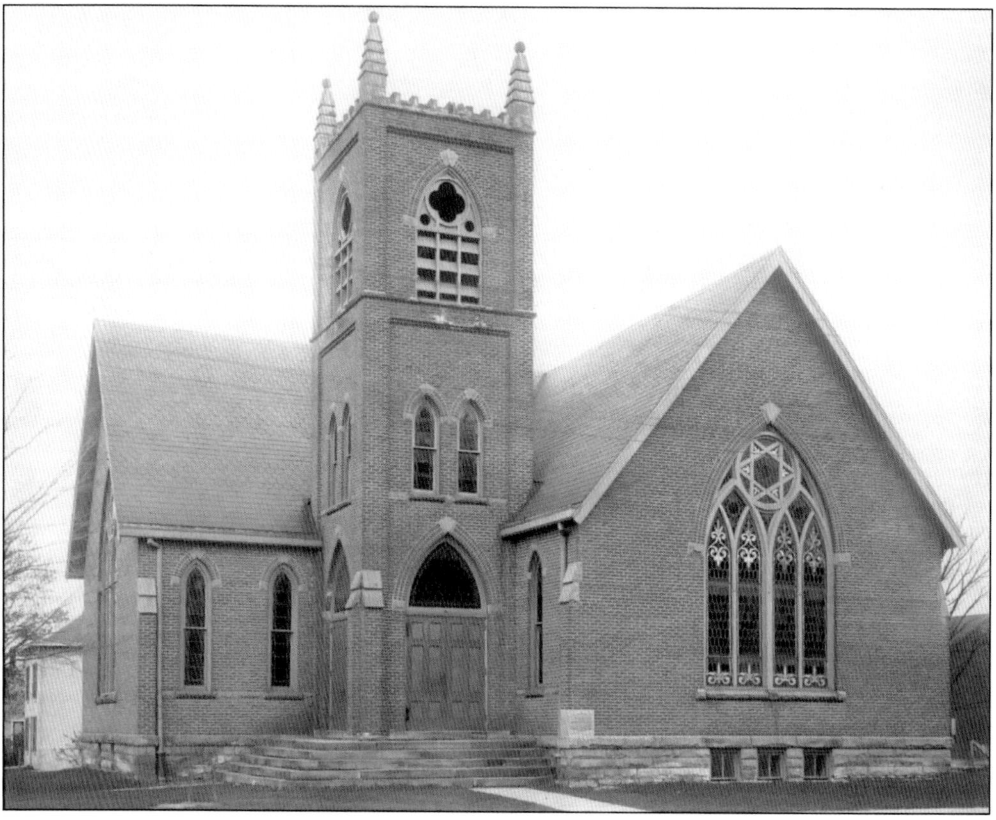

Edith Rausch stands within the burned-out Methodist church after the fire of 1930. The Milan Library can be seen in the background of this photograph, taken in 1931. The Carnegie-endowed library was donated in 1912 and built on land donated by William Galpin and A.L. Hoover.

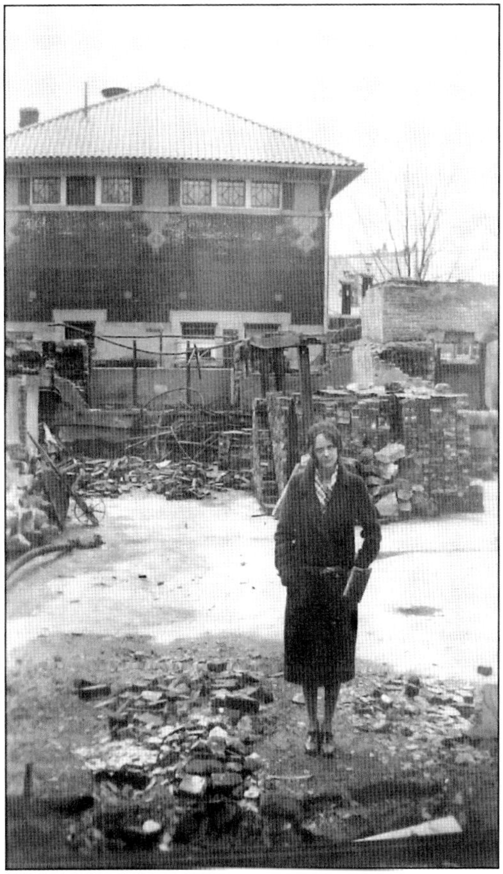

The new Edison Memorial United Methodist Church, built in 1937, is located on the southwest corner of Center and Church Streets. The church is pictured here under construction.

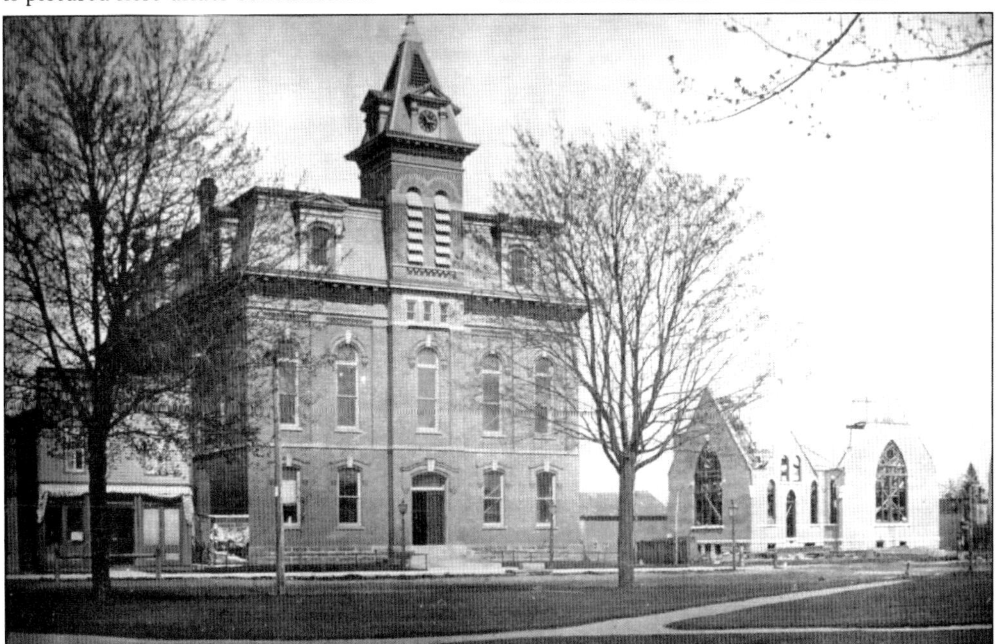

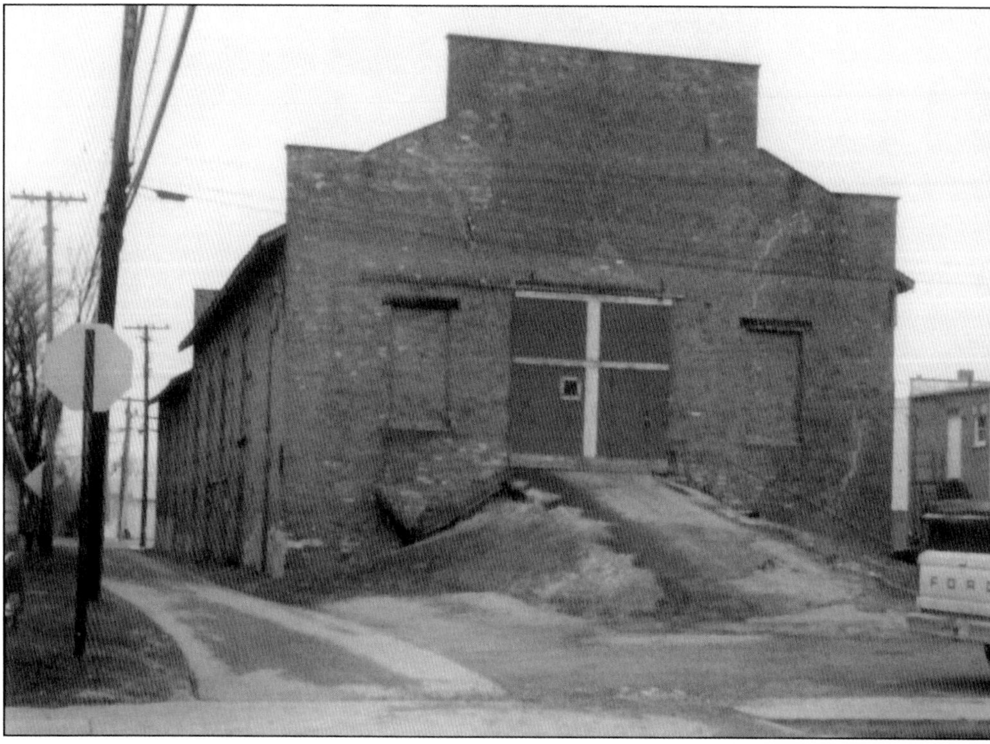

The Seventh-day Adventist temple was built in 1849 by George Lockwood and known as Lockwood Temple. Construction of the temple included a hall and stage for the group's meetings.

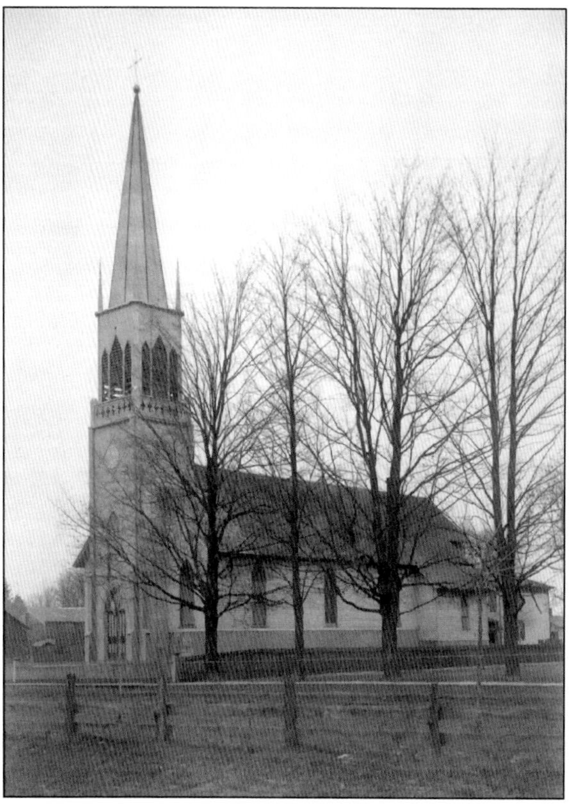

The property for St. Anthony's Catholic Church was purchased in 1862, and the home on the site was remodeled into a school and temporary worship site. Construction began on the church in 1866; it was dedicated to St. Anthony of Padua on November 16 of that year.

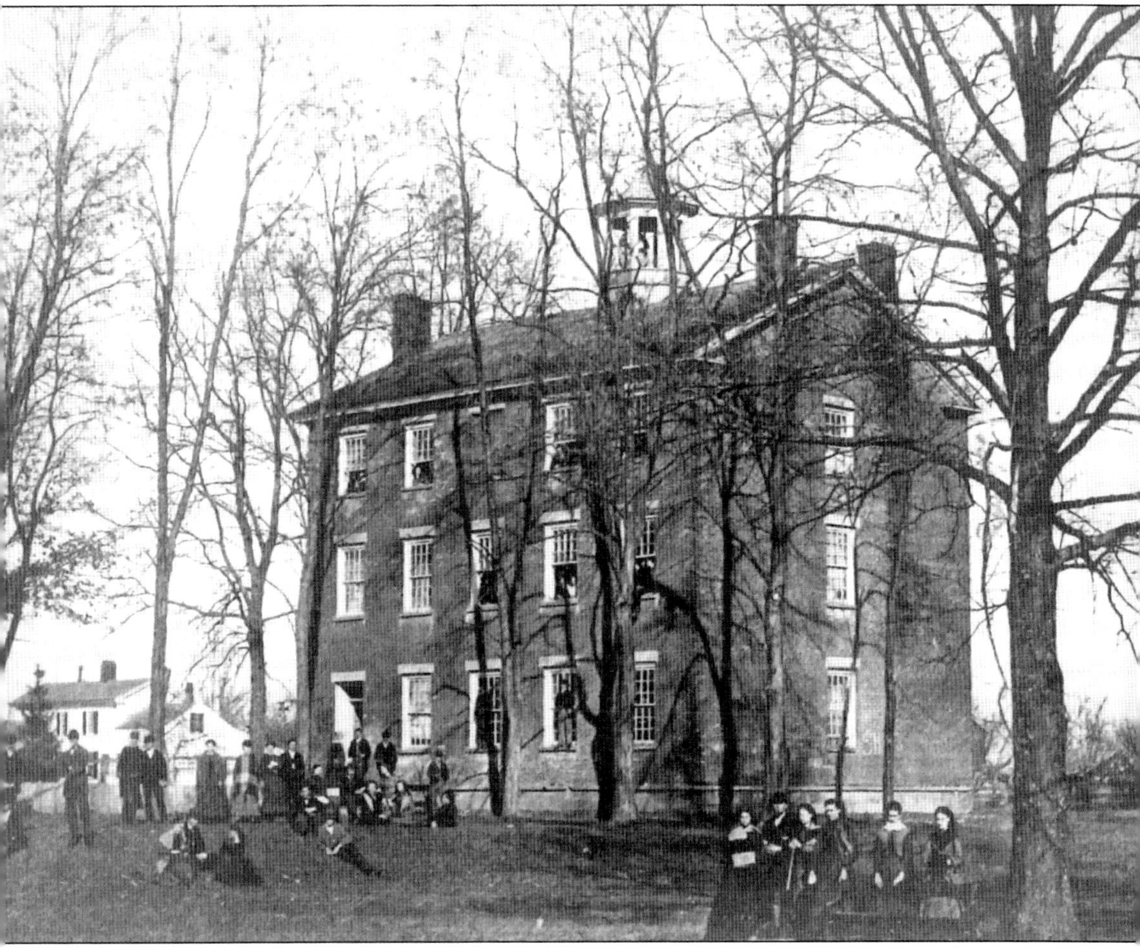

The Huron Institute was formed by the Huron Presbytery due to the need to have higher education. In 1831–1832, the Ohio legislature incorporated the Huron Institute, and the Rev. Everton Judson convinced the community to raise $2,000 of the $4,000 needed. In 1858, the name changed to the Western Reserve Normal School and it operated as an institute for preparing teachers for classroom work.

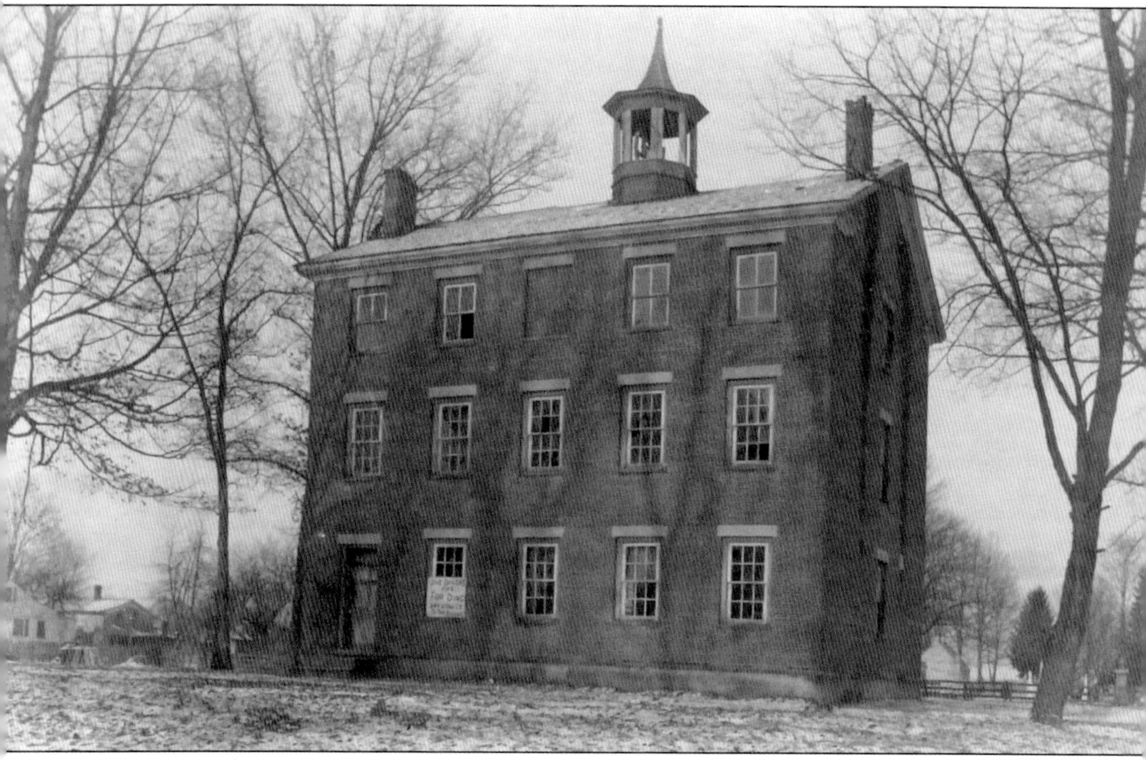

Tuition was $4 per quarter for the classical courses and $3 per quarter for the English and French departments. It was reported that no prospective student was turned away due to lack of funds. In 1867, attendance records show a roster of 179 gentlemen and 129 ladies. Visible here is a board in a window stating, "Five dollar fine for doing any damage to this building."

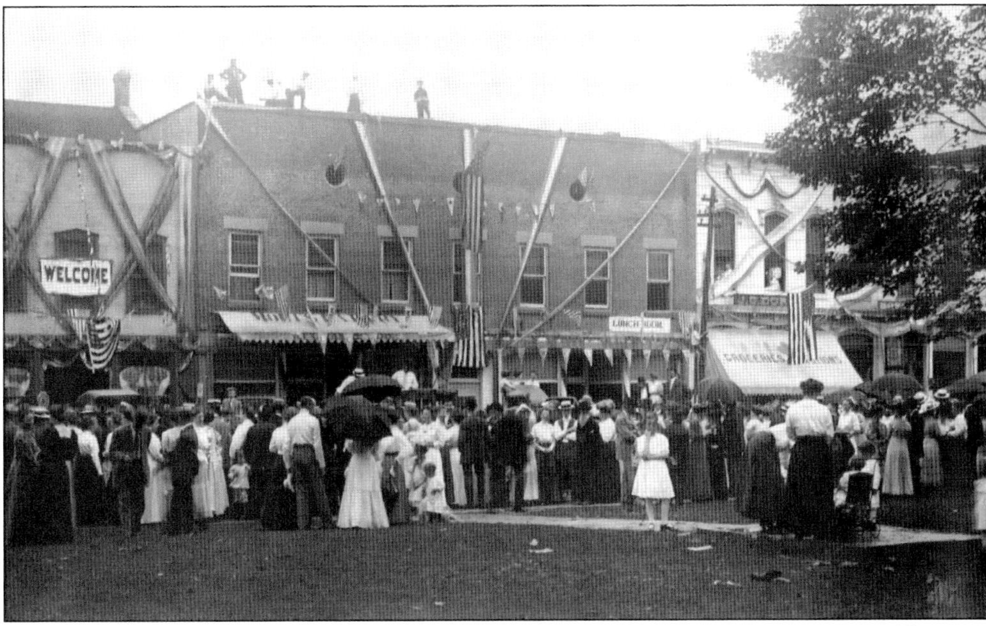

The school operated until its closing in March 1889. On January 30, 1909, it was sold to T.R. Washburn for $131.80. Its razing in 1910 was cause for the Milan homecoming and normal school reunion celebration pictured here. A boulder now marks the location of the school by the entrance to the Milan Cemetery.

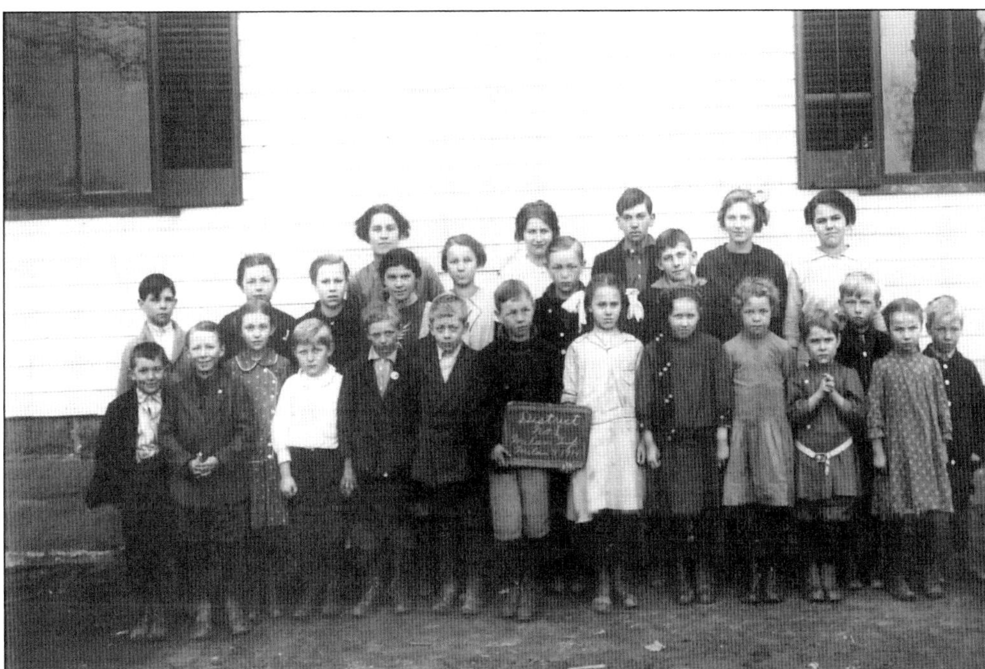

The Milan Township District No. 1 schoolhouse was known as the Petersburgh School. The first school in Milan was located in a log Moravian church, but it was replaced with the Old Yellow School at the corner of Huron and Church Streets.

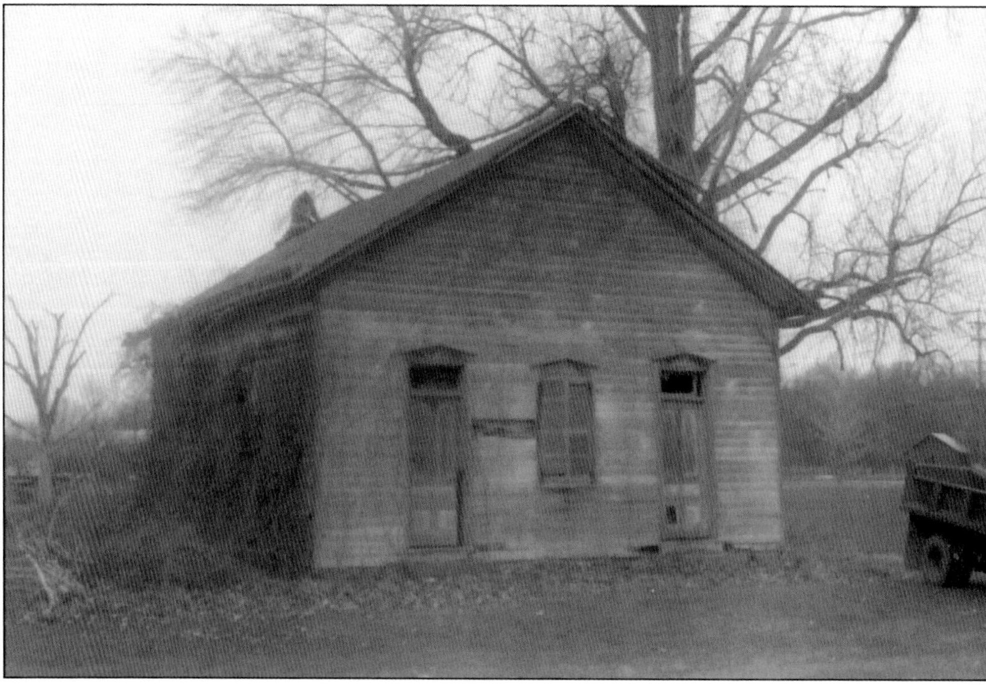

Pictured here is the North Milan School No. 8 prior to its razing. The Old Yellow School served as both a school and a meeting place for the Methodist and Presbyterian congregations until the building could no longer accommodate their numbers.

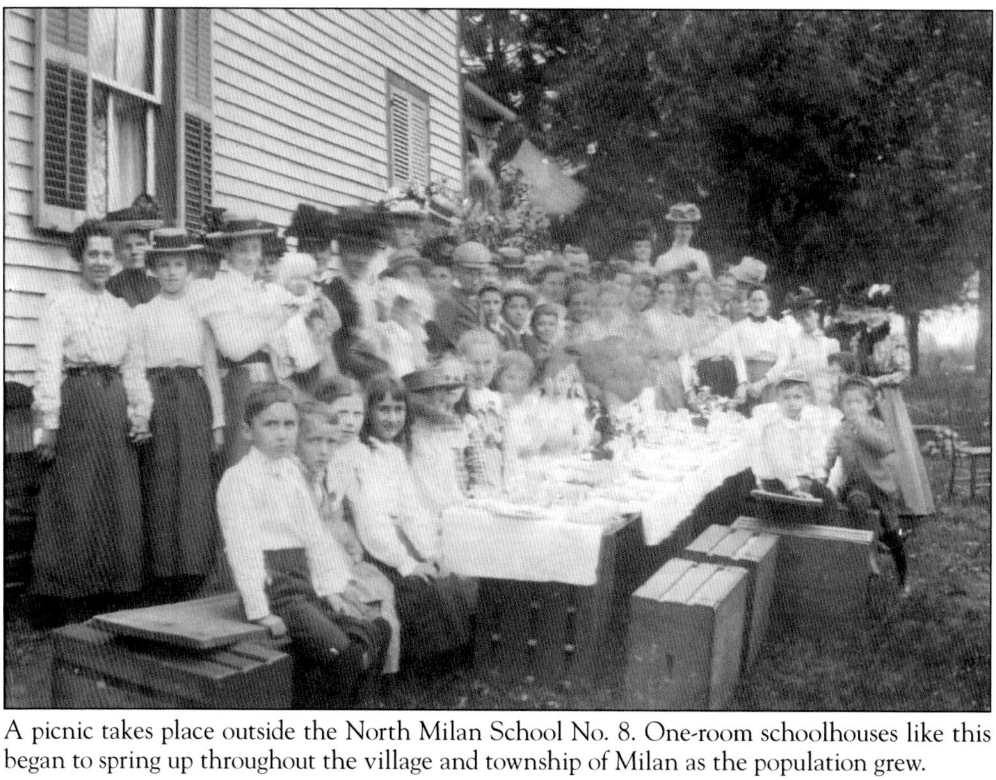

A picnic takes place outside the North Milan School No. 8. One-room schoolhouses like this began to spring up throughout the village and township of Milan as the population grew.

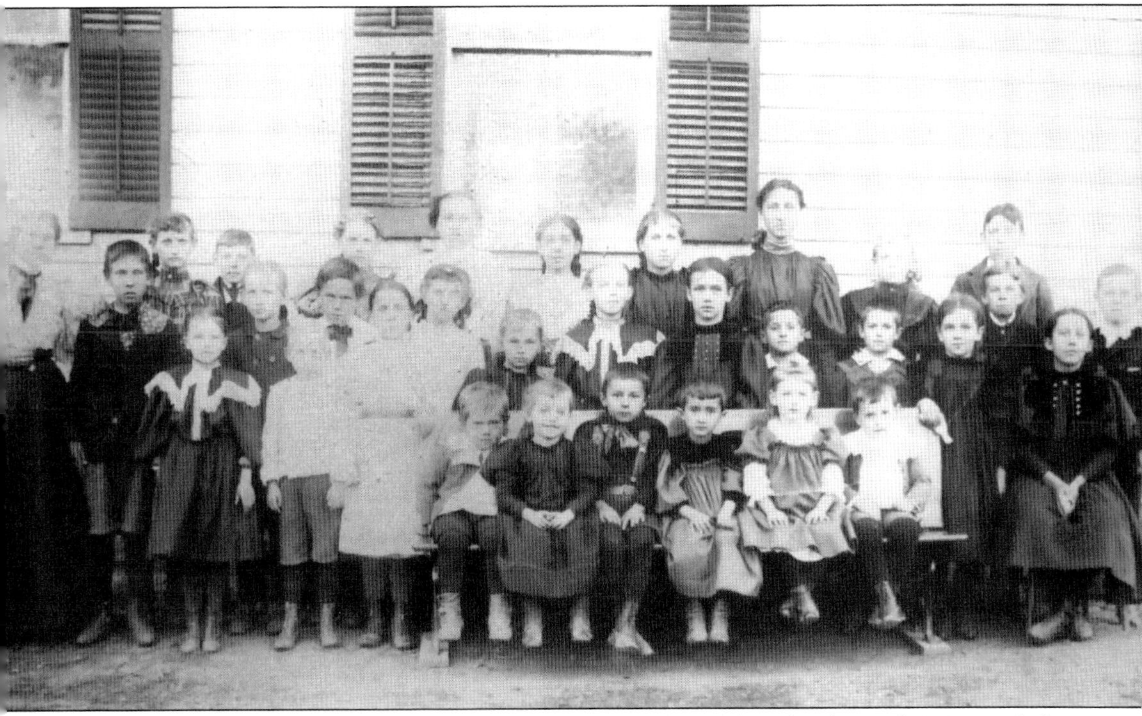

Schoolchildren pose beside the North Milan School No. 8. The Public School Act of 1849 provided state-funded support and supervision of schools. The result was the building of the Union School on Center Street in Milan in 1850.

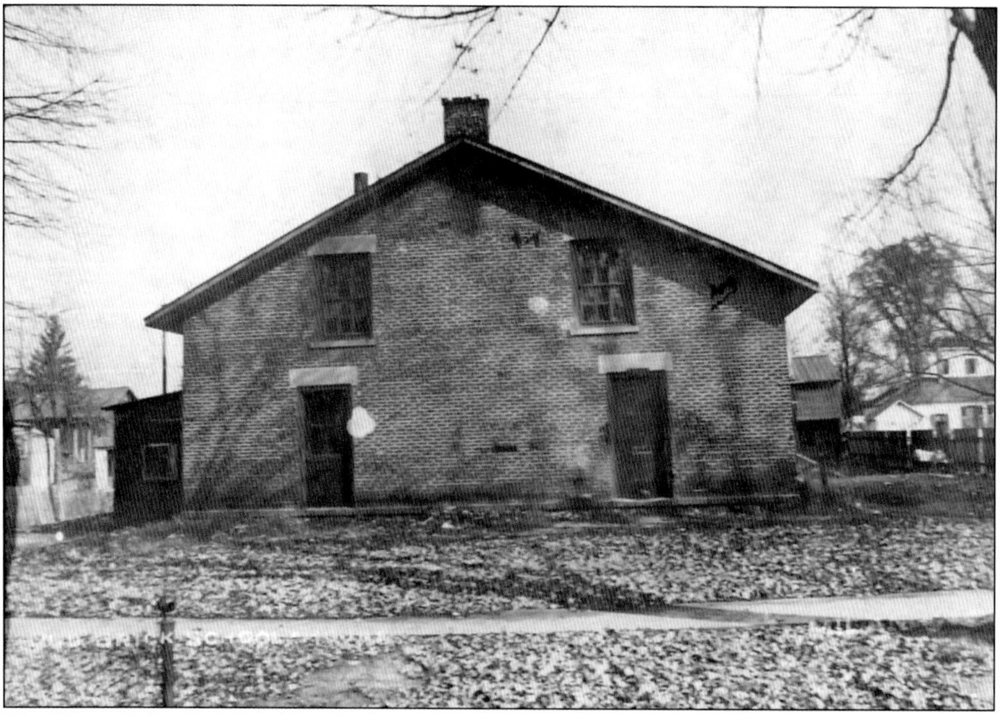

The Union School was built on the land across Center Street from the present Edison Elementary School. The building was later sold to Steven Lockwood and turned into a baseball bat factory.

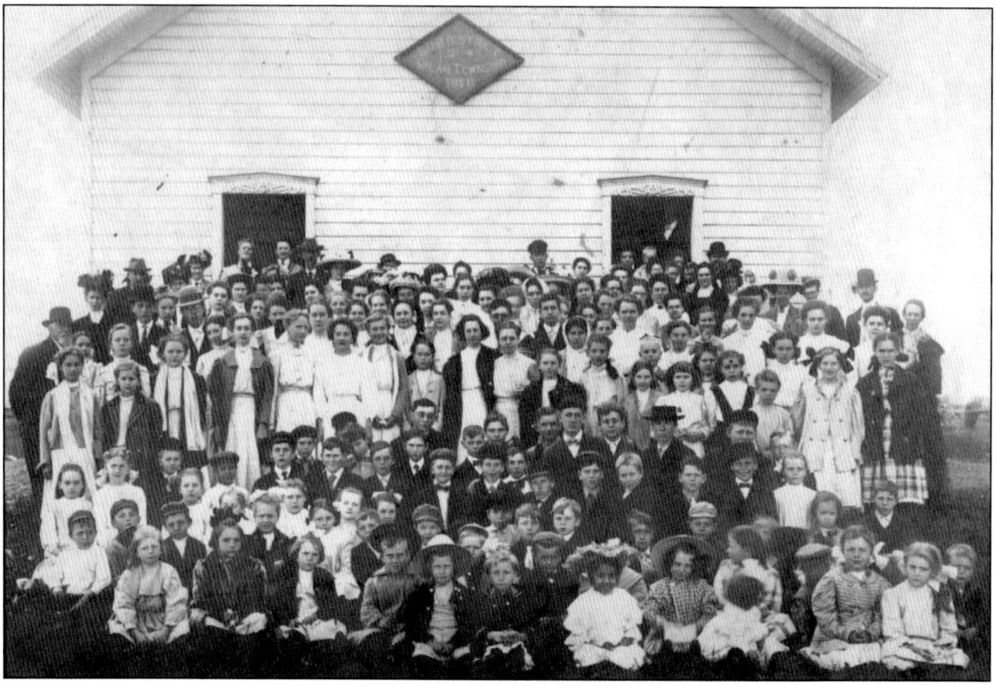

The Pages Corner School is in the background of this class photograph taken around 1910. Marion Edison Page, sister to Thomas Edison, married Homer Page and lived on a farm at the junction of Mason Road and State Route 13 known as Pages Corner.

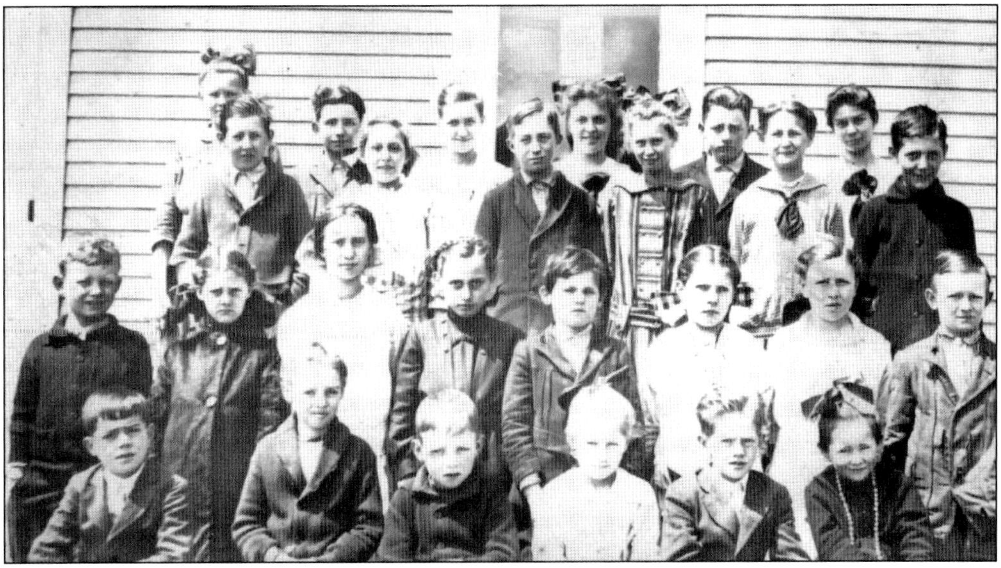

Pictured here in the late 1910s, the Merry Schoolhouse was located on Thomas Road in Oxford Township. It was the original meeting place of the Saint John's Lutheran congregation prior to the construction of the church at Union Corners.

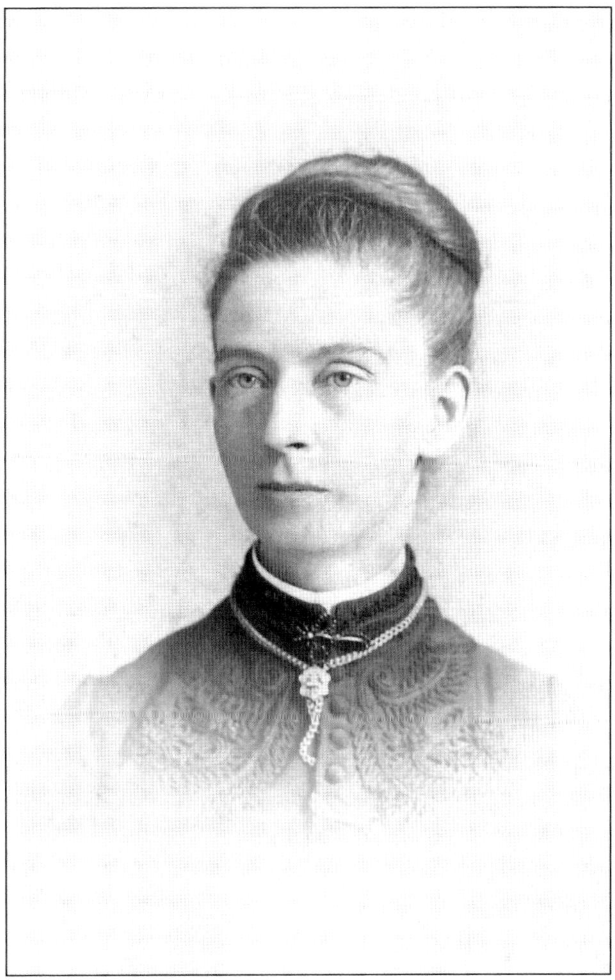

This portrait shows Milan schoolteacher Reta Traub around 1888. By this time, teaching was a socially approved profession for women, giving many the opportunity to earn an independent income.

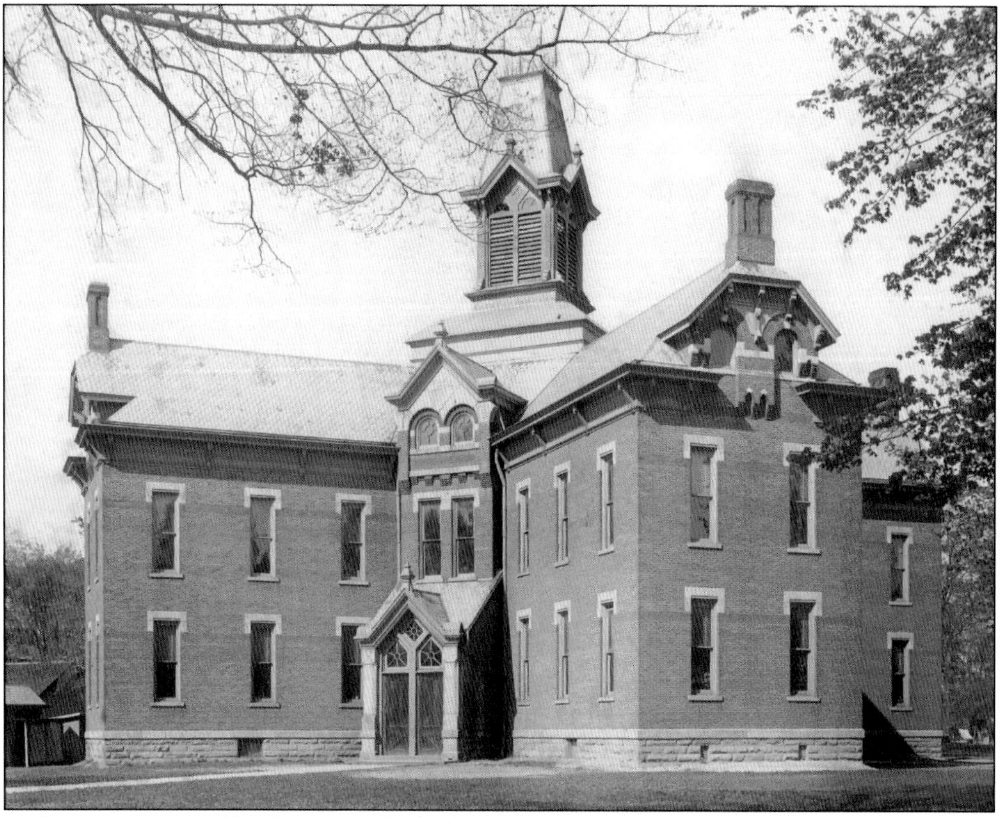

In 1884, the Milan Public School was built where the present Edison Elementary School is located. The building was replaced in 1922, and additions were added in 1953 and 1958.

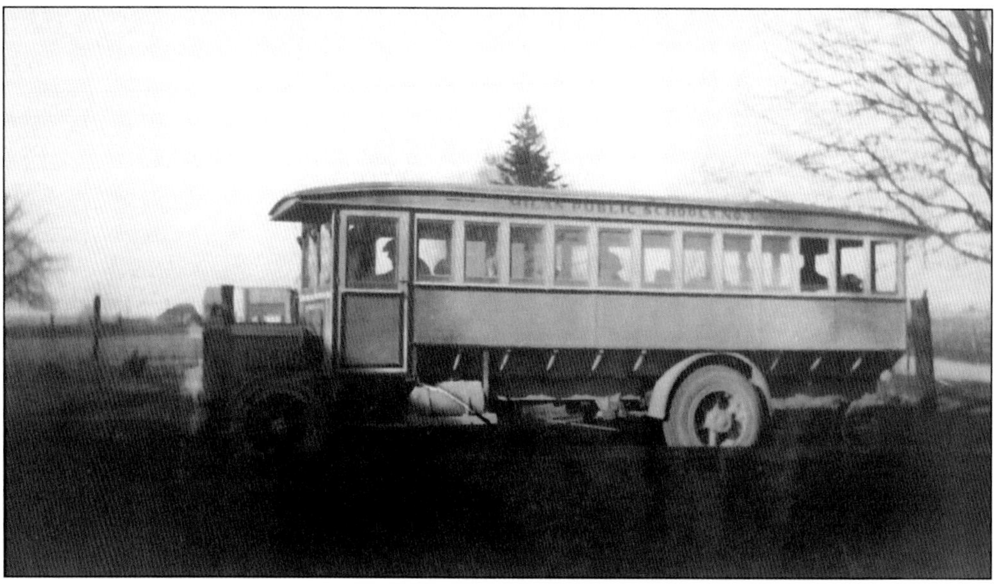

Milan public school bus no. 3 drives through muddy roads. Before motorized school transportation, schools used horse-drawn wagons with the entry-exit point at the rear so as to not startle the horses. This was possibly a precursor to the rear emergency exit doors on modern school buses.

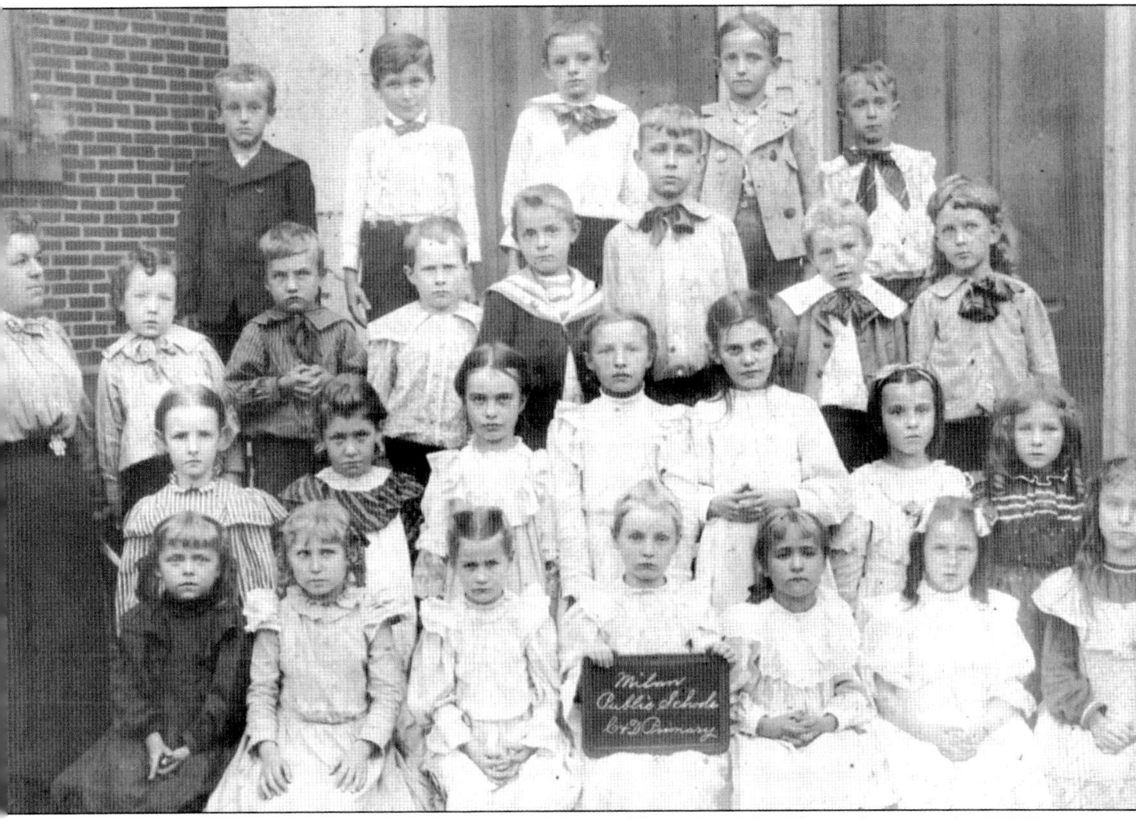

This class photograph was taken outside the Milan Public School building, showing the C&D primary class. In 1965, the school districts of Milan and Berlin were combined to create the Berlin-Milan Local School District, now Edison Local Schools. The site is now used as Edison Elementary School.

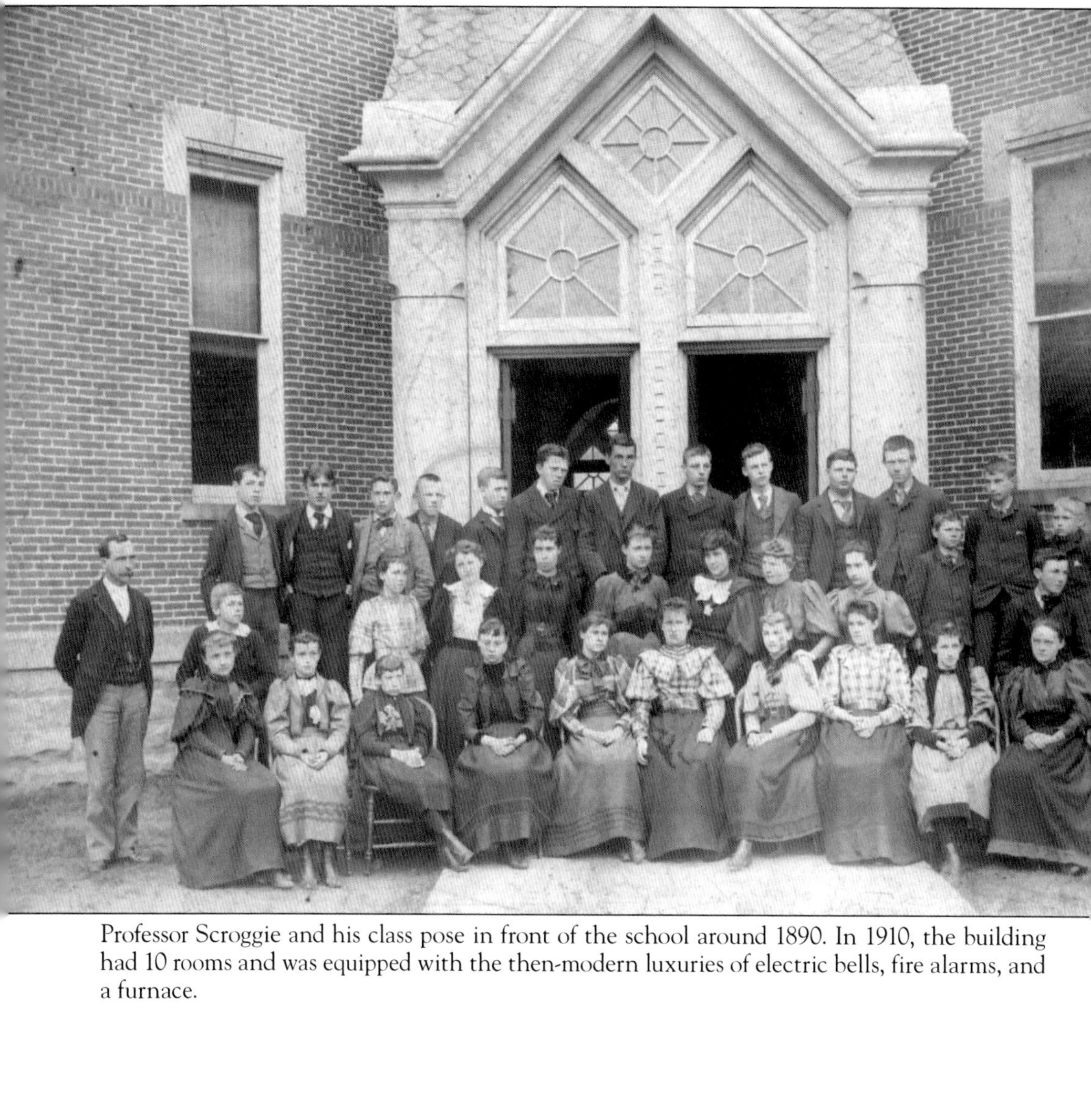

Professor Scroggie and his class pose in front of the school around 1890. In 1910, the building had 10 rooms and was equipped with the then-modern luxuries of electric bells, fire alarms, and a furnace.

Three

The Milan Canal and Shipbuilding

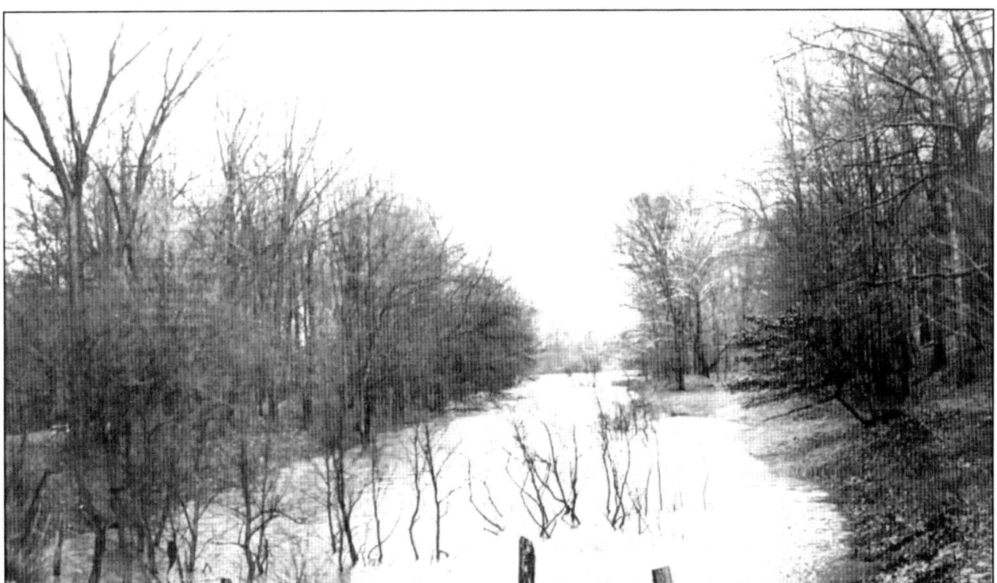

The forming of the Milan Canal began because the area of wheat-growing land in north central Ohio had marginal access to mills and markets. It was only three miles to the north that the Huron River became navigable to Lake Erie for moderate draft vessels. Water travel was faster with less cost and waste for farmers. This is a view of part of the Milan Canal.

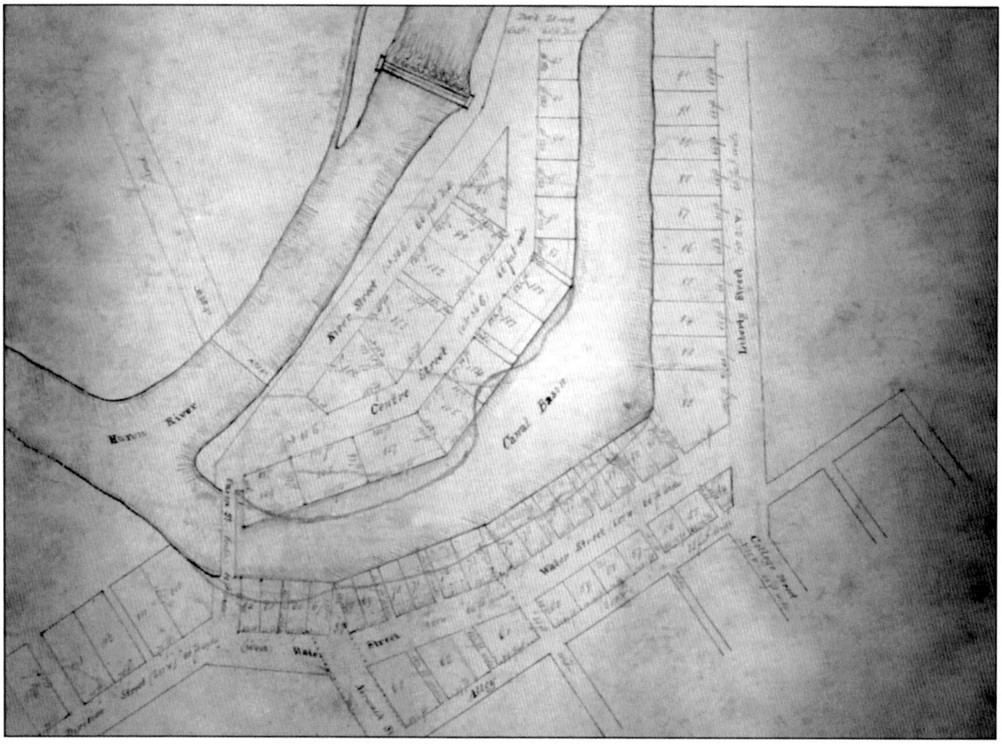

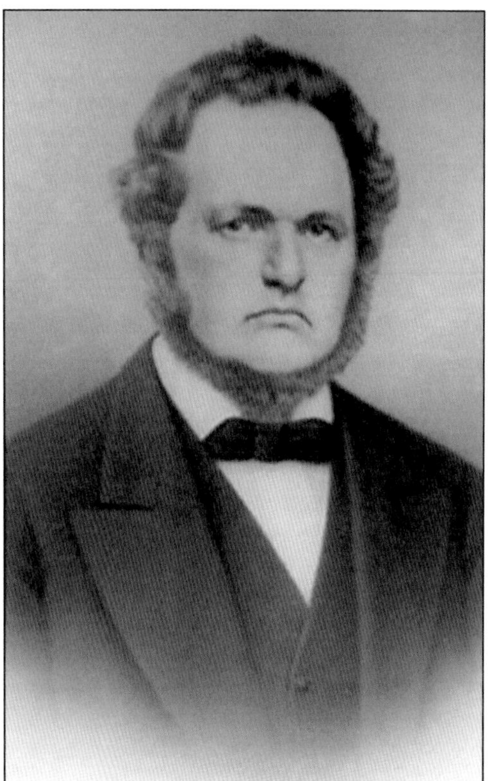

Shoaling at the inlet of the Huron River resulted in the formation of the Huron Harbor Company in 1823. Citizens from both Milan and Huron jointly addressed the problem to improve the harbor for lake vessels. In 1824, interested citizens of Milan commissioned a canal feasibility survey for sloop navigation for the three miles connecting Milan to the Huron River. This resulted in the idea that the gentle natural bend in the river would be turned into the basin while the original location of Merry's millrace would be the new river course.

In 1823, Byron Kilbourn secured an appointment as an Ohio state surveyor, and for 10 years he was active in surveying canal routes in the state. In October 1833, Kilbourn was hired as the project engineer for the Milan Canal, but he left Milan in April 1834 after having been paid $500. A towpath was constructed along the west bank of the canal to pull ships down its length to the turning basin at Milan. The original estimate for construction was $5,800. (Courtesy of the Wisconsin Historical Society, WHS-62389.)

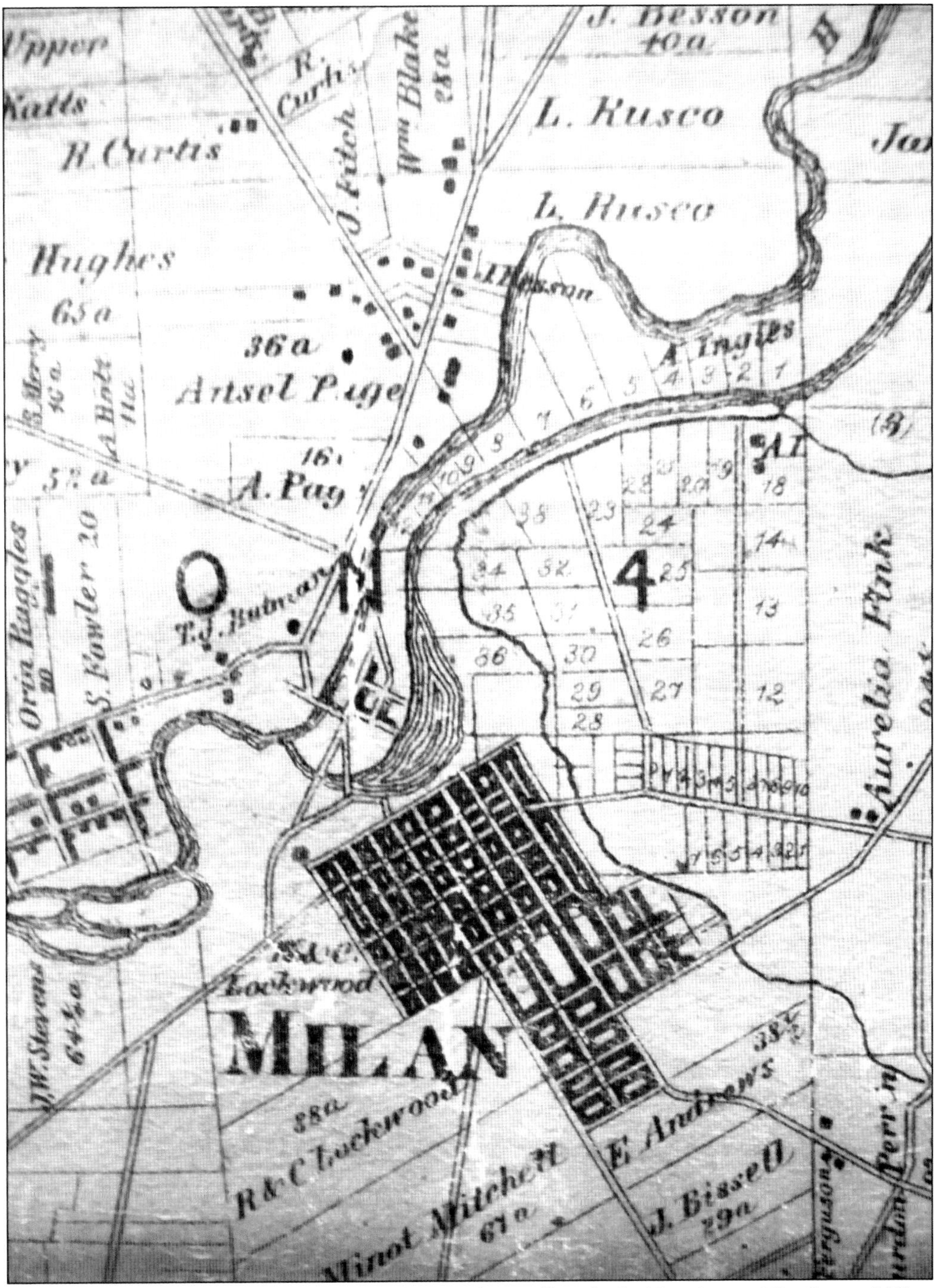

This Nunan Map shows the entrance to the canal as well as the holding basin. The State of Ohio granted a charter in 1827 with stock offerings of $35,000 at $50 a share. Funds were hard to come by, as six years passed before they entered into a construction contract for the three mile canal. By 1839, another 800 shares had been sold, with the state owning 500 ($25,000) and loaning an additional $15,000. When finished, the Milan Canal cost over 15 times the original estimate.

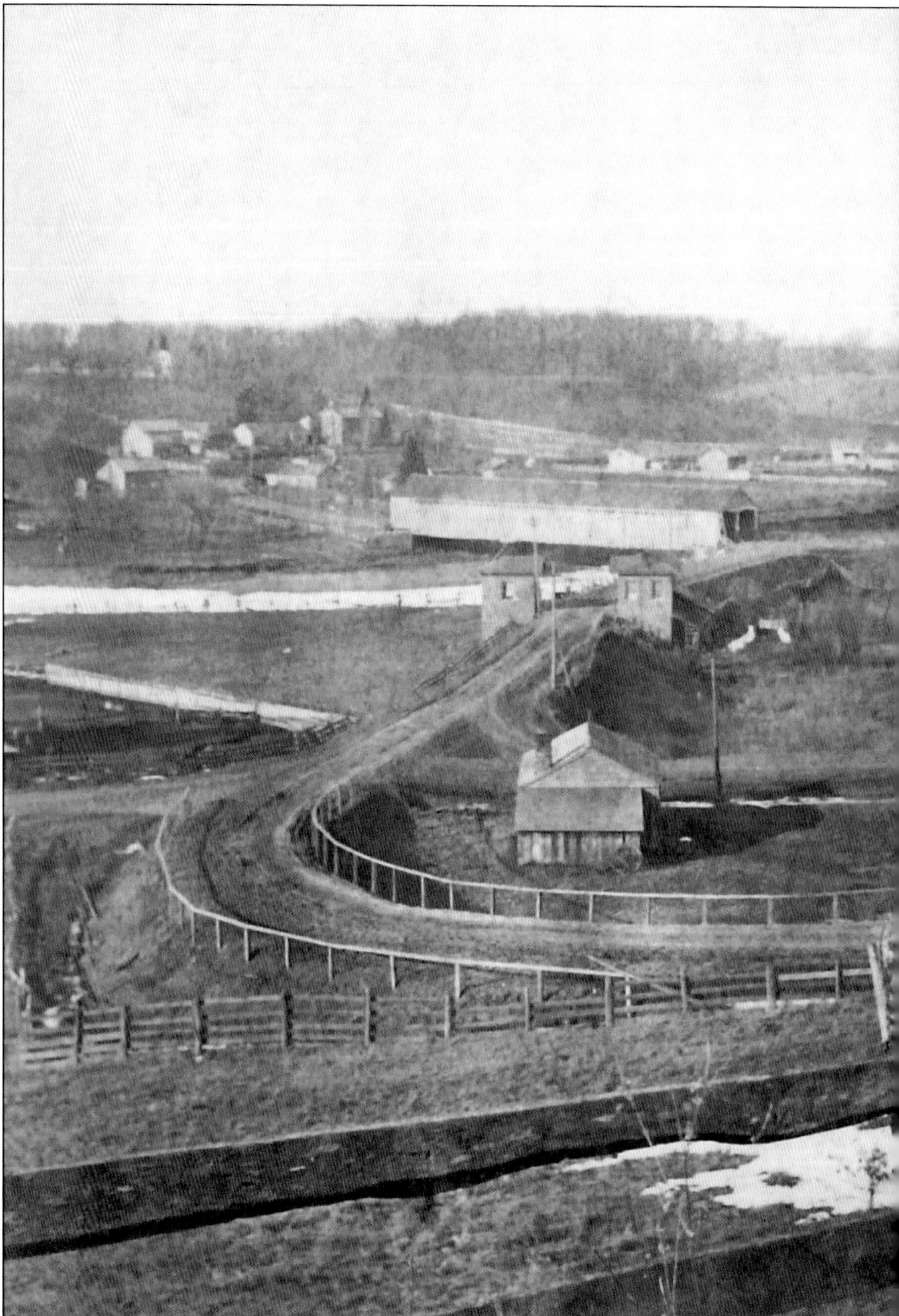

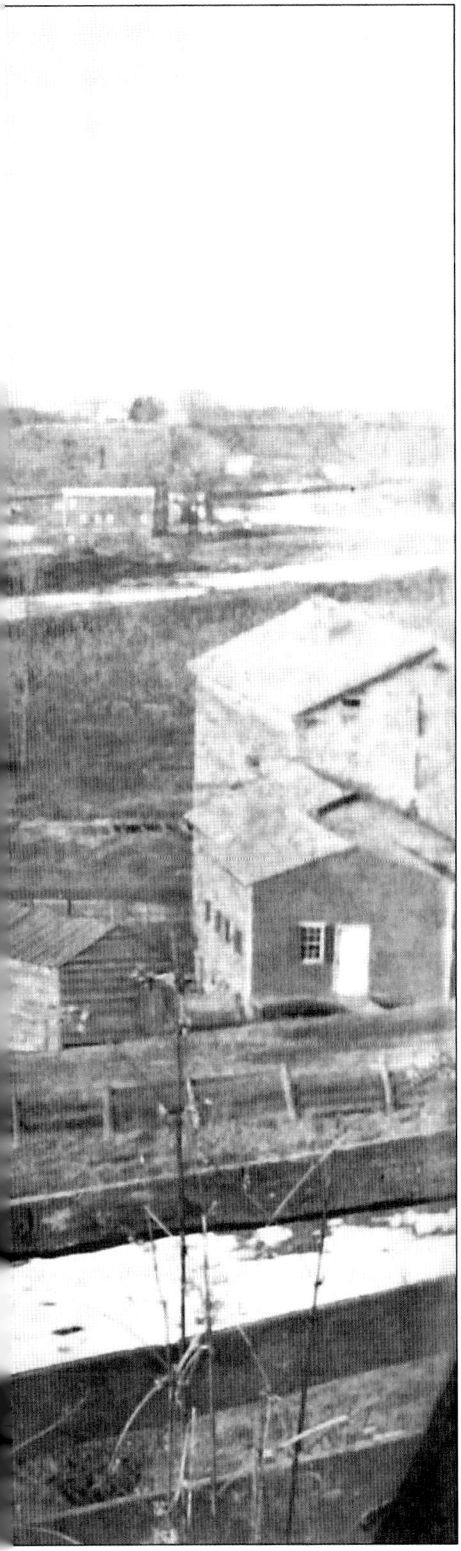

In 1836, a covered bridge was built over the Huron River, which remained until 1882 when an iron bridge replaced it. The area between the basin and the new river course was the shipyard and loading dock.

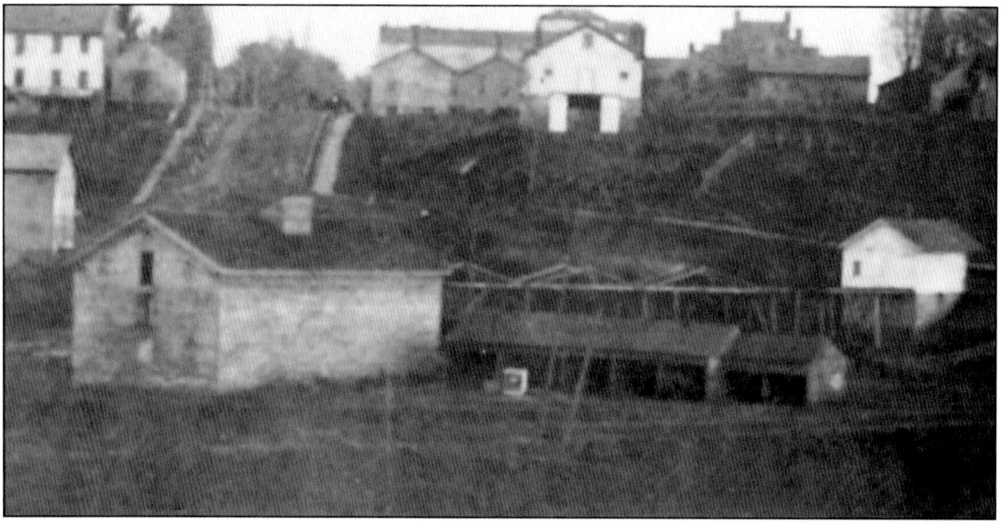

The Milan Canal opened for lake travel on July 4, 1839. The fertile soil of the area, a canal deep enough for lake ships, and the connection to the Erie Canal and New York City made the Milan Canal an instant success. Warehouses soon lined the canal basin at the foot of the hill at Milan, capable of storing 400,000 bushels of wheat. An ingenious system was devised by businessman George Lockwood to get the grain from the farmers' wagons on the roadway up the hill to ships waiting by the wharves at the base of the hill. It was done with small railroad cars elevated on timbers that ran from the receiving offices to the upper floors of the warehouses.

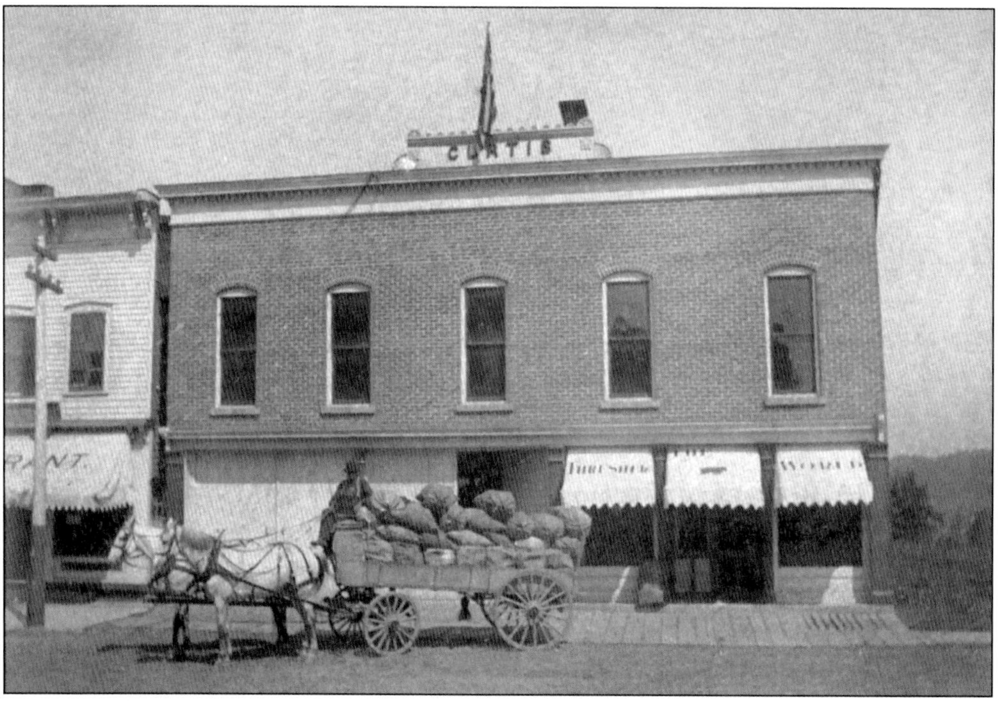

The original canal basin was designed to be 1,200 feet long by 300 feet wide to accommodate the ever-larger lake vessels. The initial study showed a slope of seven to eight feet with two sets of locks and a dam to divert river water into the canal. In 1845, due to the growing size of the ships, the canal and basin were deepened to seven feet for the passage of larger vessels.

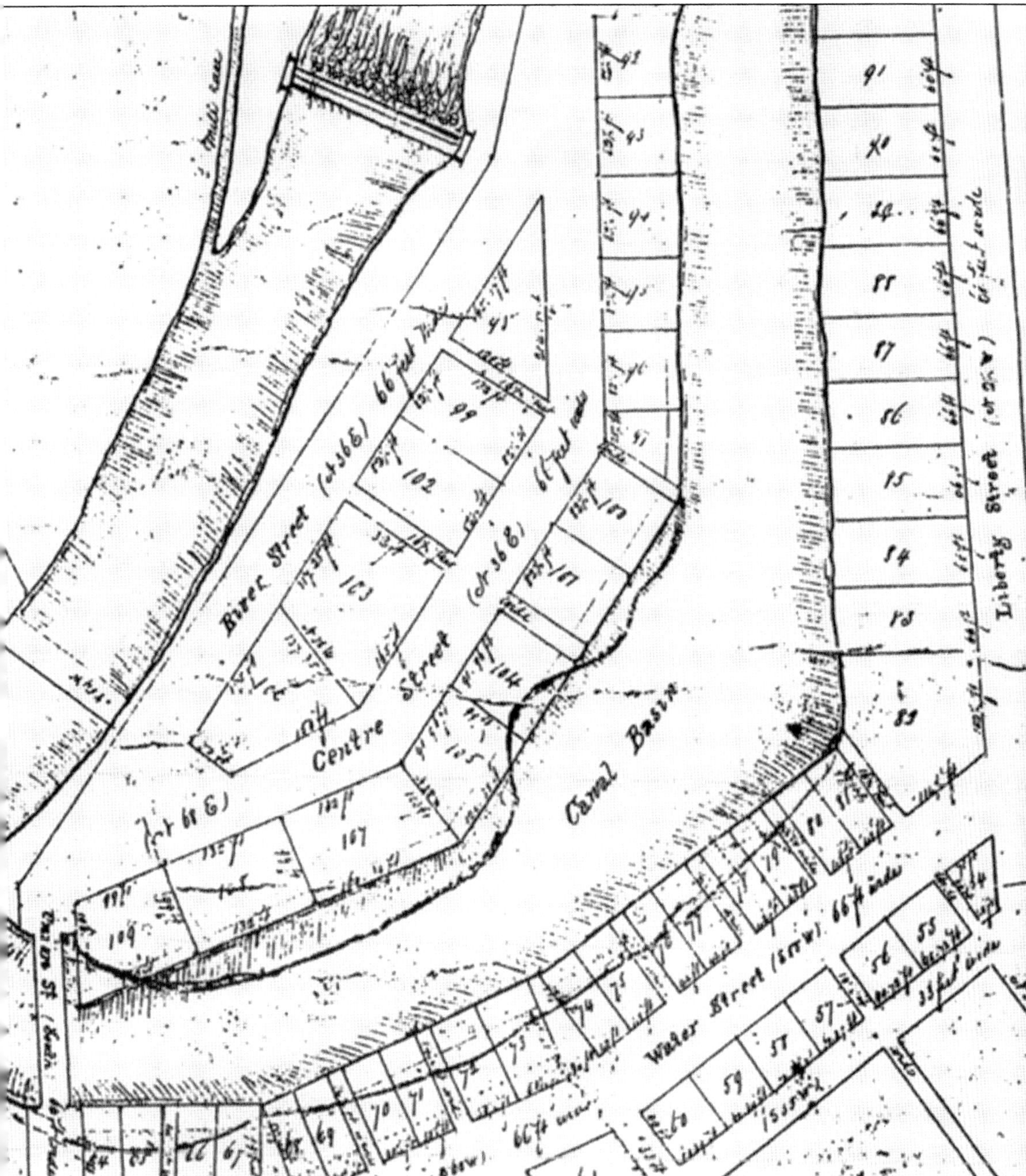

Early on, ships were built north of Milan at Abbott's Landing. The location was significant to the further planning of a canal, as the Huron River was proven navigable to this point. Between 1827 and 1828, the schooner *Mary Abbott* was built and navigated to New York City from this location. During that same period, the schooner *Louisa Jenkins* was constructed at Lockwood Landing. By 1840, the shipbuilding center had moved to the northern side of the new canal basin. It had two streets, a loading dock, and 18 lots.

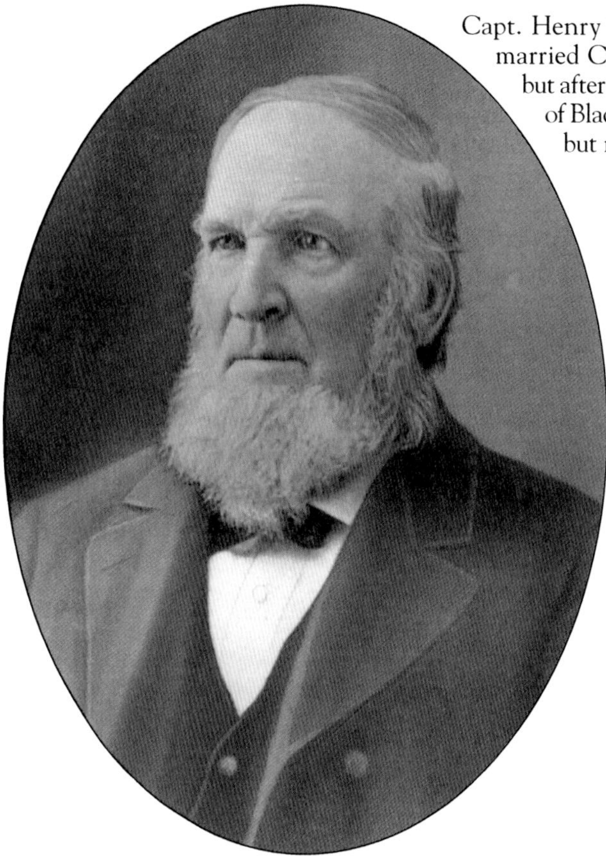

Capt. Henry Kelley was born March 1, 1816. He married Caroline Young of Buffalo, New York, but after her passing, he married Betsey A. Jones of Black River, Ohio. They had four children, but none survived into adulthood.

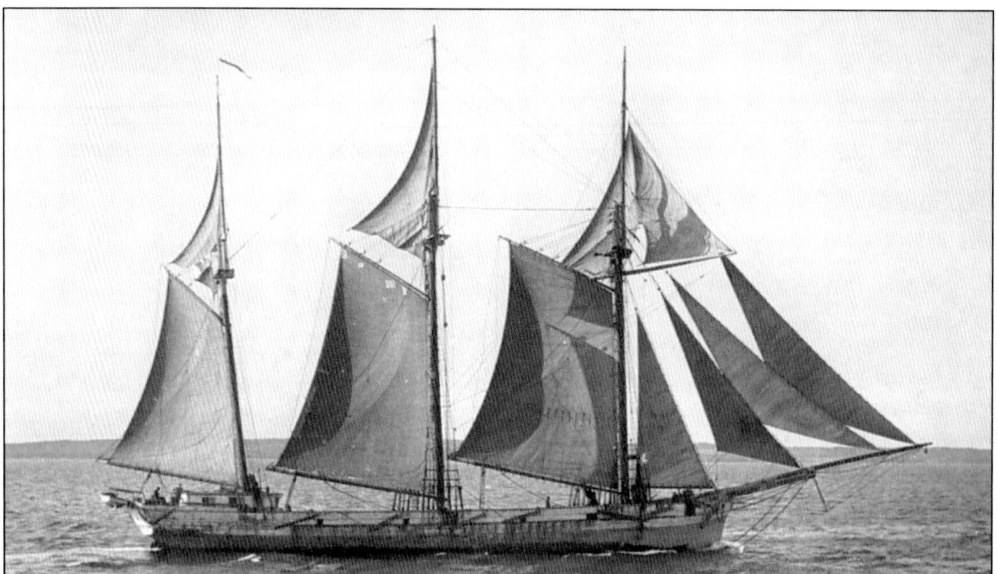

The schooner *Our Son* was built in 1871 by Capt. Henry Kelley. The ship was named after his deceased son Devillo. Captain Kelley and his wife, Betsey, adopted their son Frank when he was a little over the age of one.

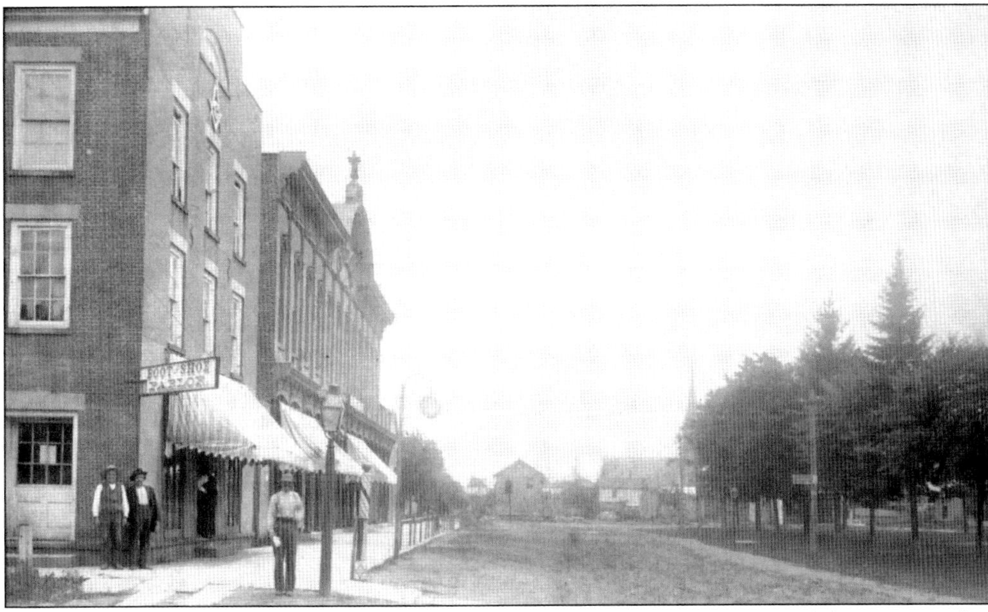

The Kelley Block was built by Capt. Henry Kelley in 1869–1870. The front of the structure has cast-iron Corinthian columns and window cornices. The building remains one of Milan's iconic architectural structures.

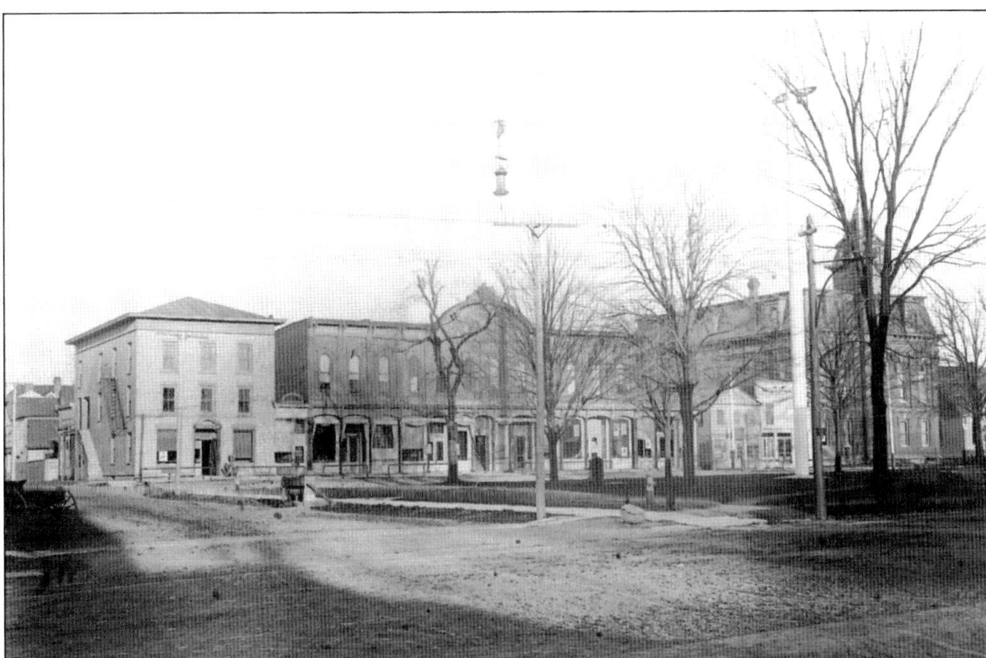

Henry Kelley died on May 8, 1903, at the age of 87. During his lifetime he served as mayor of Milan and as Erie County commissioner, and was one of Milan's most philanthropic citizens.

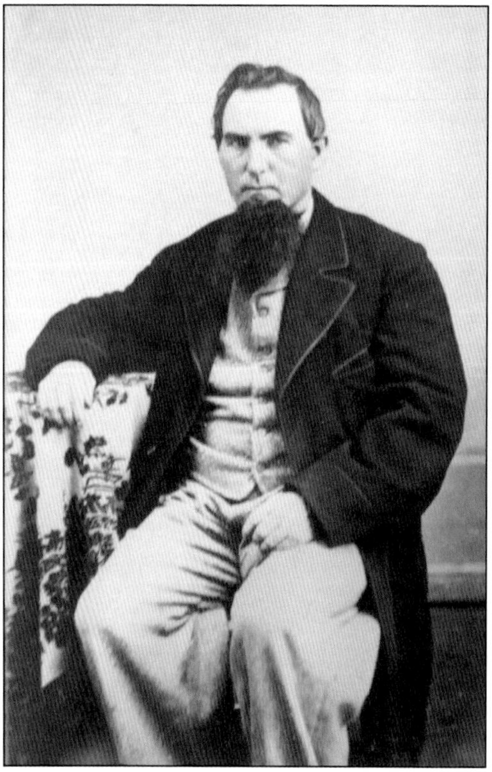

Captain Moran is best known as the captain of the schooner *Kewanee*, the ship that helped celebrate the opening of the Milan Canal and the Port of Milan on July 4, 1839.

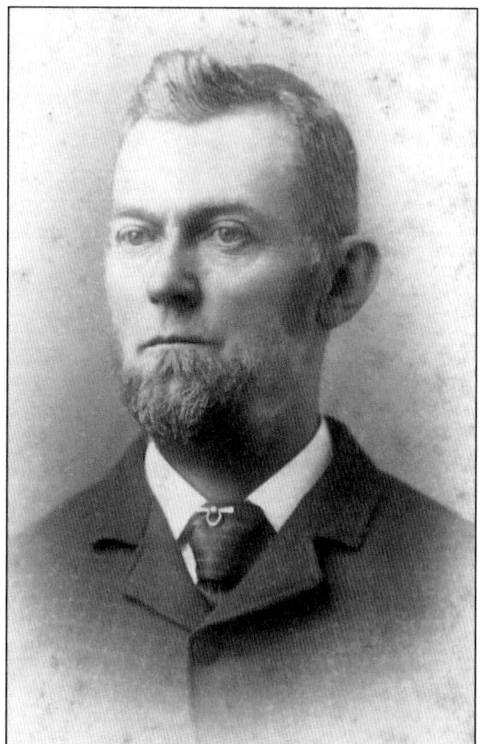

Shortly after the opening of the Milan Canal, industrious men began taking advantage of the natural supply of white oak in the area. The shipbuilding industry that had been centralized at Abbott's Landing was moved to the canal basin. Capt. John Coulter (pictured) had a large home located on South Center Street in Milan.

Capt. Hugh Hastings was the son of Robert and Helen (Johnson) Hastings. His father was of Irish descent and his mother of Scottish. He was a well-known lake captain and died on December 3, 1914. This photograph shows him as a young man.

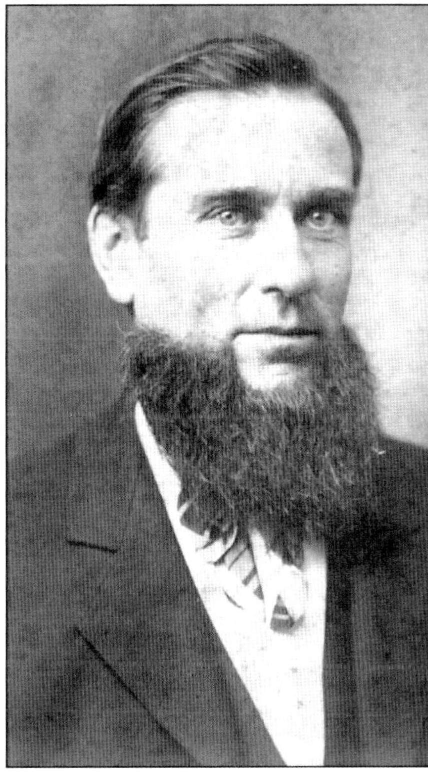

An older Capt. Hugh Hastings sits with his wife, Elizabeth. Elizabeth Hastings died in her home in Milan on September 21, 1920. Her obituary states that she was a former school teacher and "a woman of unusual intelligence."

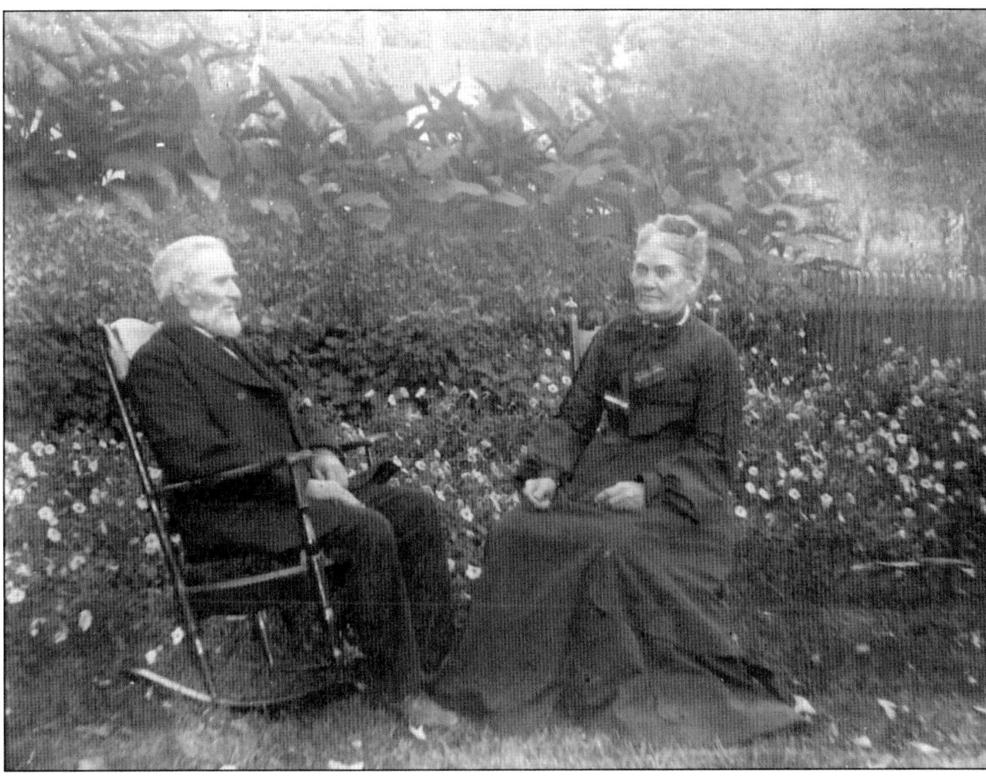

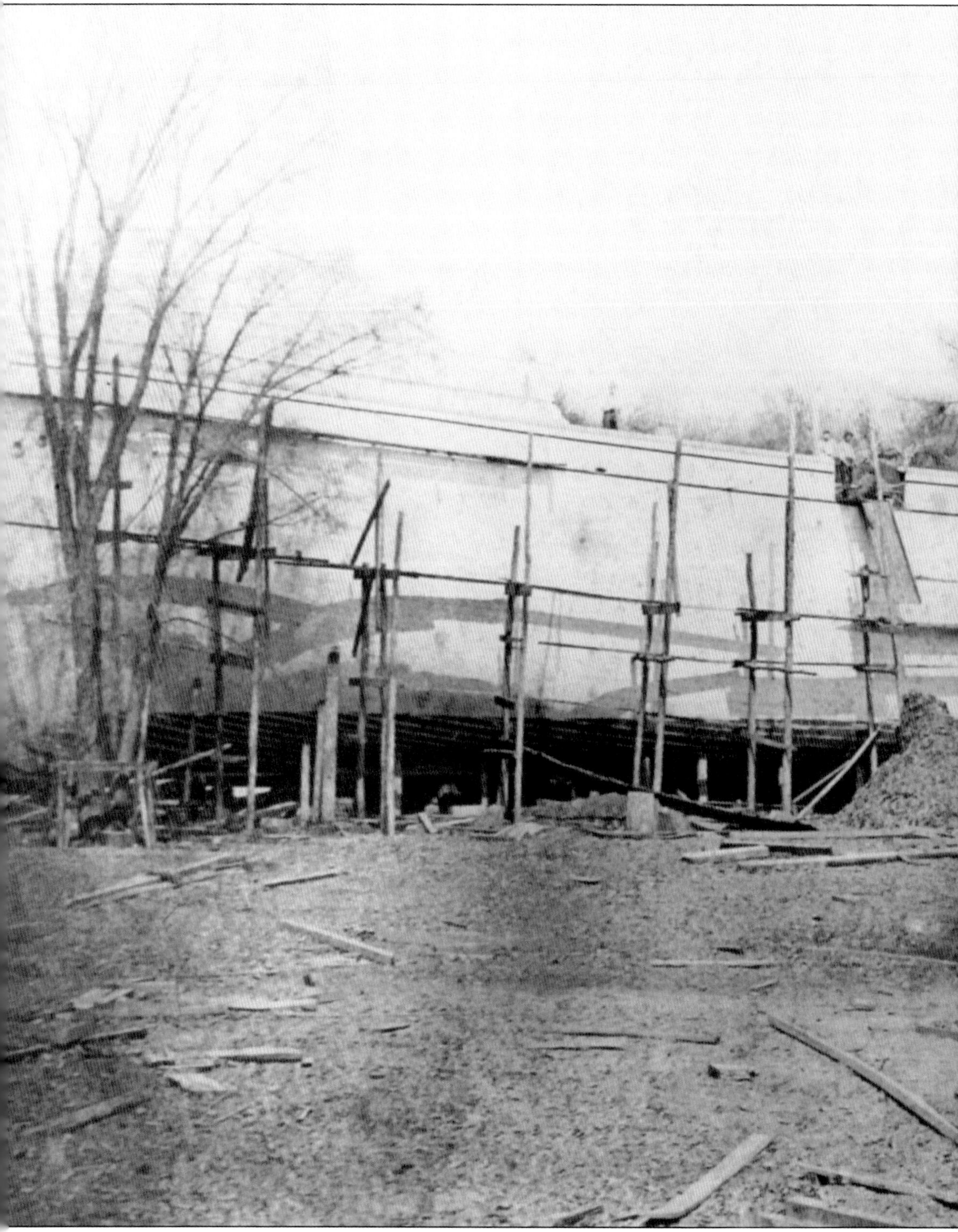

Between the years 1856 and 1860, twenty ships were built in Milan, with an additional 17 between the years 1861 and 1867. Ships built in Milan were limited in size due to the constraints of the canal and lock dimensions. As the demand grew for larger vessels, Milan shipbuilding declined

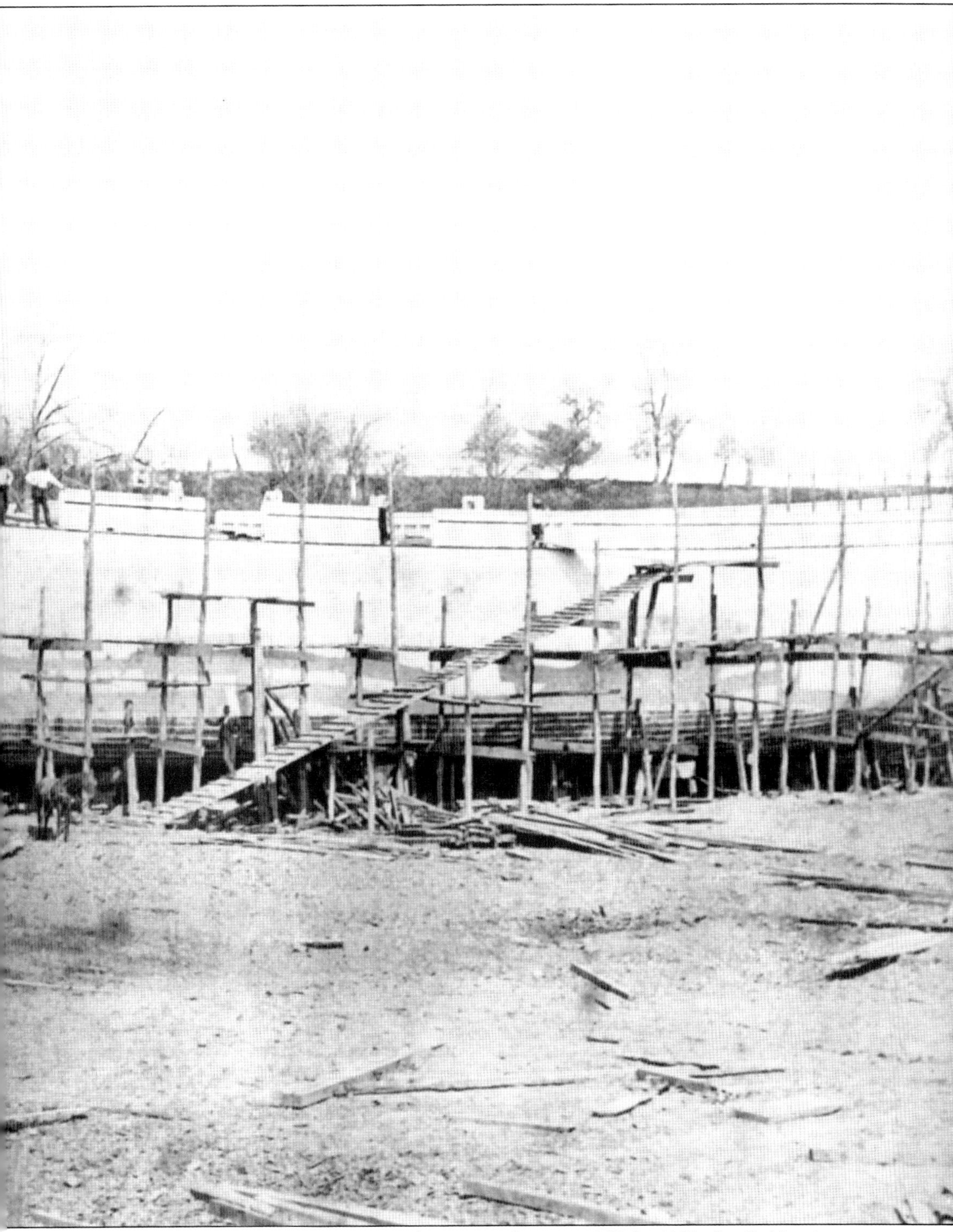

and eventually moved back to Abbott's and Fries Landings in 1868. In 1883, the *Golden Age* was built at Fries Landing. It was the largest schooner built on Lake Erie.

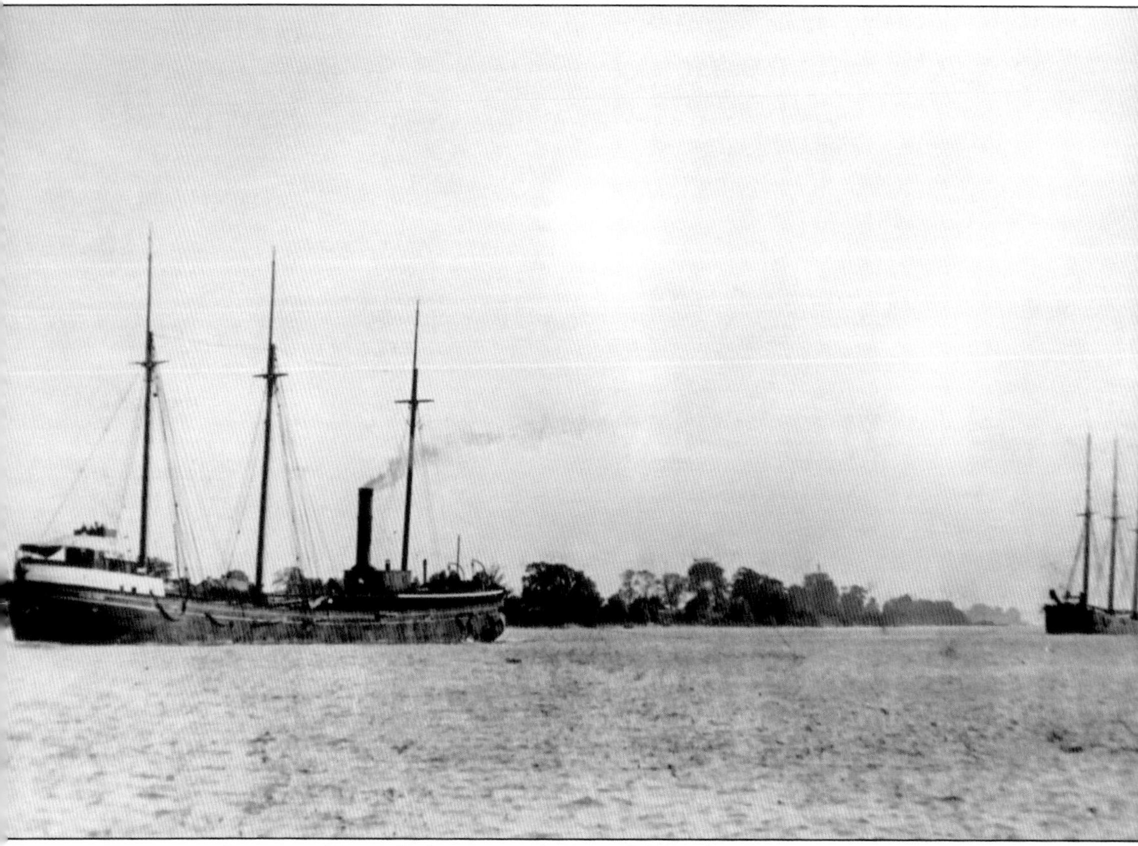

Commerce began to slow with the encroachment of the railroads. Rail shipping was growing, and the service was faster and cheaper. Lake schooners dropped prices in an effort to compete, but the last Milan Canal Company dividend was paid out in 1851. In 1864, ice floes damaged the river lock system, and the feeder dam broke in the winter of 1867–1868, draining the basin.

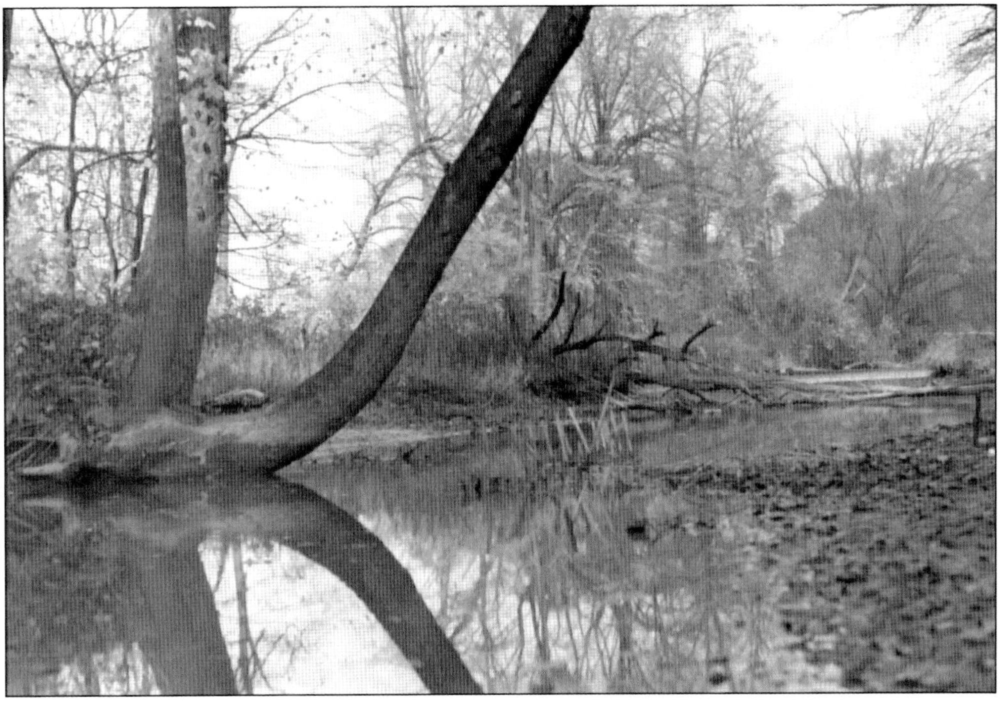

A.P. Mowry built the *Idaho* in 1863 at a cost of $25,000. It had a length of 135 feet and was 11.5 feet deep. The *Idaho* could hold 350 tons of cargo and came to the first lock of the canal trying to get to the dry dock at Milan for repairs in 1873. However, navigation for the year had shut down, and the vessel became abandoned in the lock, with little hope for money to finish any work. This photograph shows the ribs of the abandoned ship.

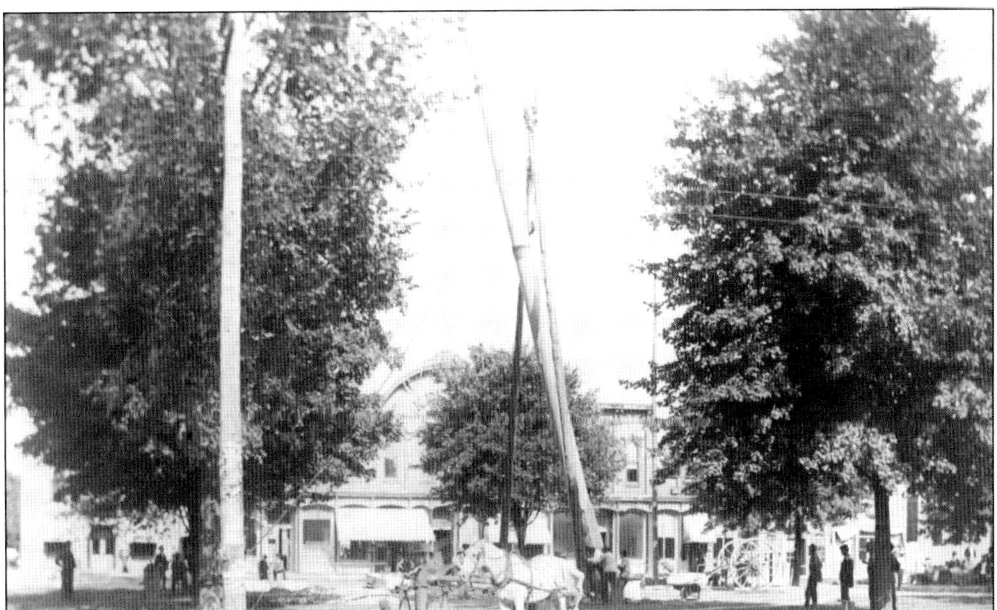

The mast of *Idaho* is raised in the town square around 1890. The last vessel built in a Milan shipyard was the *Mystic* in 1866.

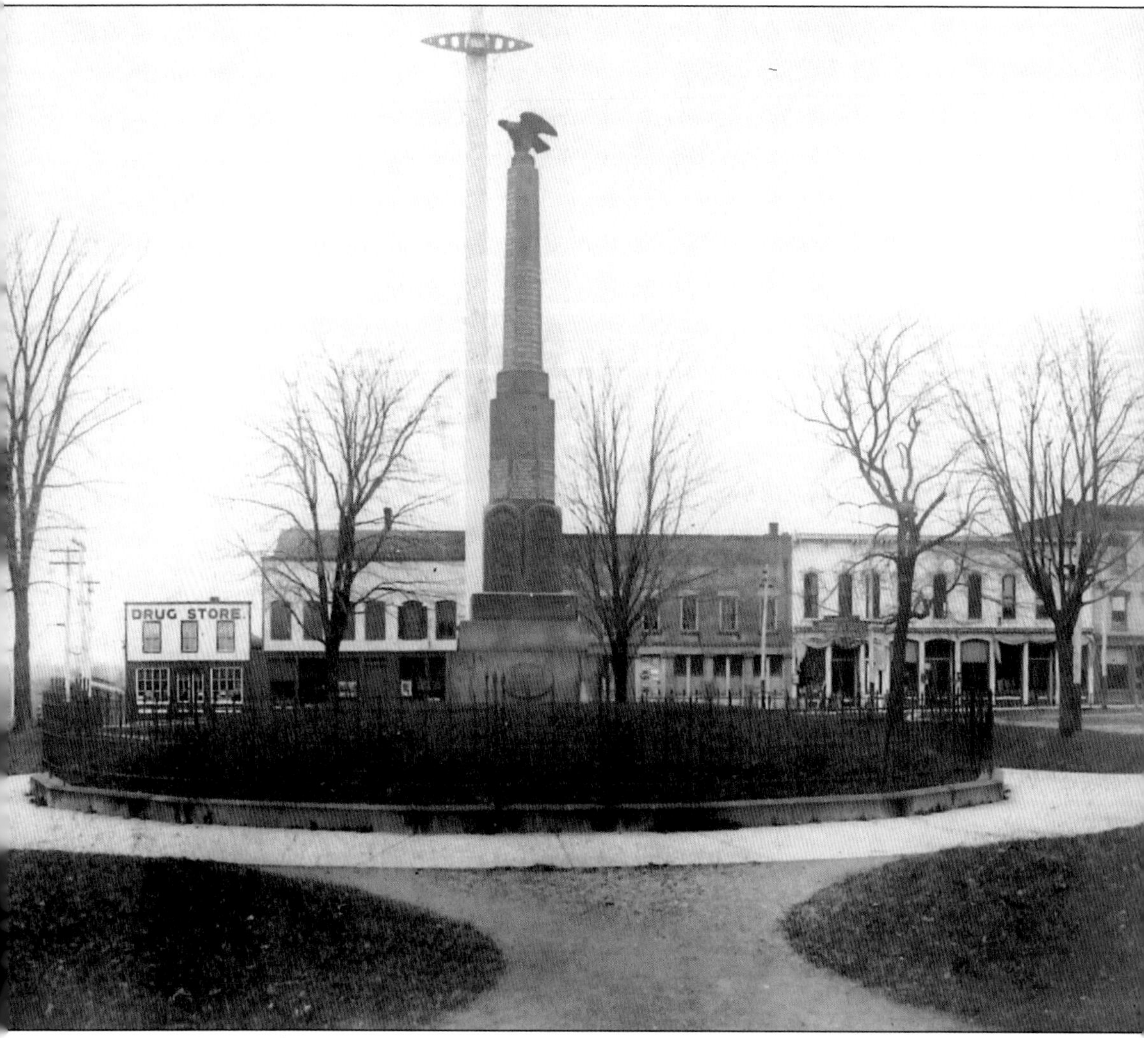

Pictured here is the mast of the *Idaho* being used as a flagpole alongside the Civil War monument in the town square. The north side of the square is visible in the background.

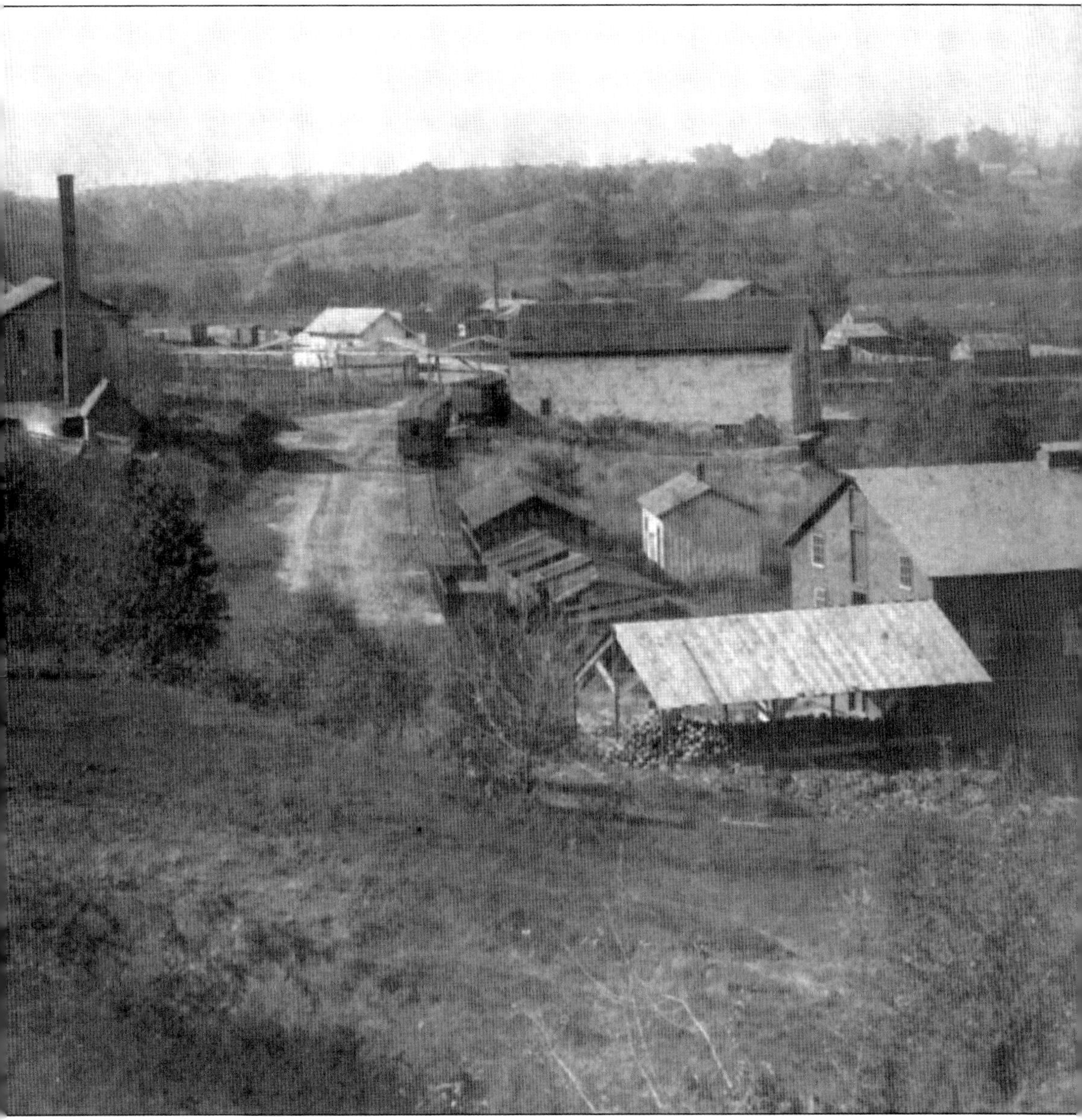

After the demise of the Milan Canal, the existing warehouses found new uses. According to the *Milan Advertiser*, their trestles were rebuilt in 1882 to accommodate the Wheeling & Lake Erie Railroad.

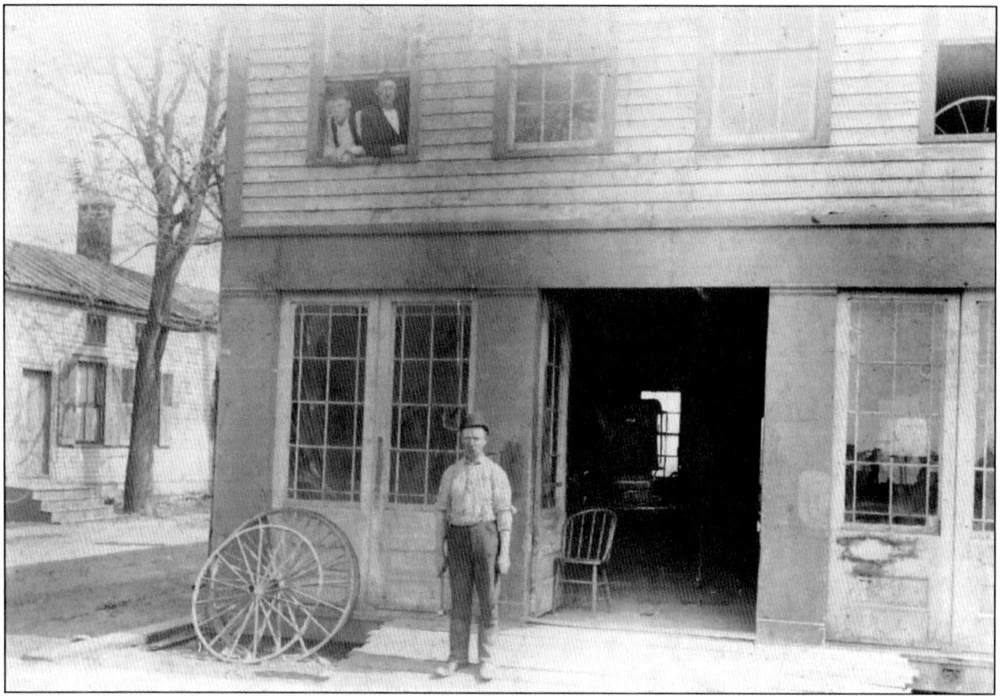

Pictured here is Jim Smith's wagon shop in Milan. On May 18, 1847, it was reported that 600 wagons lined up for six miles to unload their 20,000 bushels of grain.

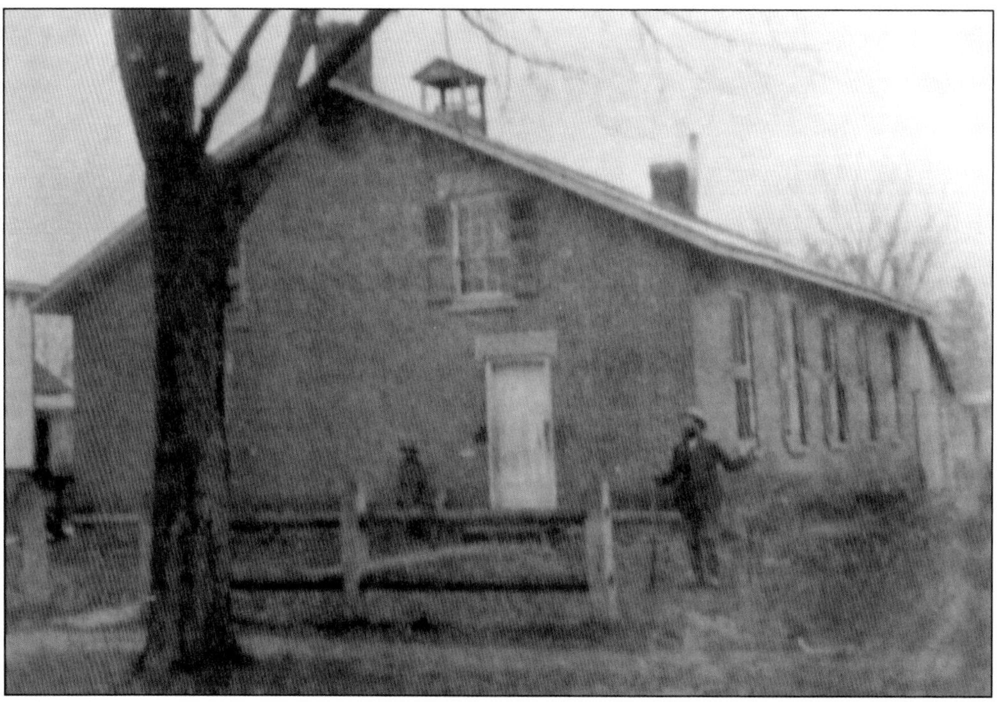

Milan's bat factory was originally the high school building. It was sold to Stephan Lockwood, who opened the factory.

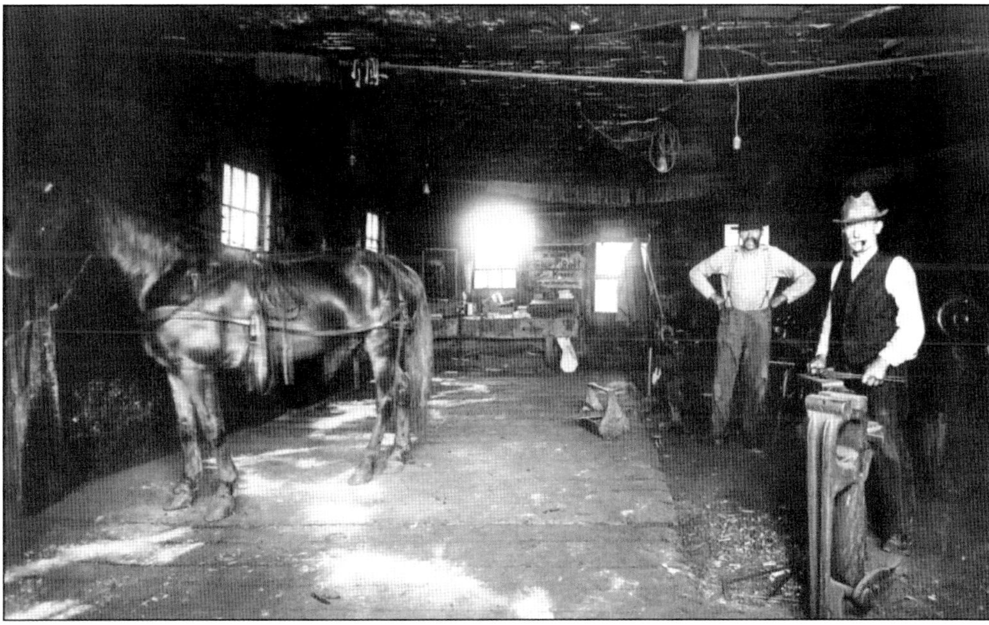

Blacksmiths Jim Smith and Leon Hunt stand in the interior of their shop. Milan had several blacksmiths, including John W. Sisty, one of Milan's earliest blacksmiths. Sisty was born in Pennsylvania on November 21, 1824, and moved to Tiffin, Ohio, with his parents in 1831. It was in Tiffin where Sisty first learned the ancient trade of blacksmithing at the age of seven. In 1847, he moved to Milan, where he became the resident blacksmith and continued blacksmithing until he was 80 years old.

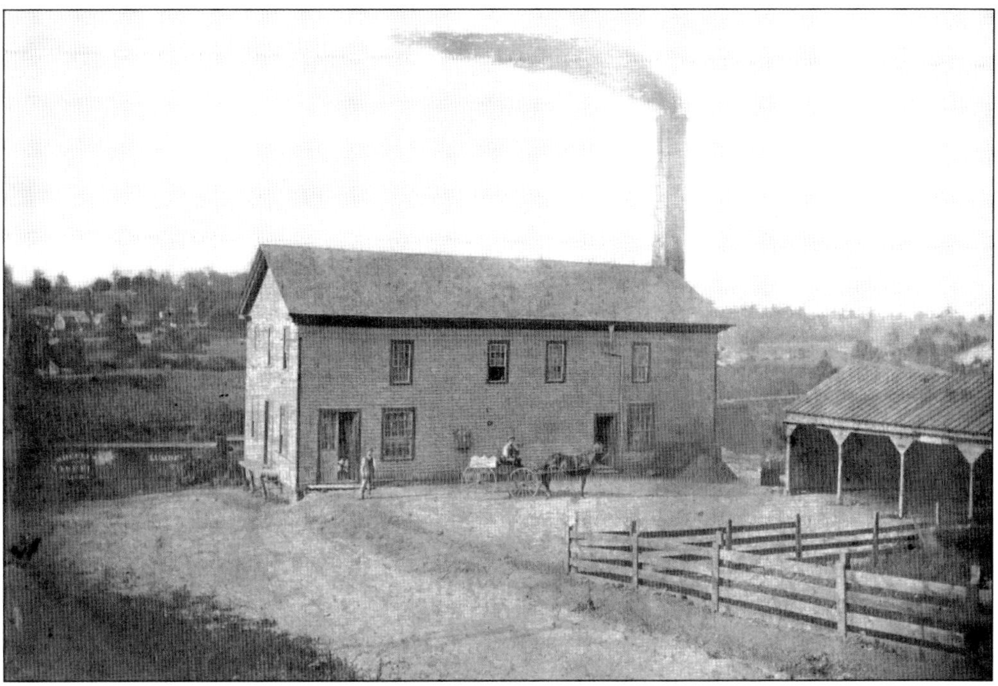

The Star Mill was built in 1849. Thomas and Samuel Winchester were the first in a long list of millers to occupy the business.

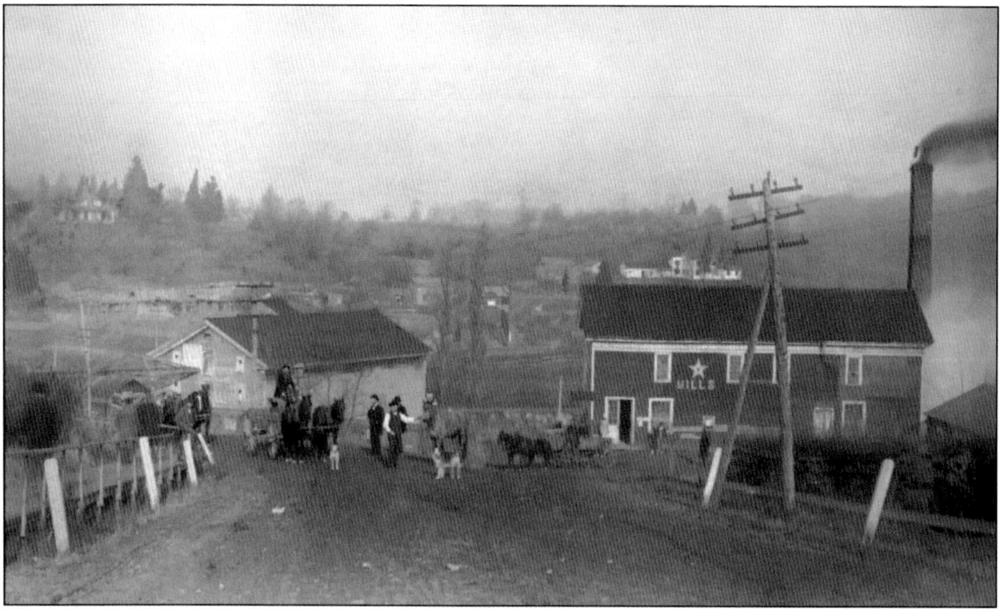

Samuel Winchester became known as "the mad miller of Milan" and was a balloonist. His first flight was in September 1855; during his second flight three weeks later, he was carried away by a strong wind and never seen again.

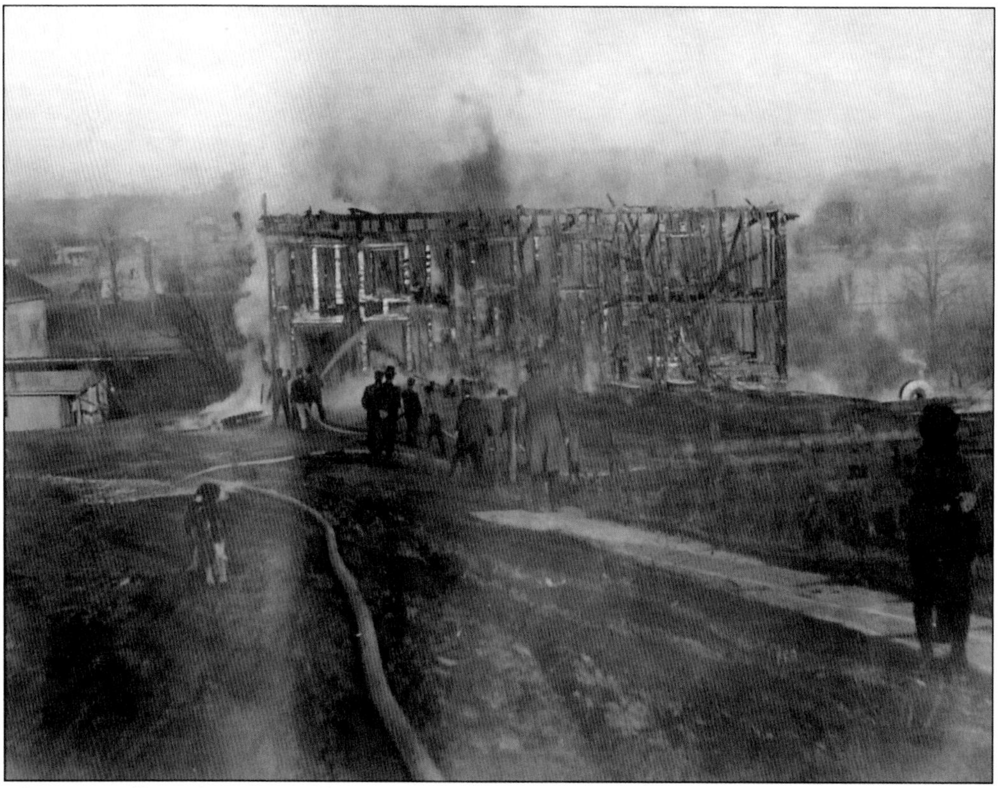
The Star Mill was later owned by Comfort Ruggles, followed by a Mr. Hanson. It burned down in 1909. The fire was a huge event in the community of Milan.

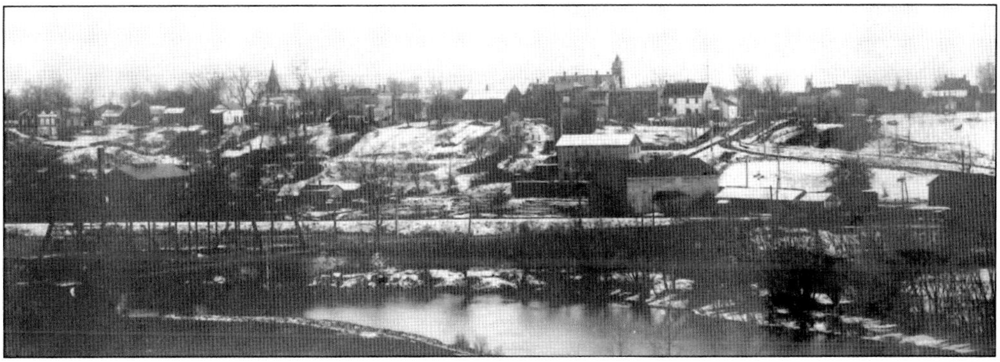

Visible in this view of the Milan Canal Basin are the Jenkins warehouse, Star Mill, and the Lockwood warehouse. The Jenkins warehouse is the last warehouse remaining in Milan.

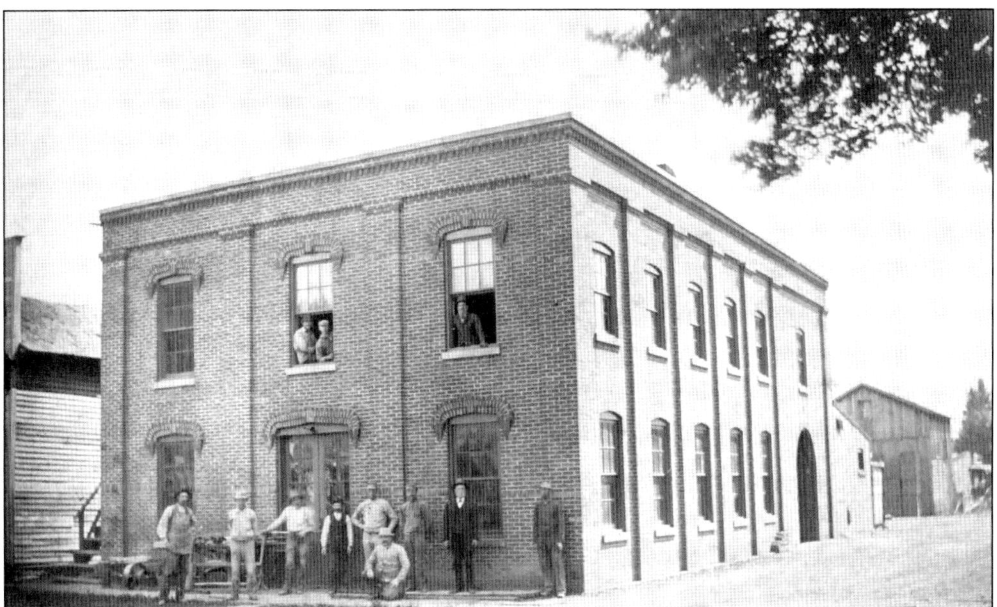

Geneva Color Works was located on the corner of Huron and Front Streets. The business made paints and varnishes and was later sold to the Sherwin Williams Company in Cleveland. Among those pictured here are owners Charles Mowry (fourth from left) and A.J. Mowry (second from right).

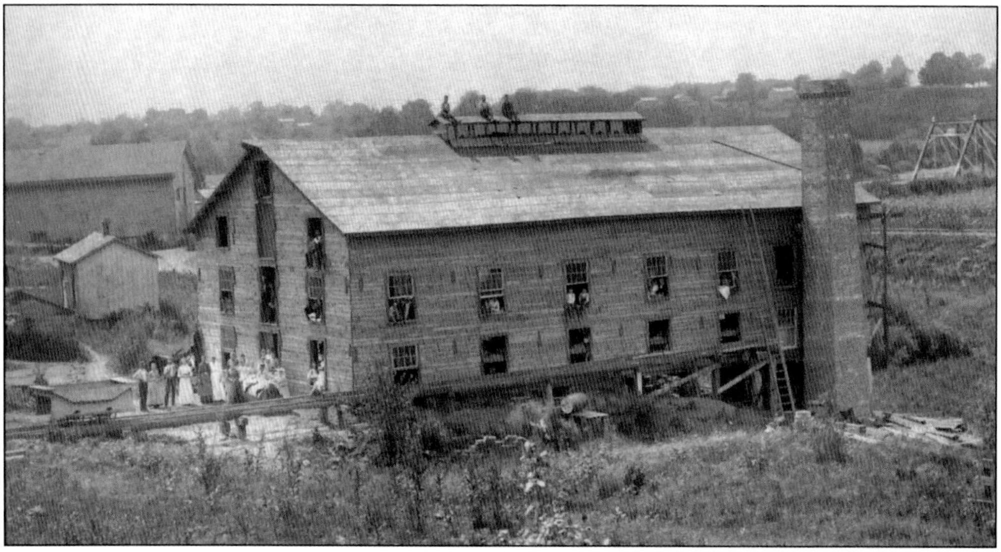

The warehouse once owned by Ralph and George Lockwood was later turned into the canning factory. This mill was located halfway down depot hill, near the W&LE railroad tracks. It burned down in 1910.

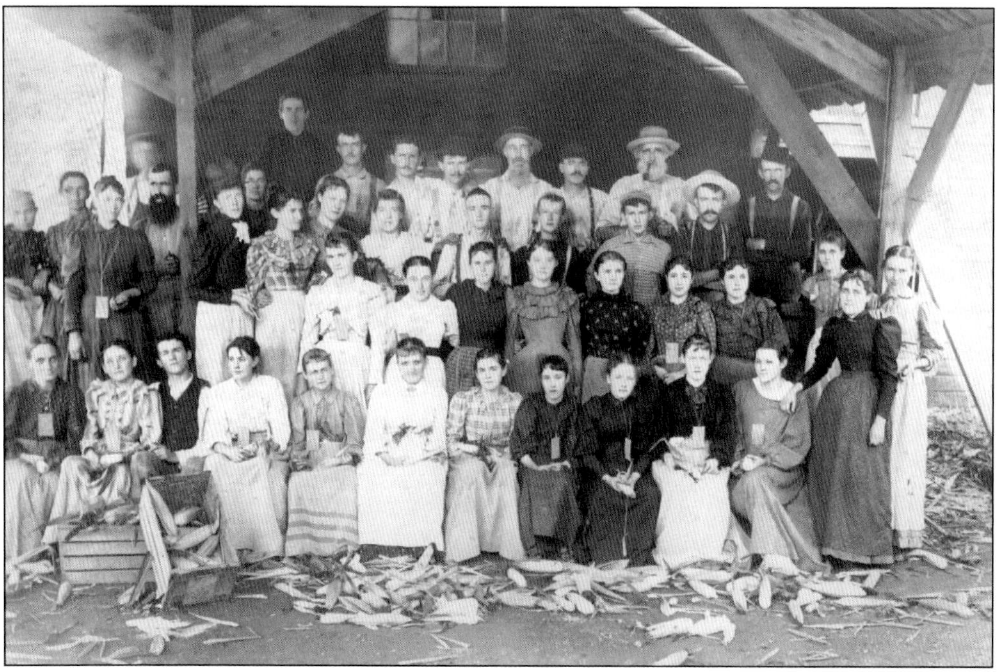

Canning factory employees pictured here in no particular order include Sarah Keen, Blanch Ewell Schadle, Henry Remlinger, Lizzie Clawson, Cora Downing Munger, Mary Kramer, Marie Detsch, Carrie Emmons Morrow, Ella Bottomly Houseman, Sadie Green Frary, Fannie Remlinger Fox, Fena Tyson, May Bailey Miller, Lizzie Wahl Sanders, Lea Sims, Anna Strickfaden, Mayme Keller, Mimi Detch Schwab, Sarah Oakley, Mrs. Wakefield, Charles Wakefield, Anna Hose, Clara Keller Laws, Etta Oakley Hinkton, Harry Hammond, Alden Emmons, Iva Wood, Louie Coleman, George Walbridge, Henry Strickradt, Horace Oakley, John Coleman, Will Scott, Albert Mead, Ed Remlinger, and Leo Remlinger.

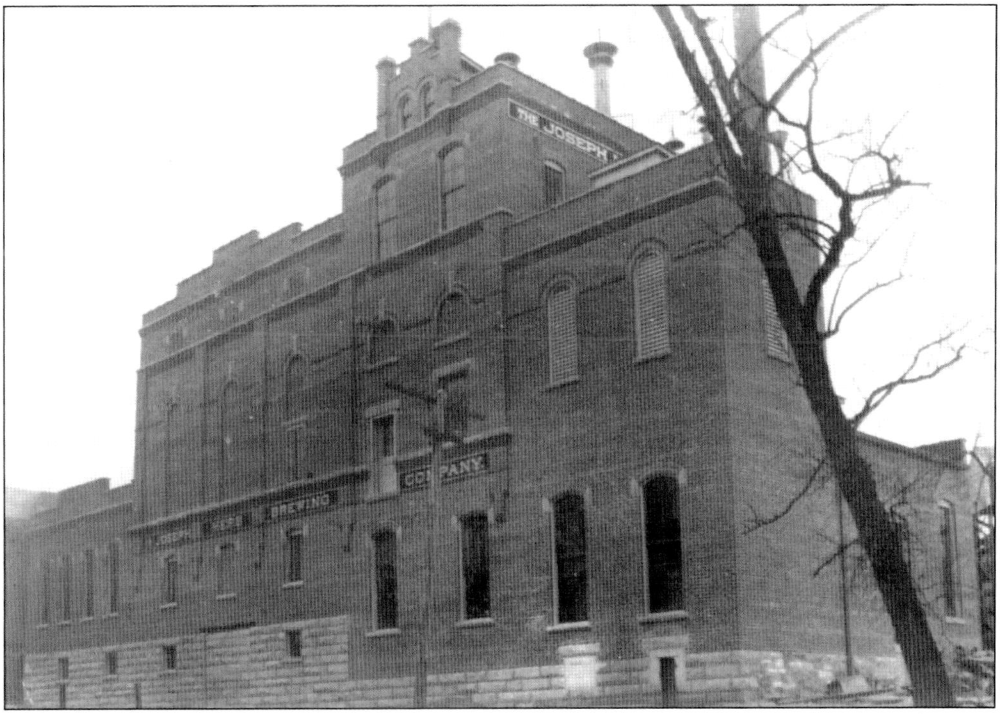

Brewing in Milan began in the 1850s with John Schell. In the early 1900s, the Joseph Herb Brewing Co. was followed by the Milan Brewing Company, which began brewing Milan Pure Beer. The Milan Brewing Company continued brewing prizewinning beers for many years. Prohibition temporarily killed the craft, and the company converted to a mushroom plant. After the repeal of Prohibition, brewing was back until it went out of business in the 1950s. The still-standing structure now operates as the Growers Chemical Corporation.

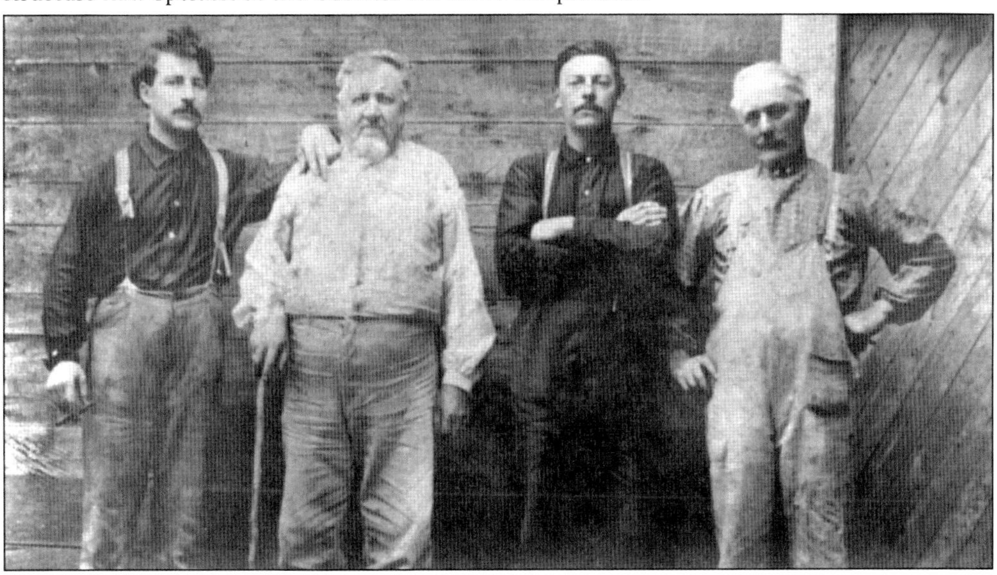

Pictured from left to right are Joseph Herb, John Beeckley, Charley Herb, and John Coyne beside the old frame brewery. The Herb brothers created the pond that supplied water for the Milan Brewing Company.

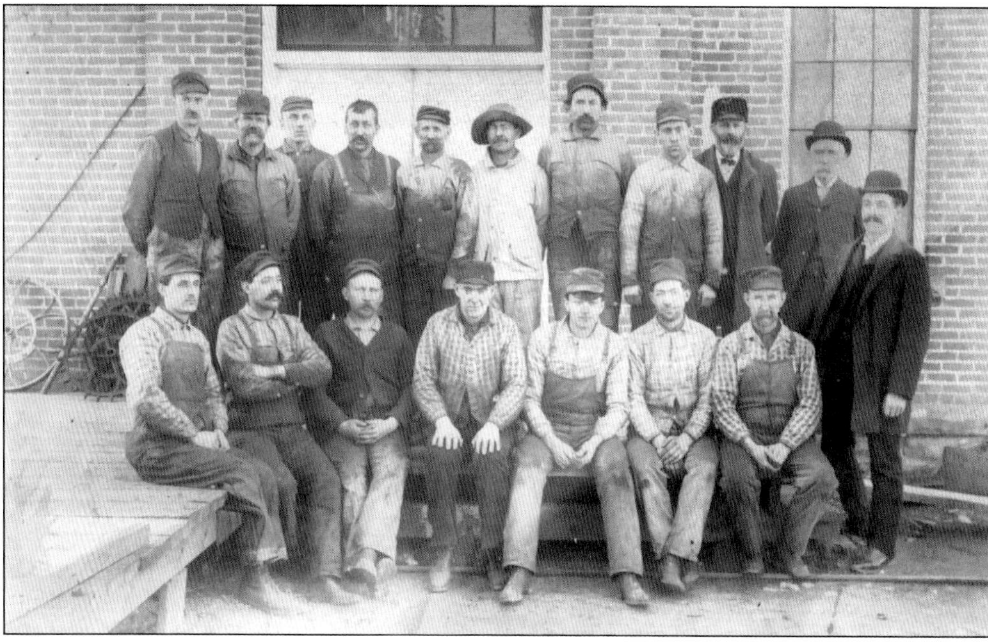

The potato digger was envisioned by Issac W. Hoover of Avery, in Milan Township. He submitted a model to the Federal Patent Bureau in 1885, and once granted the patent, began manufacturing his machine in a shed. Although first sold to neighbors and local farmers, they soon attracted nationwide attention. Hoover and his brother-in-law Albert Prout created the Hoover & Prout Company, but Prout left the business in 1910, turning into the Hoover Manufacturing Company. Pictured here are employees of the plant with Issac W. (standing, second from right) and his son A.L. Hoover (standing, far right).

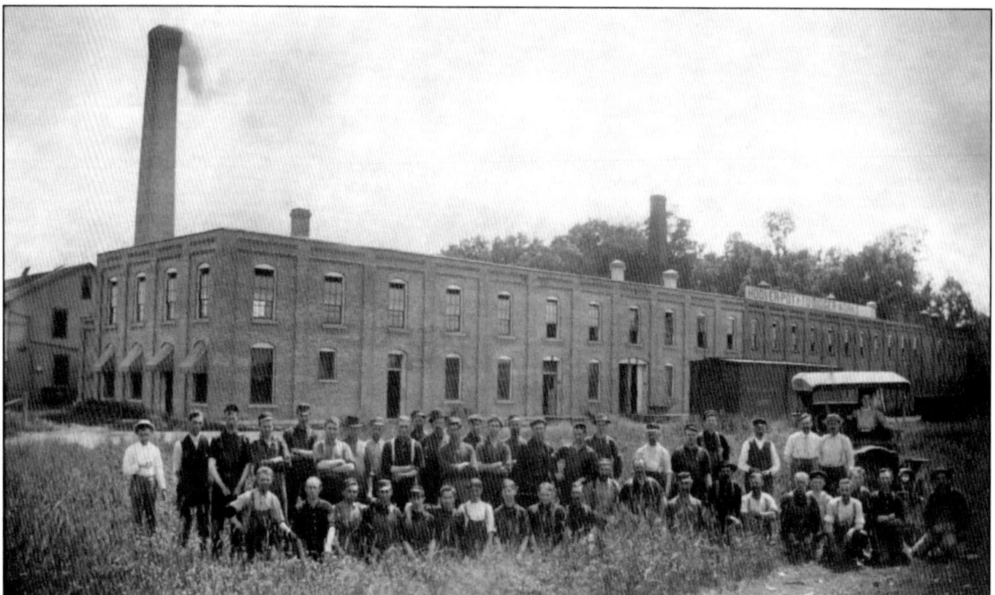

Hoover workers pose in front of Hoover Potato Digger Works. By 1913, the original design had been modified to accommodate a gasoline engine, and Deere & Company was the sole distributing agent for Hoover products. By July 1926, Deere had bought out Hoover.

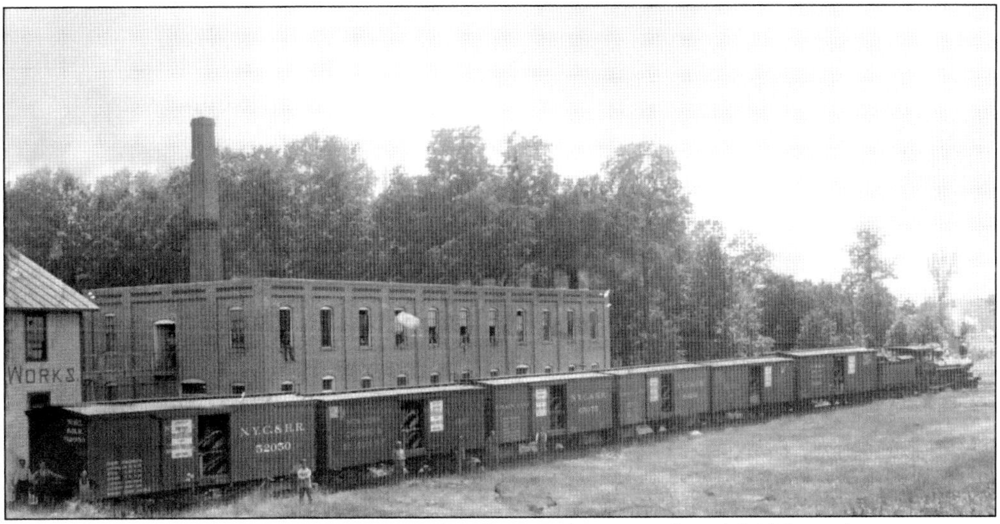

The extensive Hoover Potato Digger Works plant in Avery produced 5,000 machines per year. Pictured here are railcars loaded with Hoover diggers. The still-standing structure now operates as the Schlessman Seed Company.

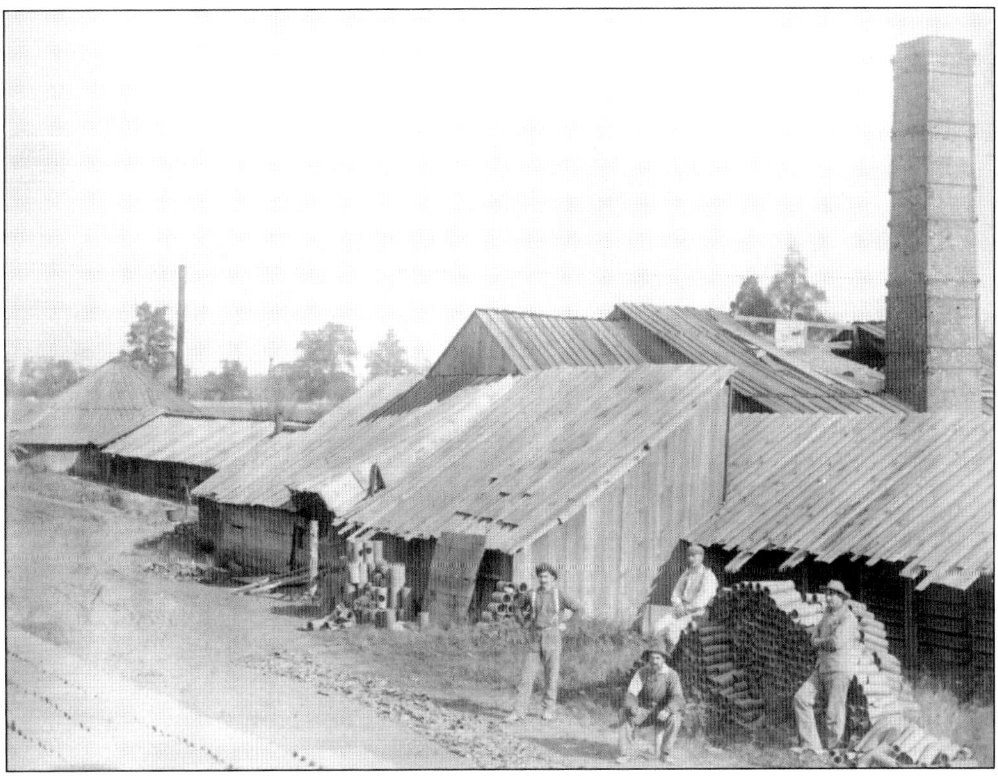

Lavey Pottery and Tile was located on State Route 113, half a mile east of Milan. Tiles are pictured drying before being fired.

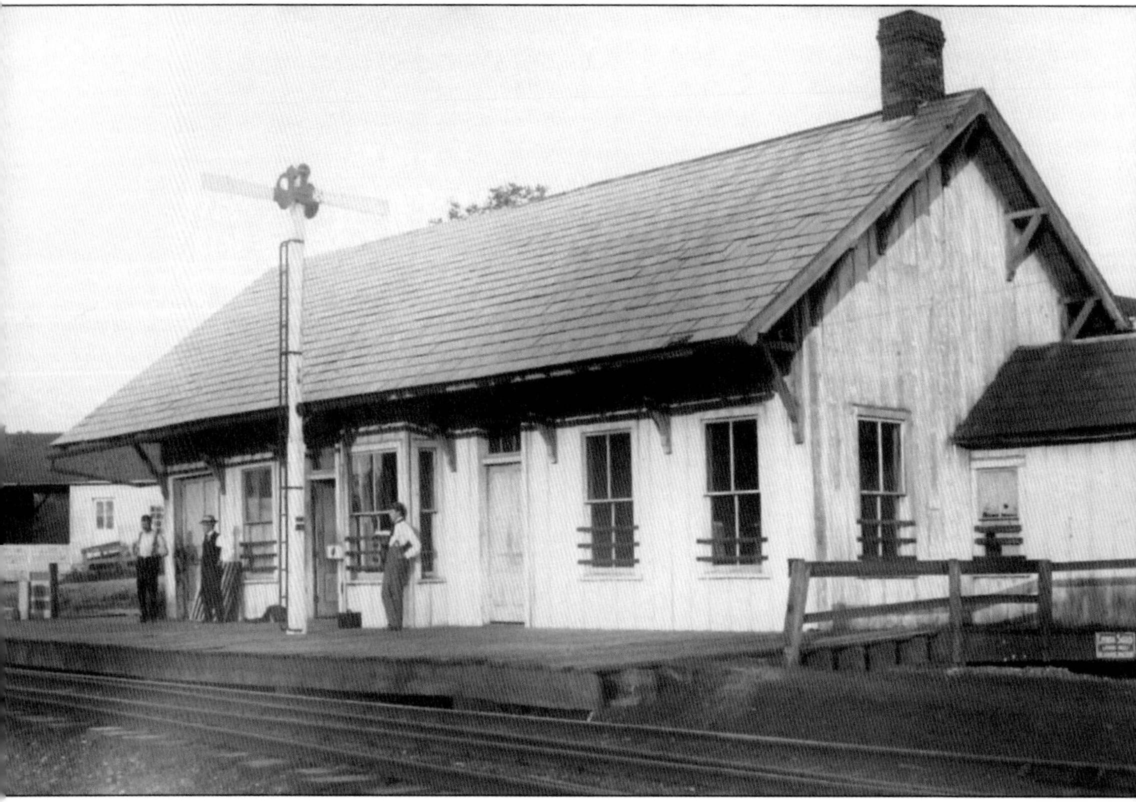

On July 21, 1881, the towpaths of the canal were leased to the Wheeling & Lake Erie Railroad for 99 years at a rate of $50 per year. Included in the lease were the locks, basin, and dry dock area. On March 28, 1906, the company was dissolved by the Erie County Court of Common Pleas. Pictured here is the Wheeling depot in Milan in the early 1900s.

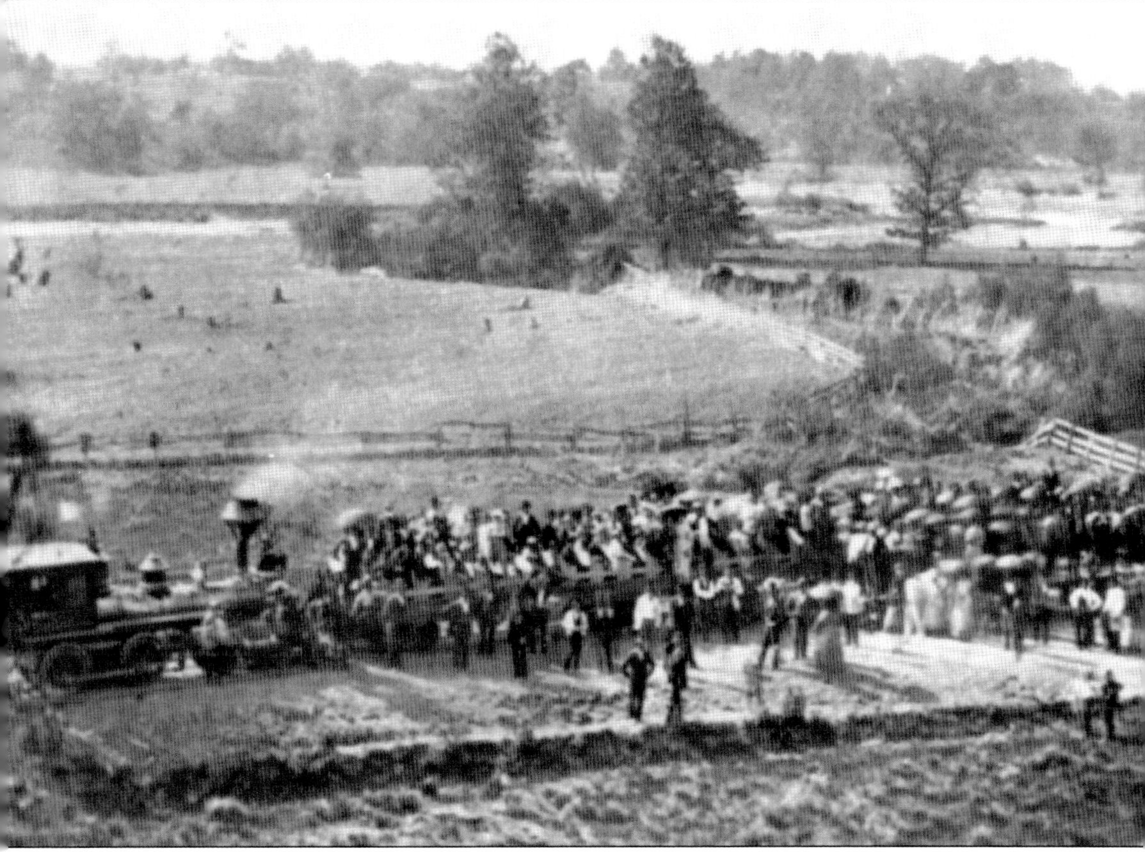

Pictured here is the opening of the Norwalk-Milan branch of the Wheeling & Lake Erie Railroad. In celebration of the completion of the railroad line, the W&LE gave free rides every hour between Milan and Norwalk on May 31, 1877.

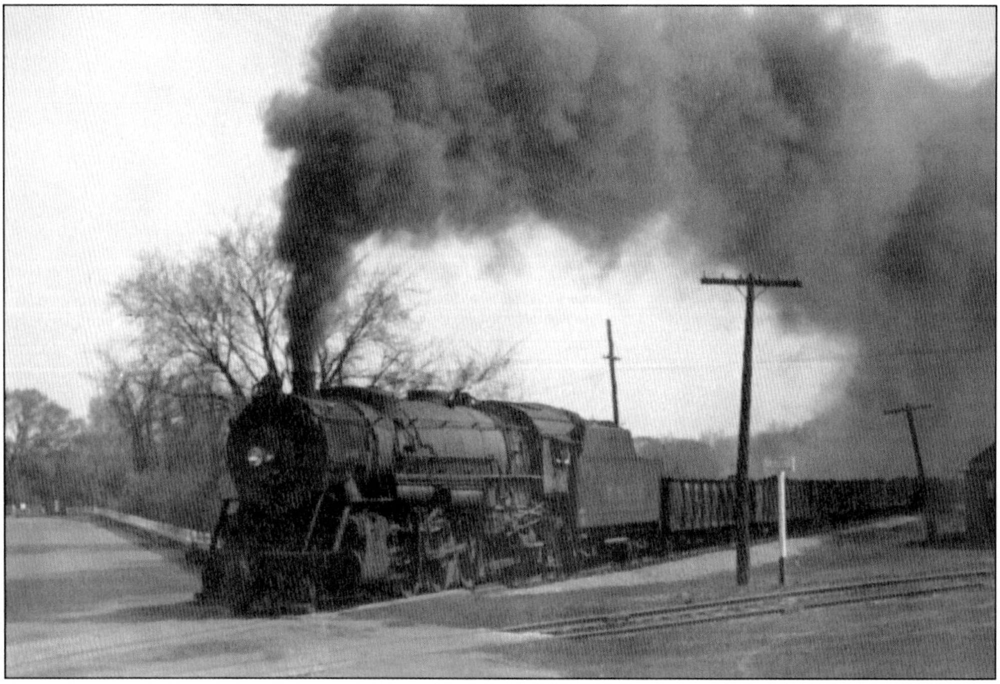

A Wheeling & Lake Erie steam train crosses Milan near the bridge over the Huron River around 1930. The first rails were narrow gauge but were changed to standard gauge by the mid-1880s.

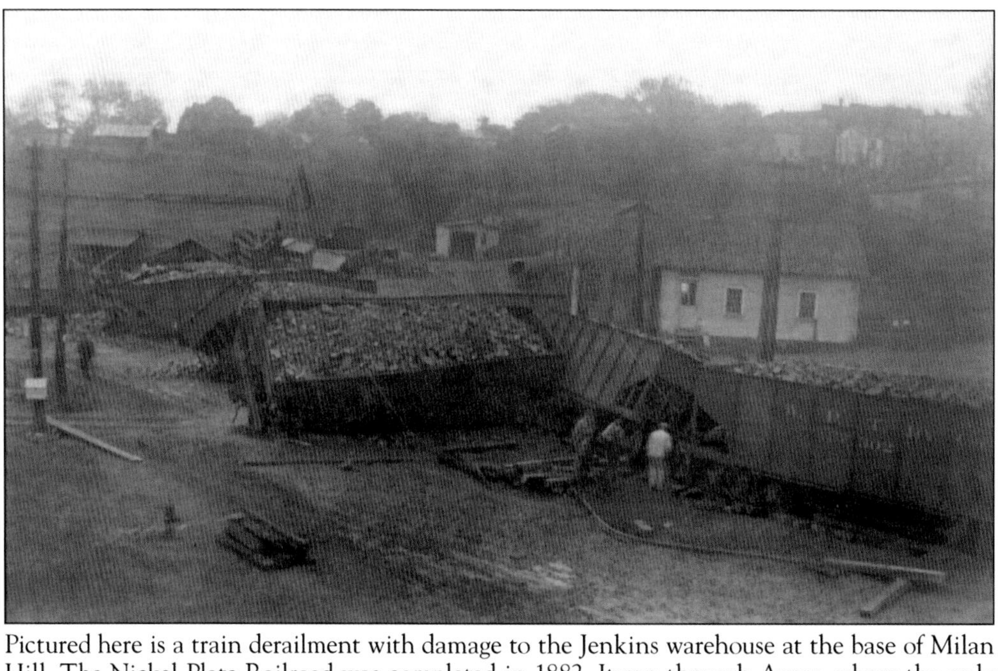

Pictured here is a train derailment with damage to the Jenkins warehouse at the base of Milan Hill. The Nickel Plate Railroad was completed in 1882. It ran through Avery, where the only station in Milan Township was located. A grain elevator was soon added at this location.

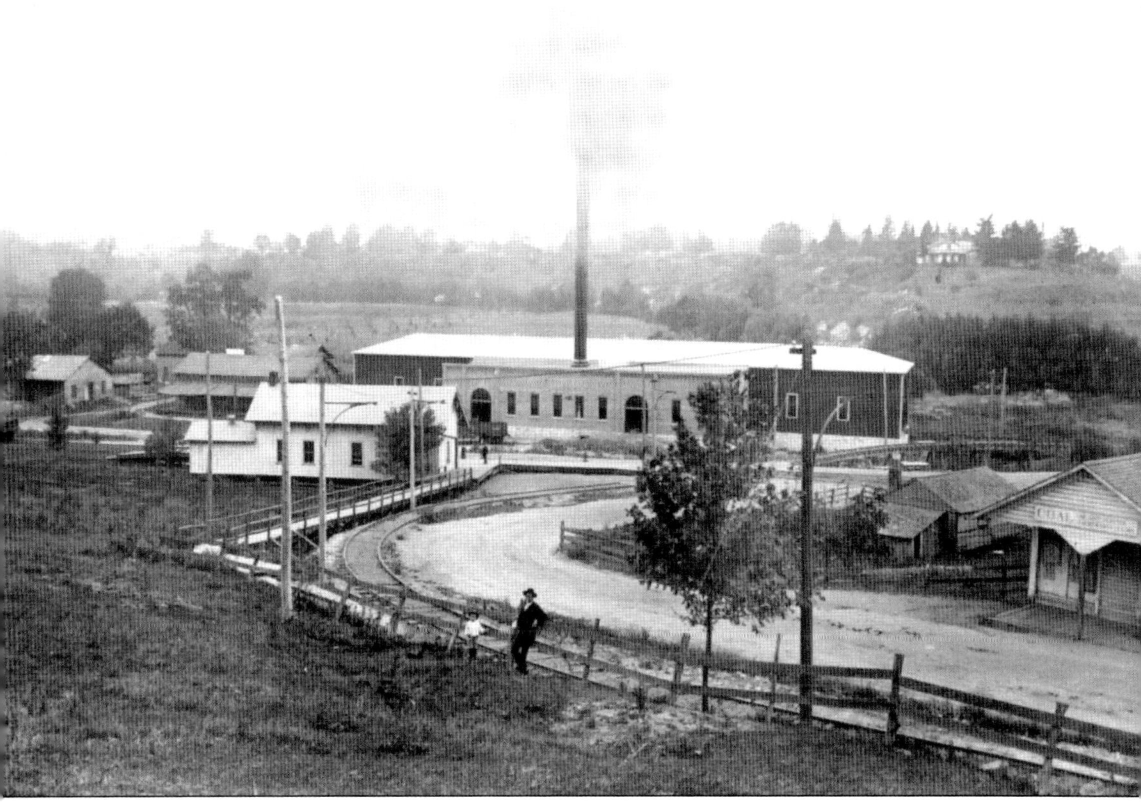

The Sandusky-Milan-Norwalk line of the interurban claimed to be the longest electric railroad in the world. Regular service began on July 12, 1893, from the Soldiers' Home in Sandusky to Milan. Pictured here is the Milan power station at the base of the old canal basin.

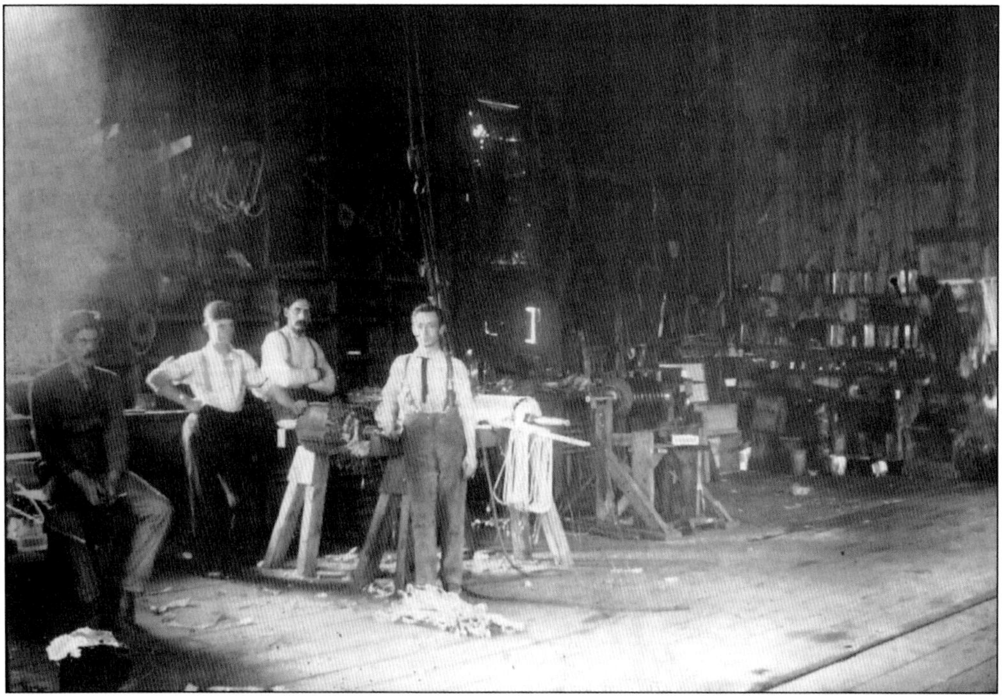

Honey Keller is one of the men pictured here in the interurban repair shop in Milan. The Sandusky-Milan-Norwalk line became part of the Lake Shore Electric, a larger network of lines in northern Ohio, which operated until 1926.

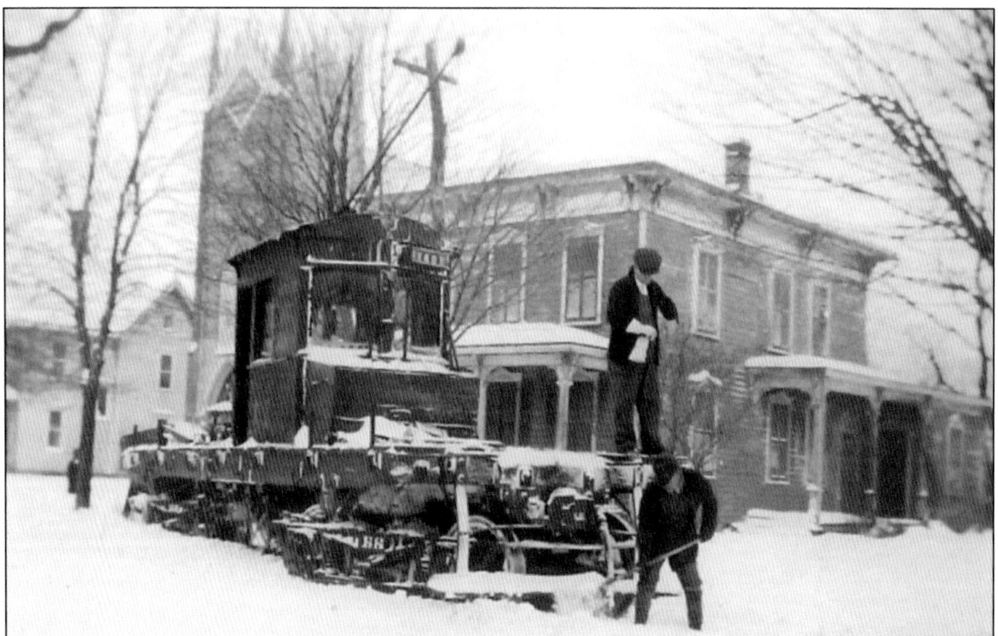

During the winter months, the interurban train was used as a snow plow to help clear the streets of Milan. It is pictured here in that capacity on Main Street in the early 1900s.

Four

HOMES AND PEOPLE

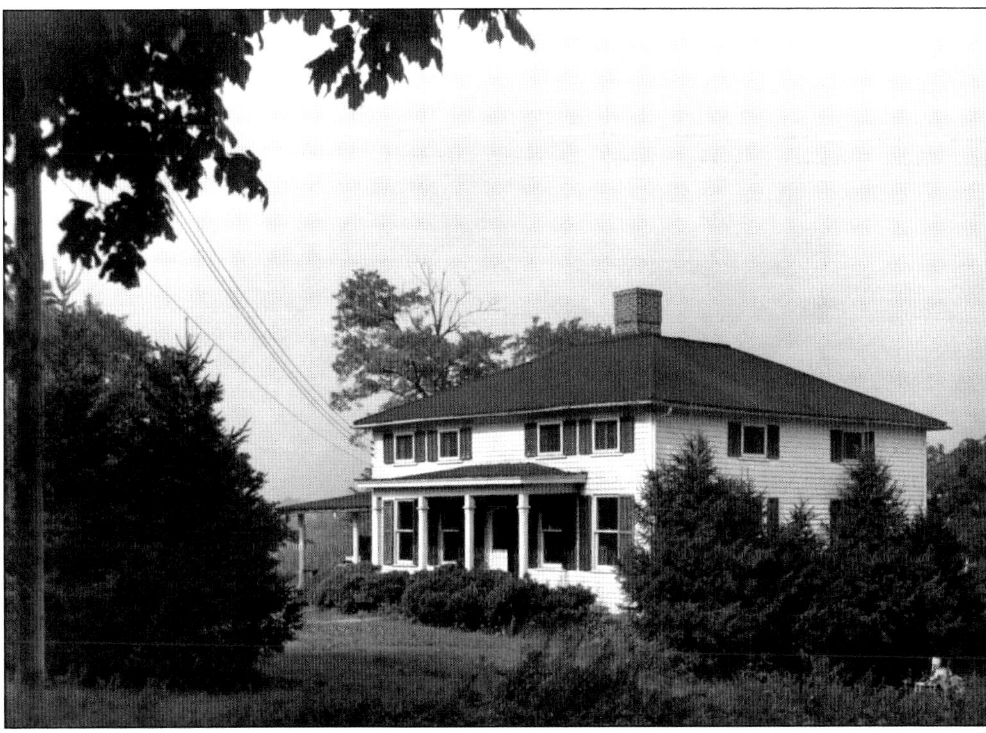

The F.W. Fowler home was built in the 1820s on Bank Street. Frederick W. Fowler was an influential town member, participating in the formation of the Milan Canal Company and later becoming a judge of the Common Pleas Court of Huron County. He died in 1868.

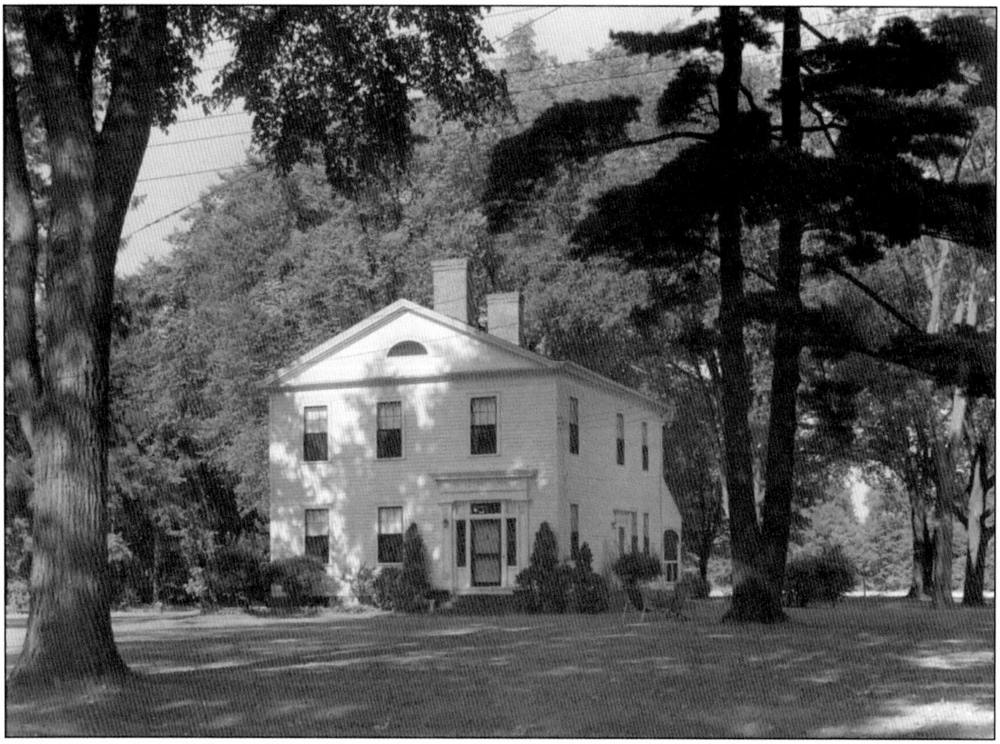

Ebenezer and Rachel (Hyde) Andrews came to Milan in 1825 from Green Farms, Connecticut. He built his home with the Federal touches of an elliptical fanlight in the pediment but also mixed in a rectangular door transom common to the newer Greek Revival style of the time.

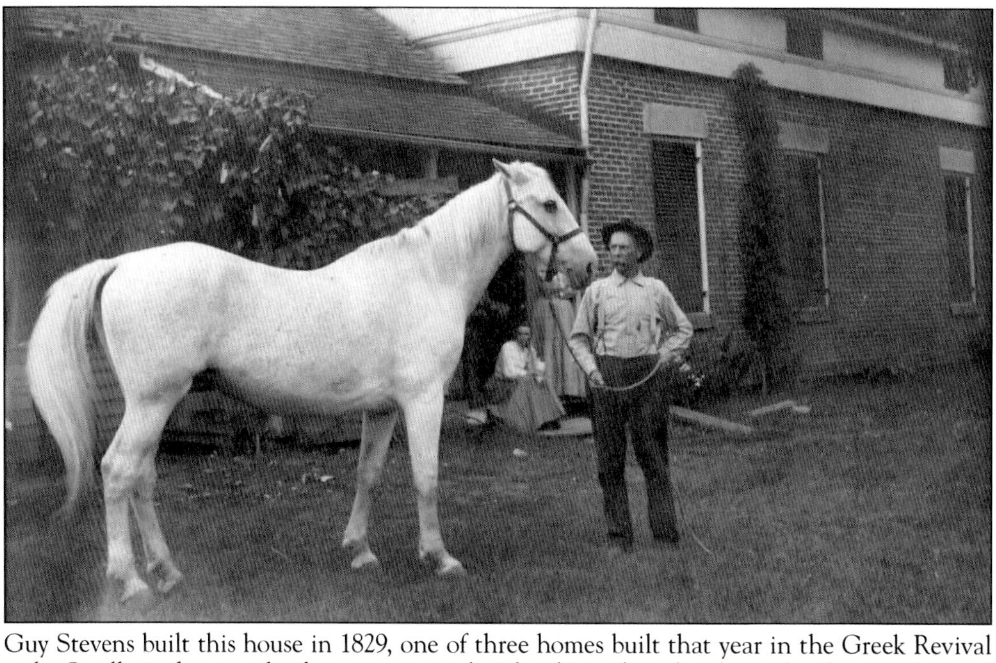

Guy Stevens built this house in 1829, one of three homes built that year in the Greek Revival style. Small windows in the frieze are topped with a hipped roof and cupola, characteristics of the Tuscan style.

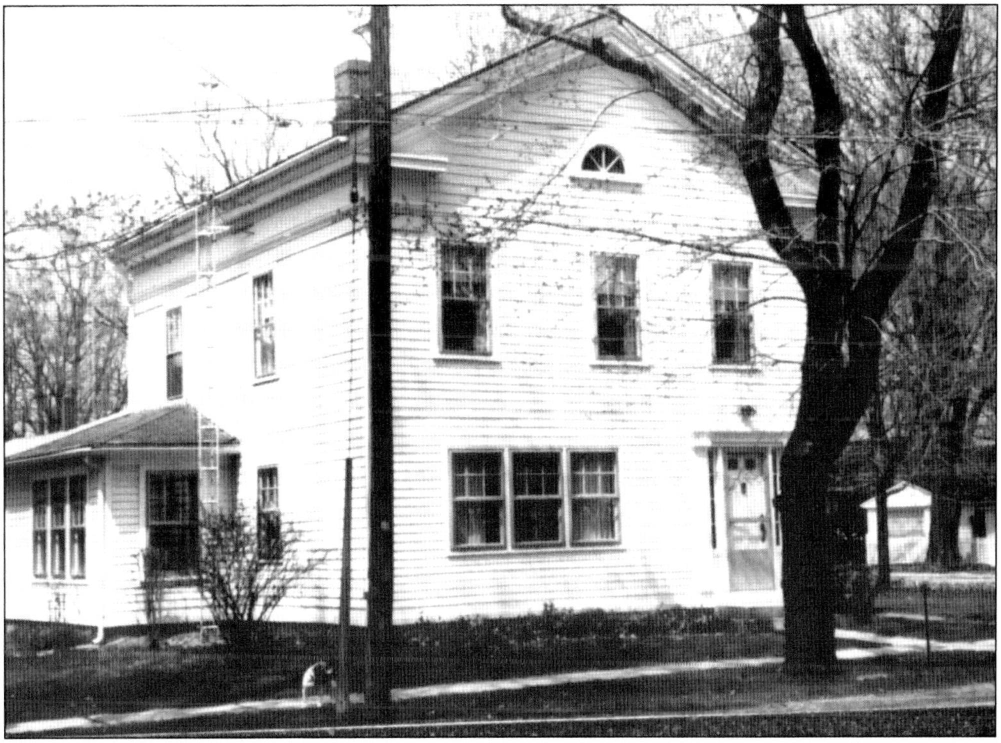

The second house of Ebenezer Merry is located on the corner of Edison Drive and Front Street. The home was built in the early-to-mid-1820s and is still occupied.

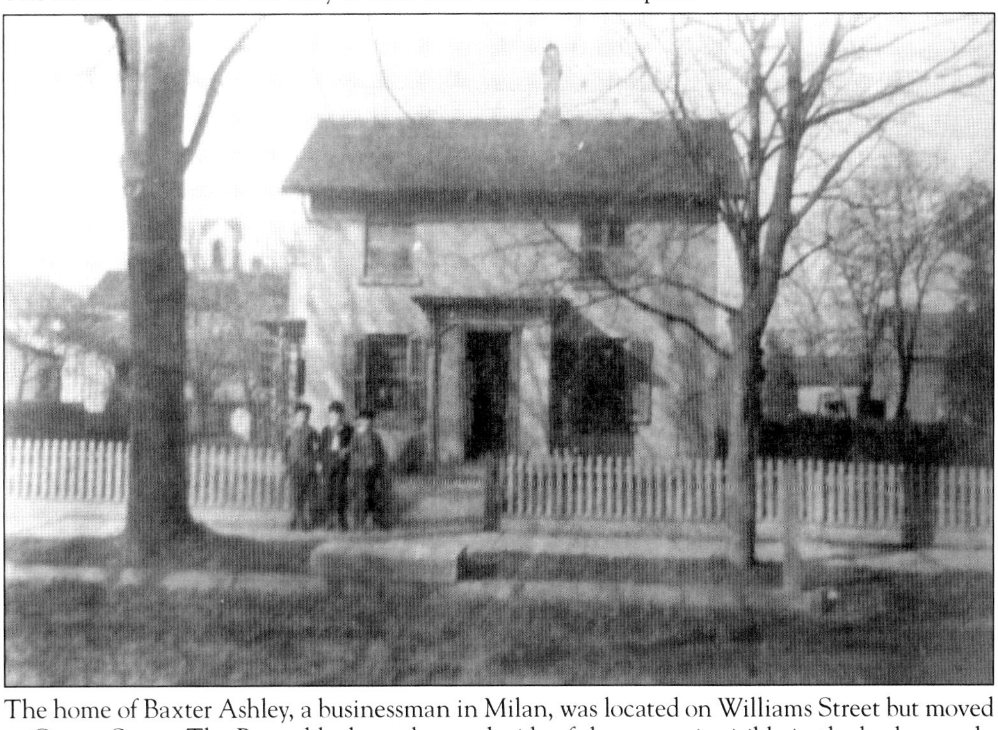

The home of Baxter Ashley, a businessman in Milan, was located on Williams Street but moved to Center Street. The Potter block on the south side of the square is visible in the background.

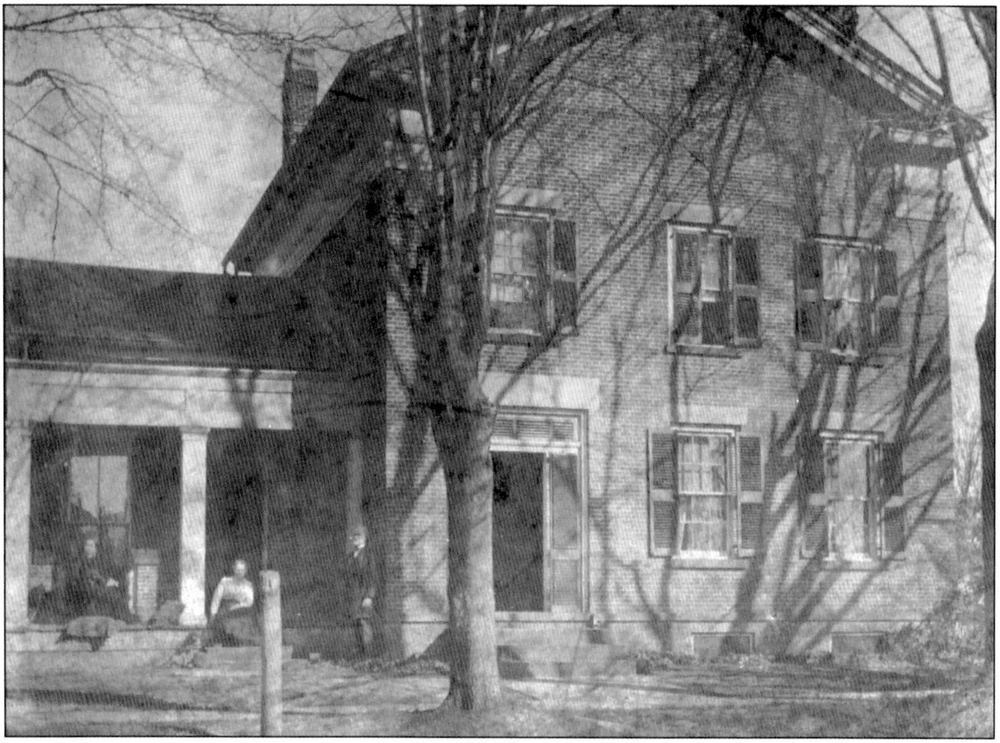

In 1846, Dr. Leman Galpin built his home in the popular Greek Revival style. Dr. Galpin gained recognition as the attending physician at the birth of Thomas Alva Edison on February 11, 1847.

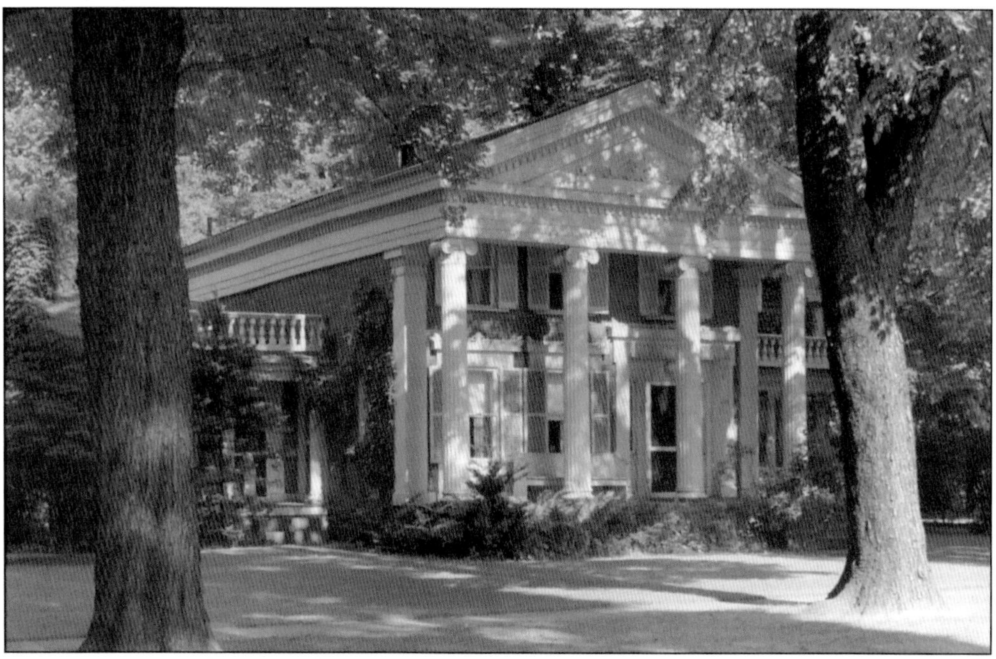

Zenas King, one of the first builders of iron bridges, built this home in 1847 while living in Milan. The temple front and hand-carved fretwork on the pediment are interesting features.

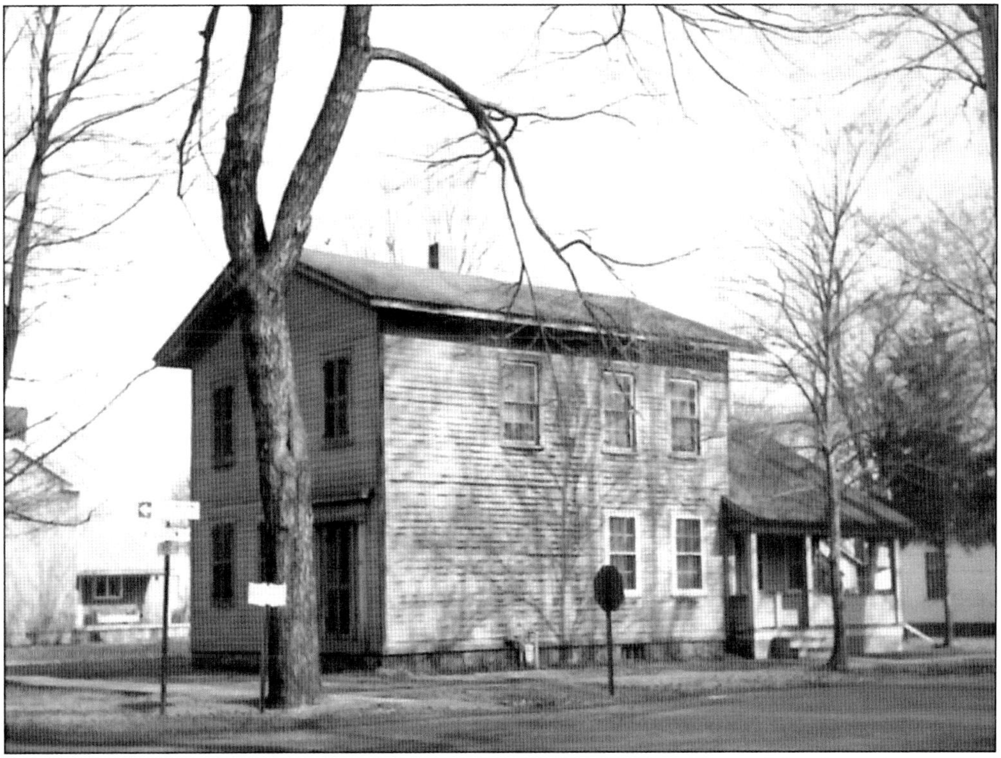

The Sayles house was built in the mid-1840s. It is built in the Greek Revival style and was willed to the Milan Historical Museum in 1968 by Robert Sayles.

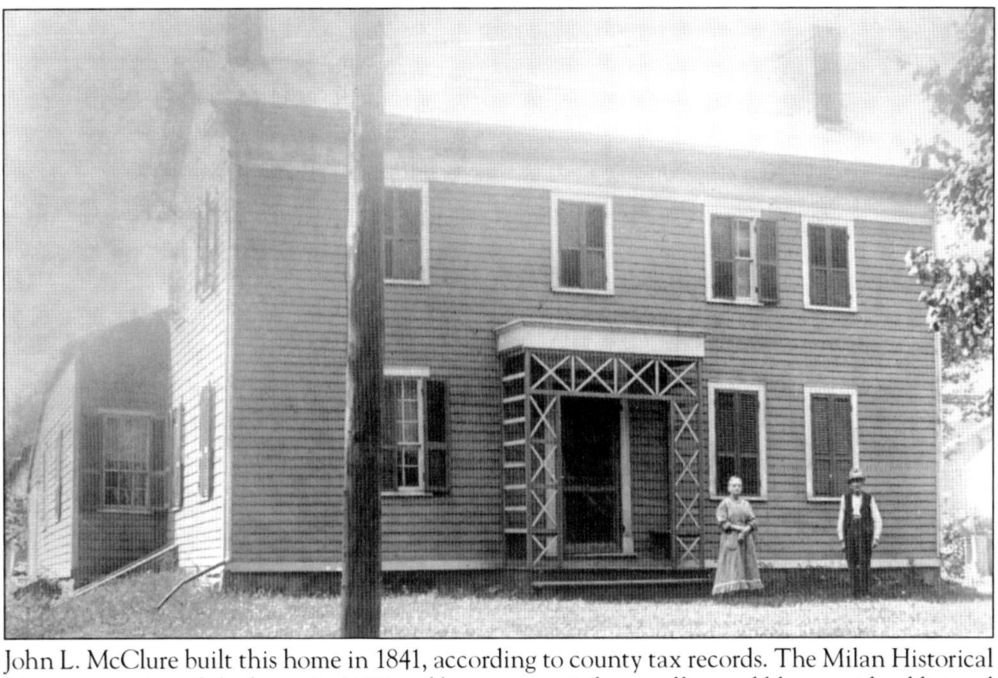

John L. McClure built this home in 1841, according to county tax records. The Milan Historical Museum purchased the home in 1989 and began using it for an office and library with additional collections storage space. Due to structural hazards, the building was razed in 2009.

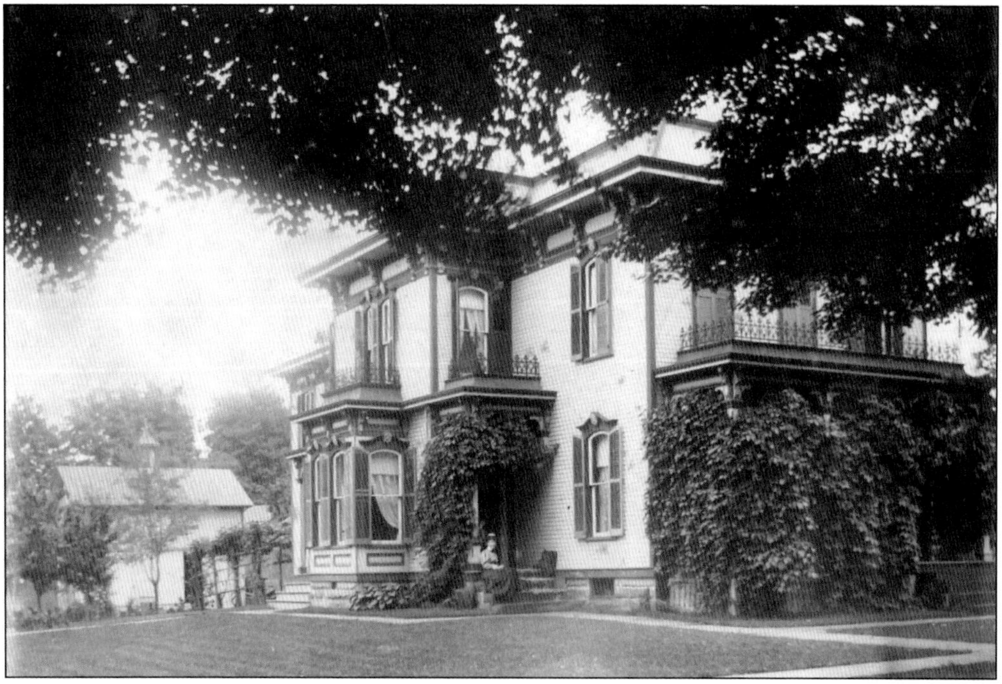

The home of Capt. Hugh Hastings is a beautiful reminder of the past glory of Milan's lake captains. Hastings's boyish dreams were of a seafaring life, and by the age of 21, he was the master of the vessel *Darian*. He later became captain of several ships operated by the Valentine Fries Company. He retired from lake service in 1900 and spent the following 15 years residing in Milan.

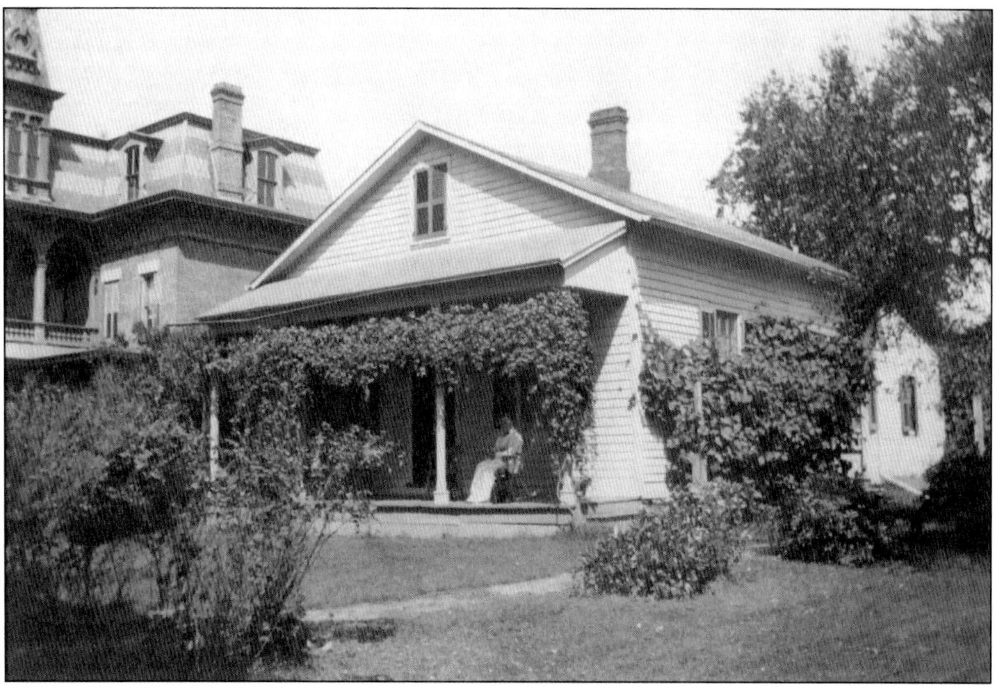

The Stoddard house is located on Edison Drive, pictured here around 1910. The home is designed in the popular Greek Revival style with a square-columned porch added at a later date.

The home of Nathan Jenkins is still occupied on Front Street in Milan. It was built in 1837, partially from the funds Nathan Jenkins secured after gaining contracts to help dig the Milan Canal. Jenkins later sold the house to Dr. E.L. Perry.

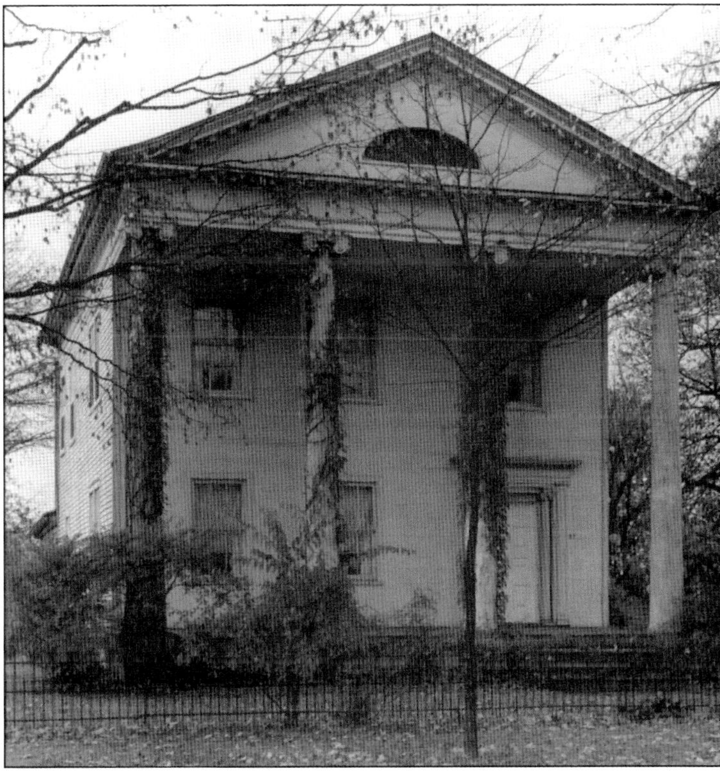

The J.C. Lockwood home, built in 1850, was extensively altered in 1870. The original Greek Revival design with a standard gable roof was changed with the addition of the large front porch, mansard roof, tower, and south wing.

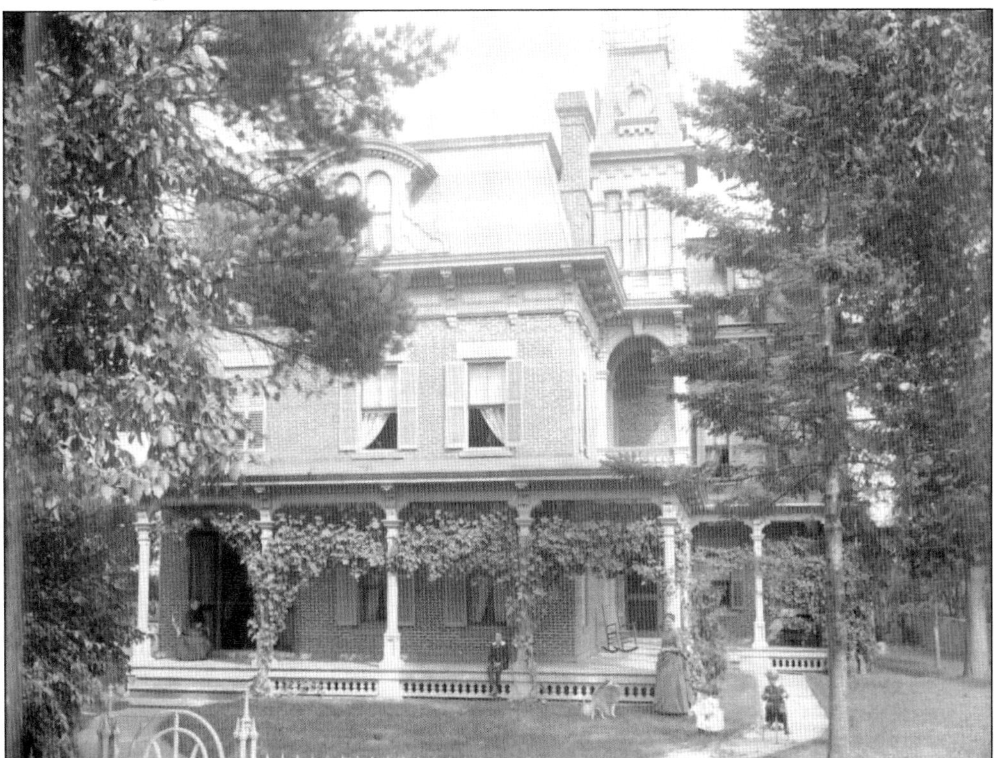

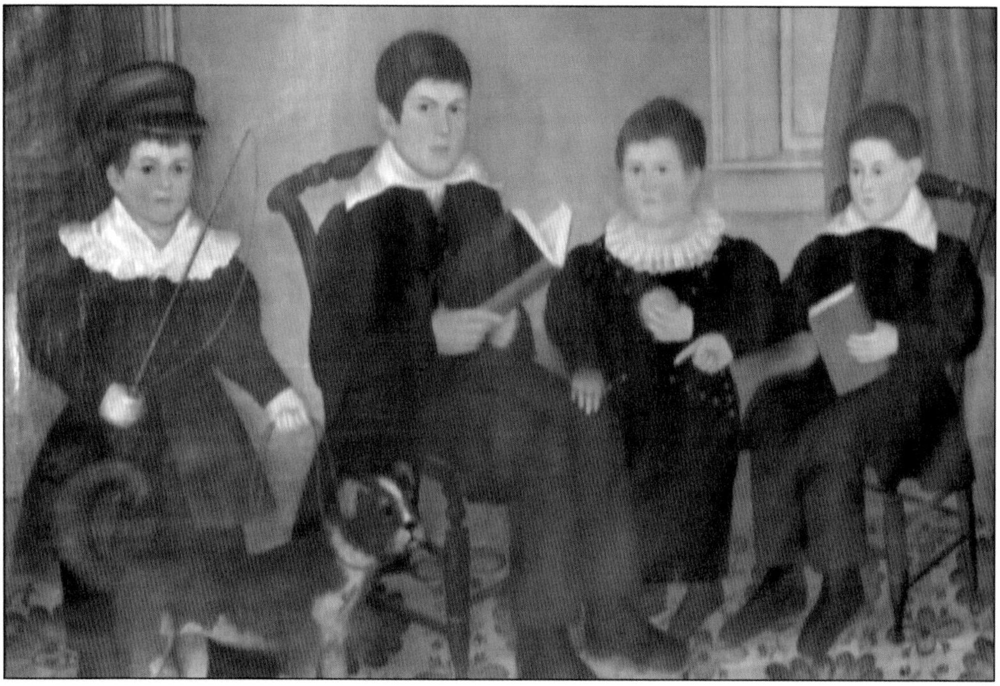

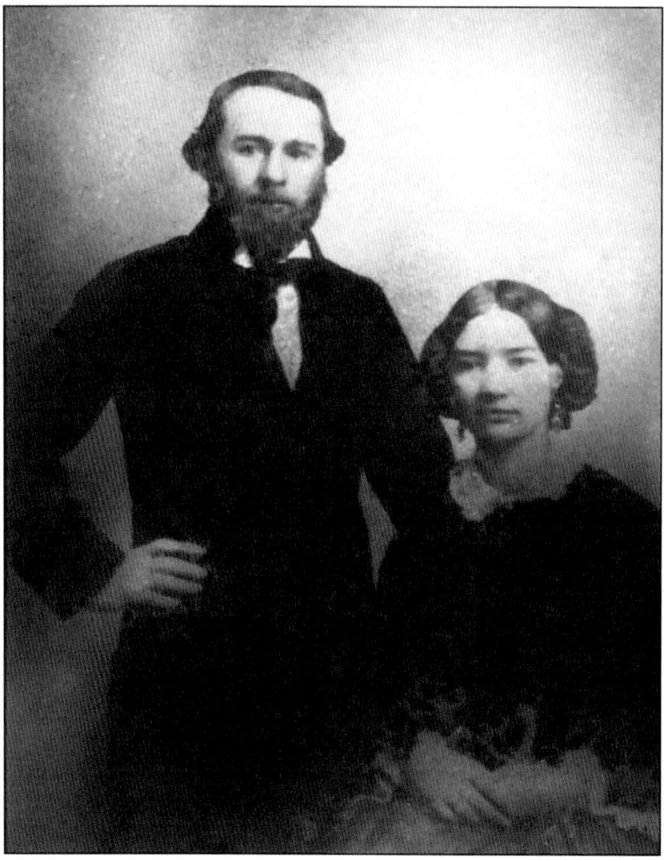

George Henry Standart was born on May 17, 1829, to Needham Standart and his second wife, Naomi Wilbor Standart. His half-brother William was born in 1825 to Needham and first wife, Margaret Hamilton. She died February 2, 1828, after a carriage accident that had occurred in October 1827. George Henry and William are pictured here with Charles Wilbur and Stephen H.

George Henry Standart poses with his wife, Myra Allen Standart, in this portrait. George had two other brothers, Charles Wilbor and Stephen H., shown in the previous painting, and a sister, not shown. George Henry died in Denver, Colorado, on April 17, 1887.

Nellie Standart, born in 1861, was the daughter of George Henry and Myra Standart. This photograph shows her at the time of her marriage to Harley Gibbs. Nellie's brother Henry Needham Standart lived in Cleveland and died in Denver, Colorado, on December 28, 1919.

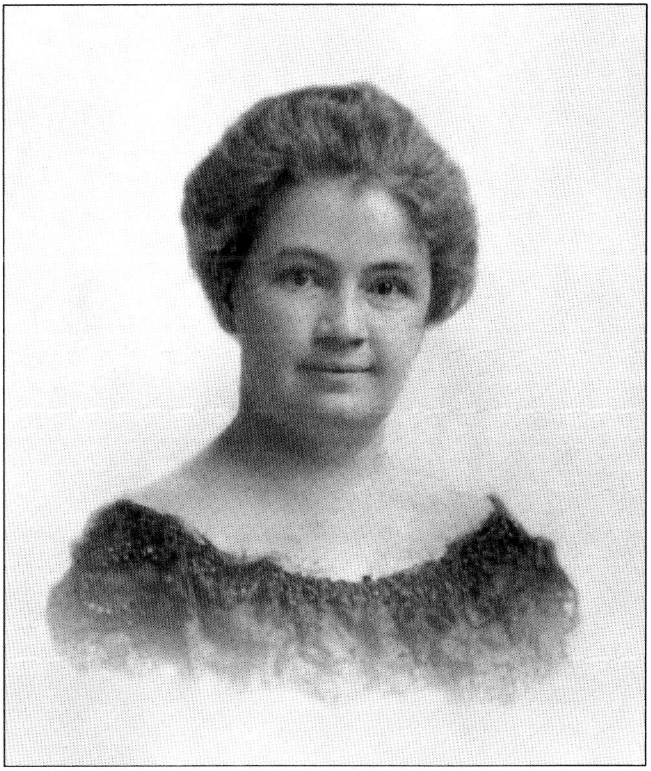

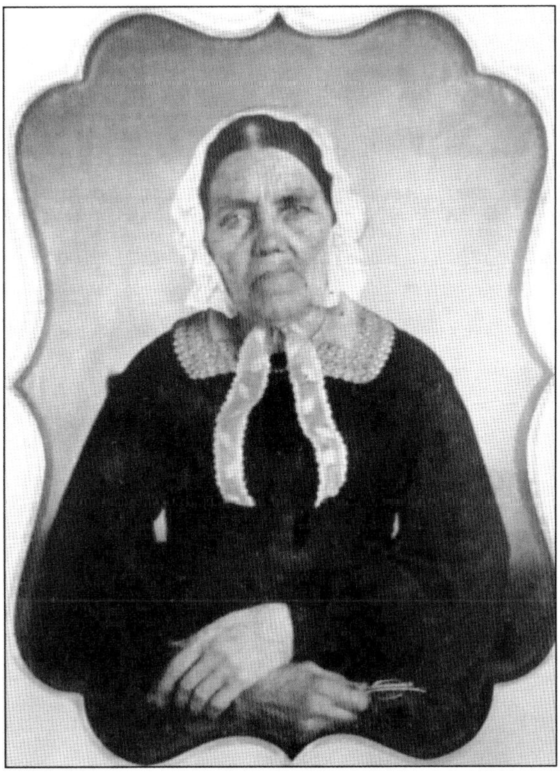

Charlotte Adams Merry, born in Tinemouth, Vermont, on August 17, 1780, was the daughter of Sarah and Aaron Adams, brother of John Quincy Adams. She died at the age of 99 on February 8, 1879.

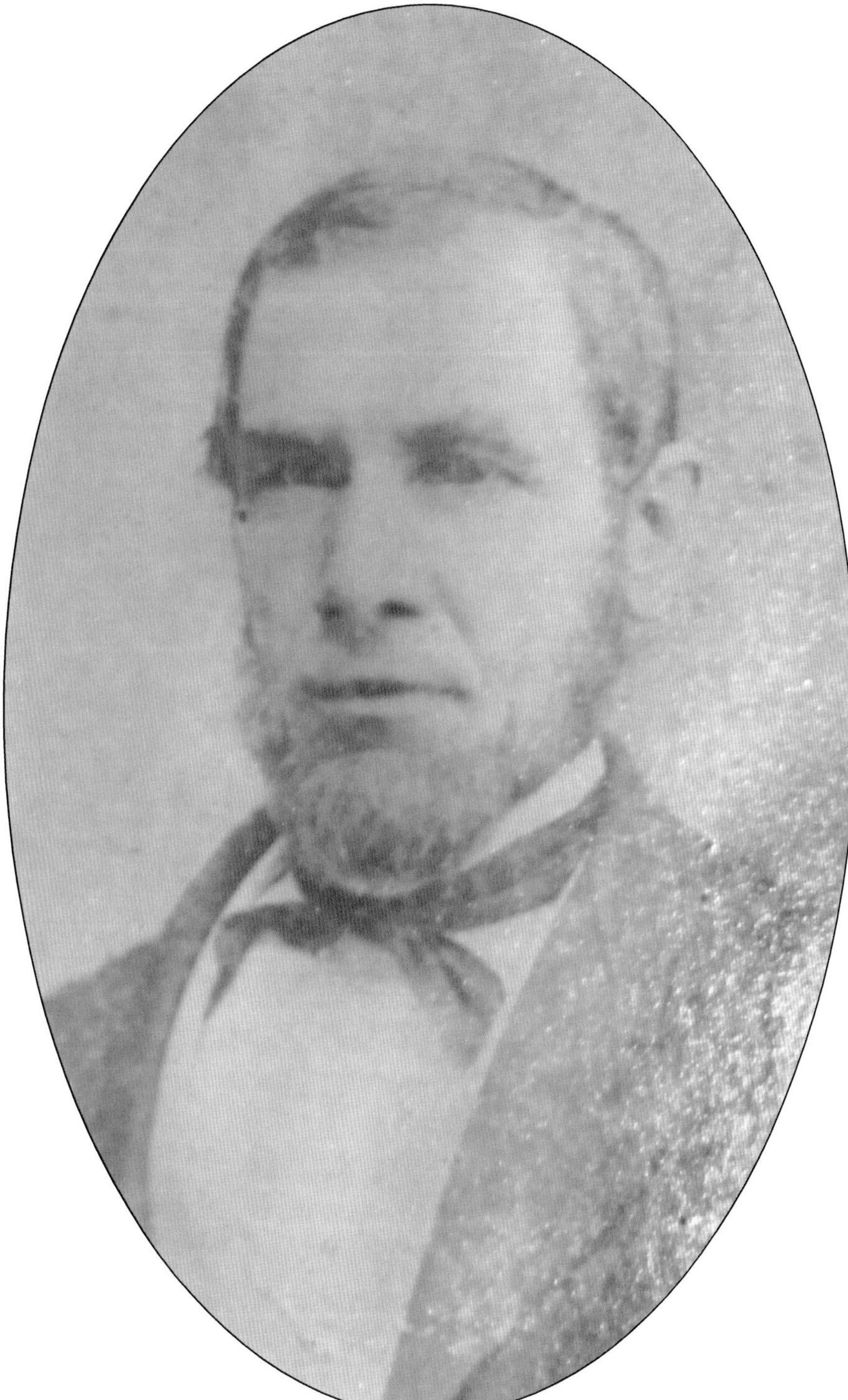

Ebenezer Merry II was born in Milan in January 1820. At the age of 24, he was chosen recorder of the county, serving from 1844 to 1850. In 1867, he was elected county auditor and served for 14 years. He died in April 1888.

This mid-1870s photograph shows Atta Moore Merry, wife of Ebenezer Merry II. Atta Moore was born in 1824 to Ruth Merry and Orasmus Milton Moore. She married Ebenezer Merry II in 1846, and together they had eight children. She died in 1898.

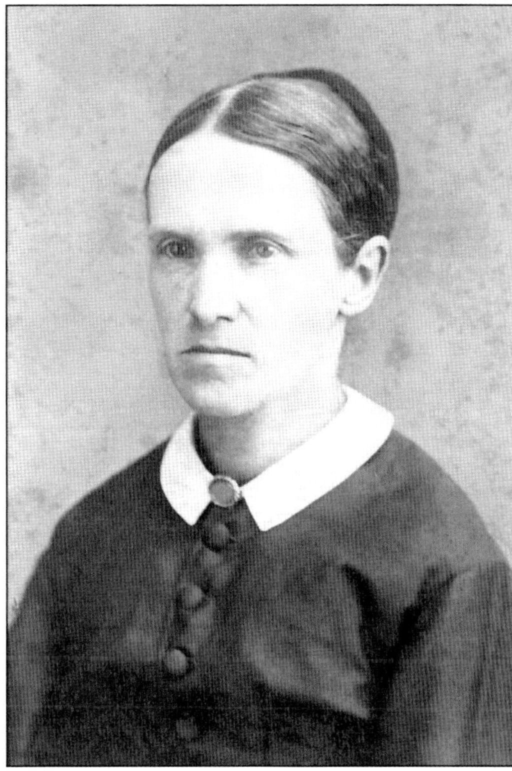

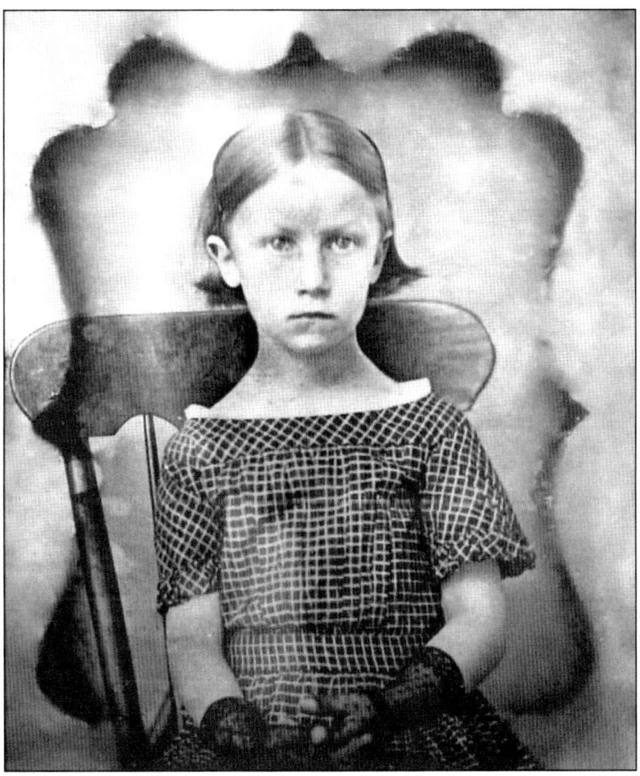

Ruth Rose Merry was the daughter of Ebenezer II and Atta Merry. She was born on August 2, 1848, the first child of Atta and Ebenezer Merry. She died in Milan on December 21, 1871.

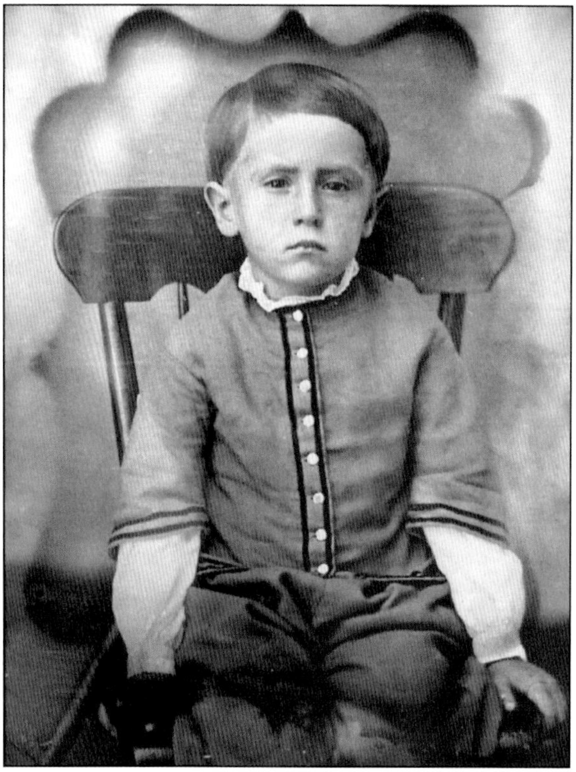

Ebenezer Junior Merry was the son of Ebenezer II and Atta Merry. He was born on September 16, 1850, and died on May 3, 1882, in Atchison, Kansas.

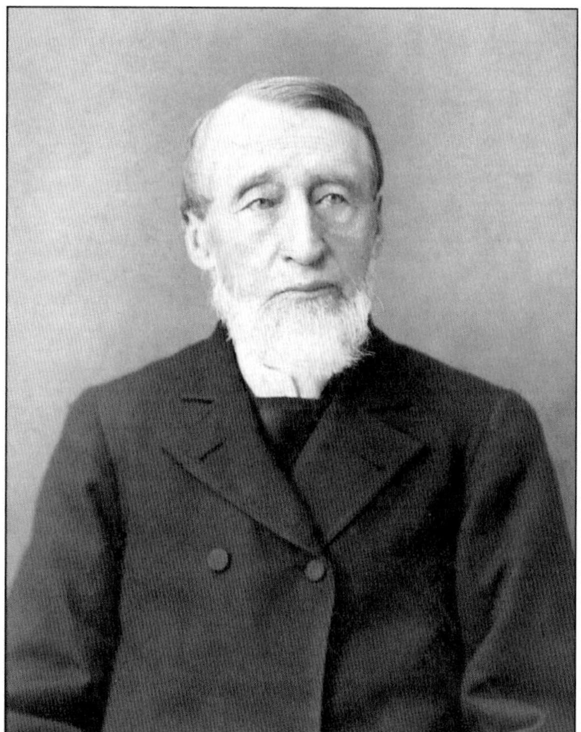

Augustus Porter Mowry was born in 1812, the son of Augustus and Polly (Hazelton) Mowry. He was married to Betsey M. Adams on December 31, 1838, in Huron by Reverend Judson, and together they had three children. A.P. Mowry owned the schooners M. *Stalker*, built in 1861, and *Winona*, built in 1862. Both ships were built by Henry Kelley.

James Cannon Lockwood was born in Norwalk, Connecticut, on November 14, 1814. He was the son of George and Mary (Cannon) Lockwood. By 14, he was working as a clerk for Nathan Jenkins, buying him out at the age of 21. Lockwood married Louise Choate in December 1835, and in 1880, he wed his second wife, Mary Van Norman. He died on November 27, 1890, having one son, Jay.

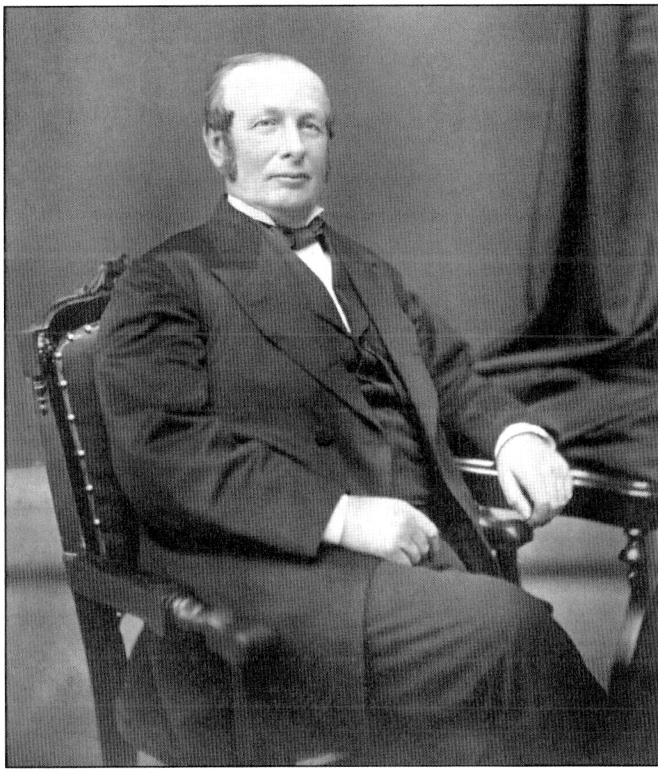

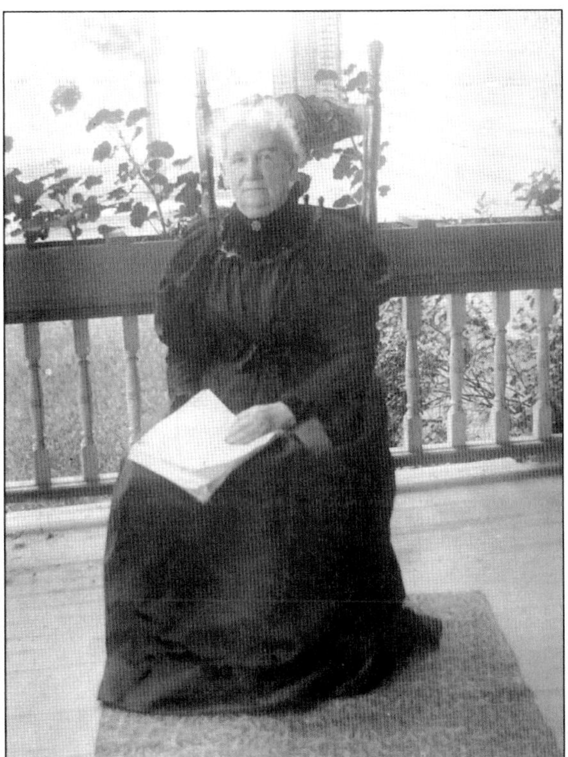

Sarah (Lockwood) Lockwood was born on October 30, 1826, to George and Mary Lockwood in Milan, Ohio. She was a sister of James C. Lockwood and married Stephen A. Lockwood in 1847. Together they had eight children. She died on April 6, 1914.

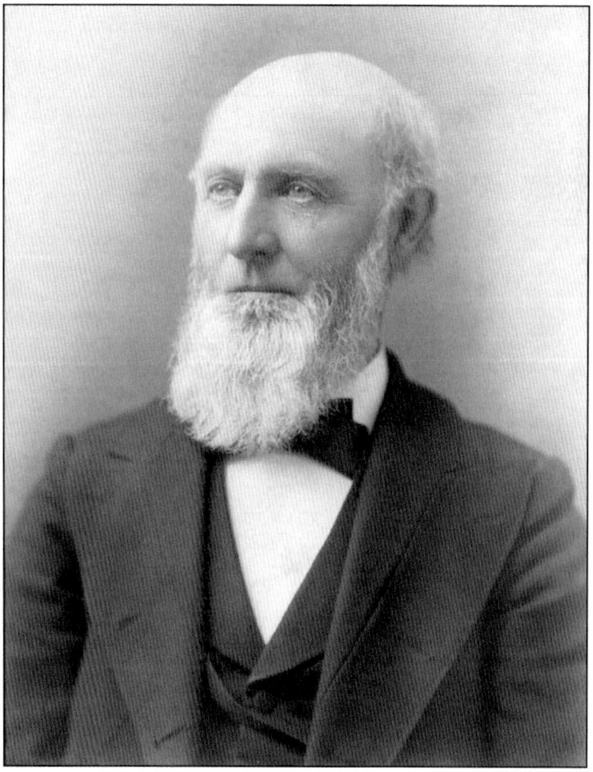

Stephen Adolphus Lockwood was born on June 11, 1820, the son of Ralph Lockwood. He was one of the first students of the Huron Institute and went into business with his brother William. Together they formed S. & W. Lockwood mercantile on the west side of the square, which was destroyed during the fire of 1852. He died on March 6, 1898, at the age of 78.

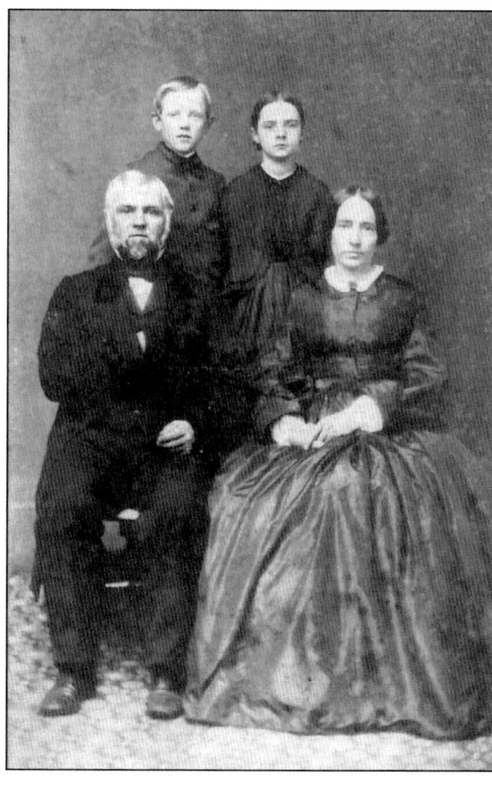

This photograph shows Dr. Leman Galpin and his family. Before becoming a prominent doctor in Milan and the attending physician at the birth of Thomas Edison, Galpin studied medicine under Dr. M. Stuart. He began his own practice in 1839 and continued to serve in Milan for 35 years. He married Electa Euphrasia Adams in 1844, and together they had two children, William and Mary.

William Adams Galpin was born on December 20, 1851, in Milan. He became one of Milan's greatest benefactors, donating half of the site for the Milan Public Library with A.L. Hoover. He also established endowments for the library and the Presbyterian church, as well as land for the Galpin Sanctuary. He married three times and had two children.

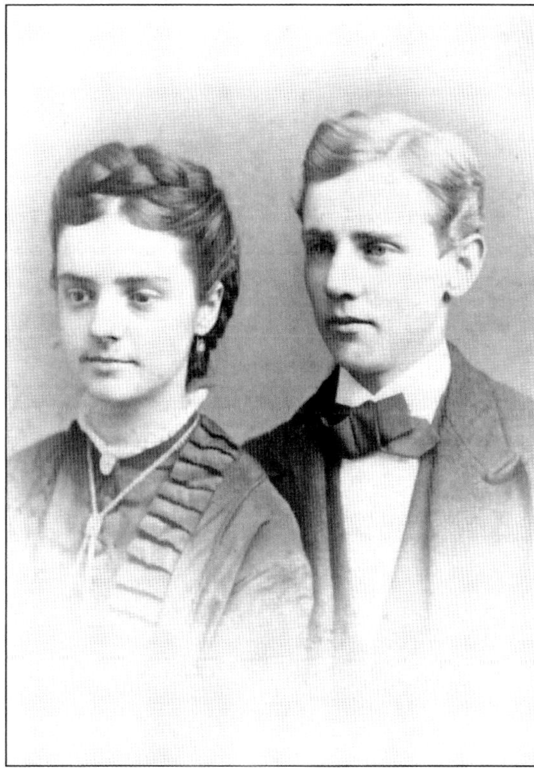

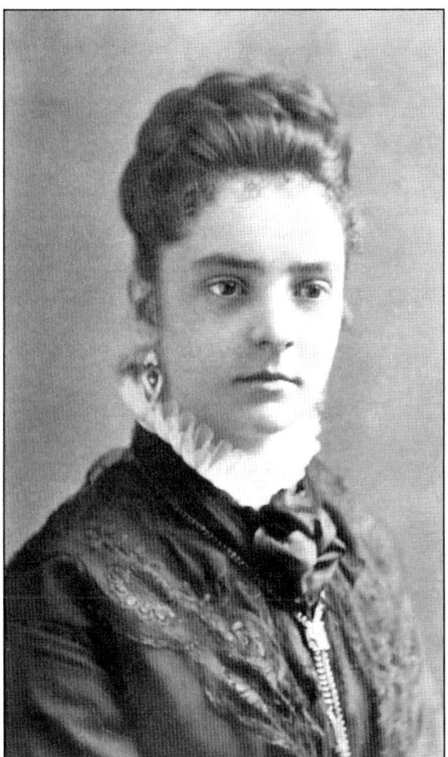

Mary Euphrasia Galpin was born on May 30, 1854, in Milan. She attended Oberlin College and married Lyman White on June 17, 1874. Together they moved to Michigan where she raised their two daughters.

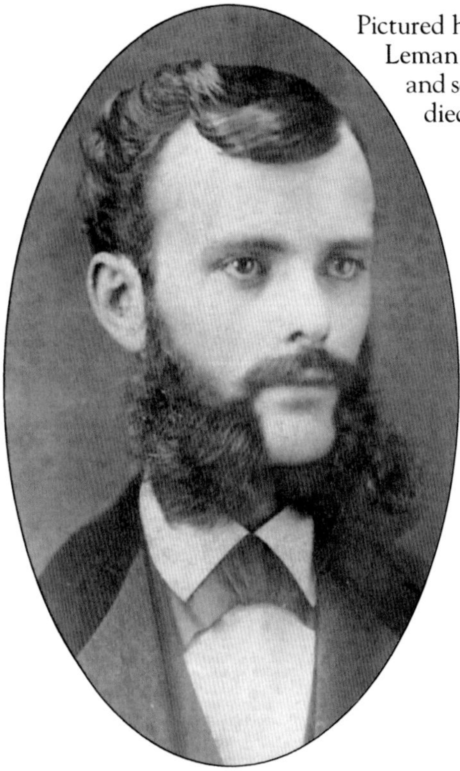

Pictured here is Lyman White, husband of Mary Galpin. Dr. Leman Galpin moved to Michigan to live with his daughter and son-in-law until his death on August 23, 1893. Lyman died on May 22, 1921.

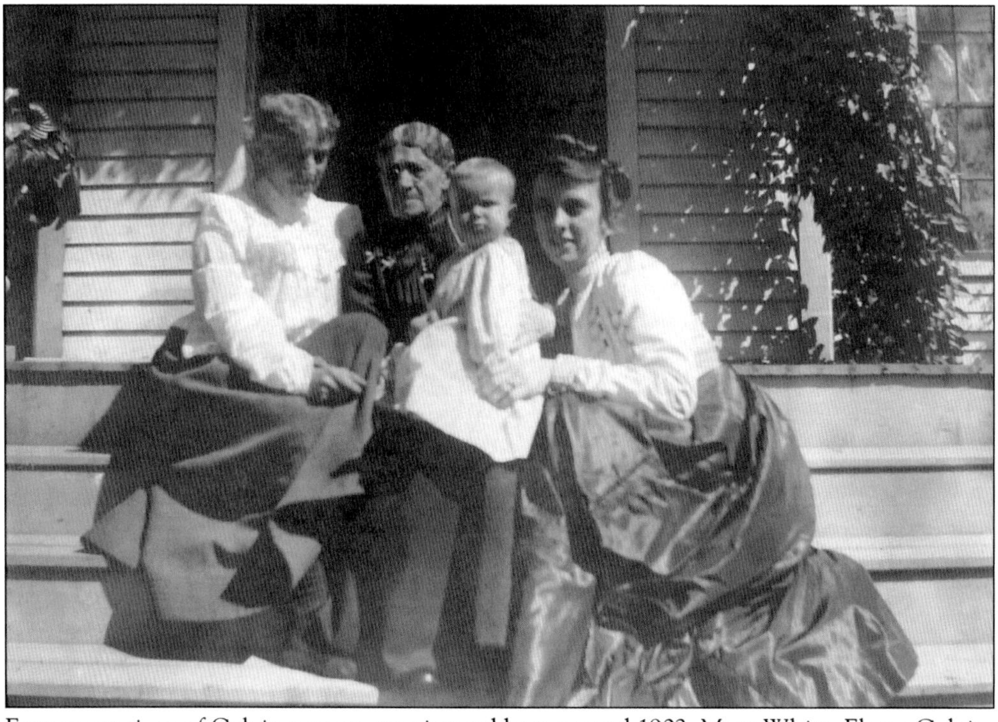

Four generations of Galpin women are pictured here around 1902: Mary White, Electa Galpin, Mary's daughter Marie, and Marie's baby, Ruth.

Maria Butman, on behalf of the ladies of Milan, presented Captain Moran of the schooner *Kewanee* with a flag during the festivities of the opening of the Milan Canal on July 4, 1839.

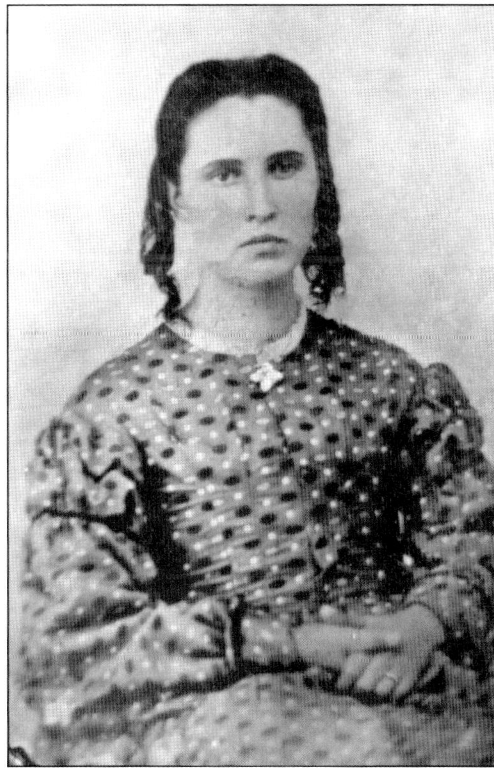

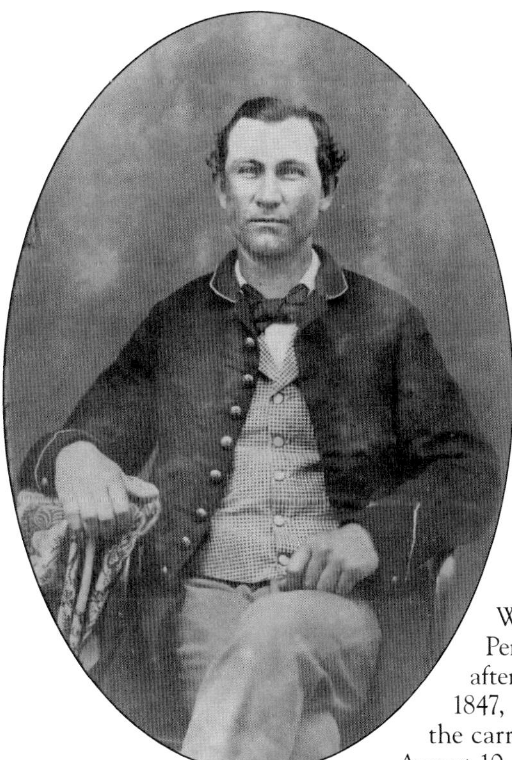

William Beers was born in Bloomsburg, Pennsylvania, on May 17, 1820. He moved to Milan after his marriage to Esther Anna Leach on April 21, 1847, in Wooster, Ohio. For years, William operated the carriage and wagon factory in Milan. He died on August 10, 1903.

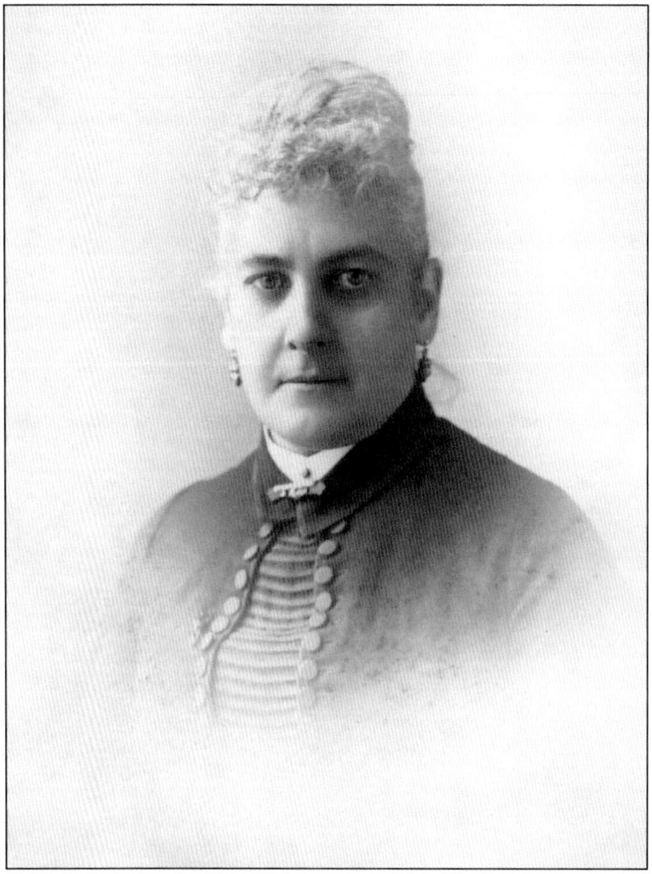

Eleanor Andrews was born in 1840, the daughter of Ebenezer Andrews and Rachel Hyde. She died in her family home in Milan on April 4, 1924.

J.L. Smith poses with his family in this photograph. Smith was one of several Milan blacksmiths and a partner of John Sisty. John W. Sisty lived to the age of 95, passing away on February 11, 1920.

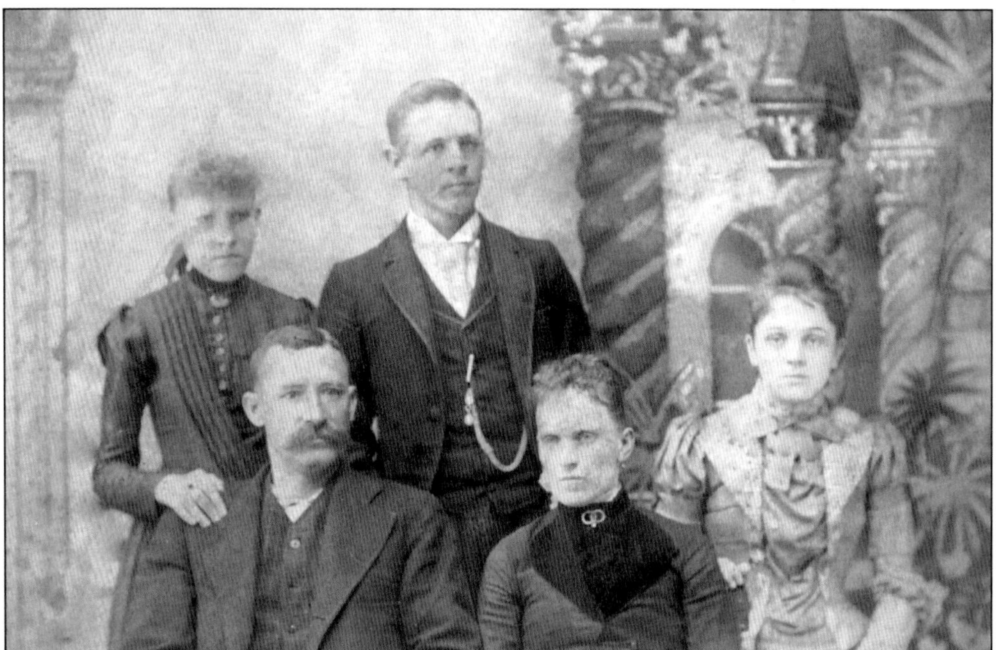

Ralph W. Sayles was born in 1852 and married Mary Elizabeth Cherry in 1871. Their son, Robert, was born in 1888 and married Florence Brown in 1913. This photograph was taken around 1890.

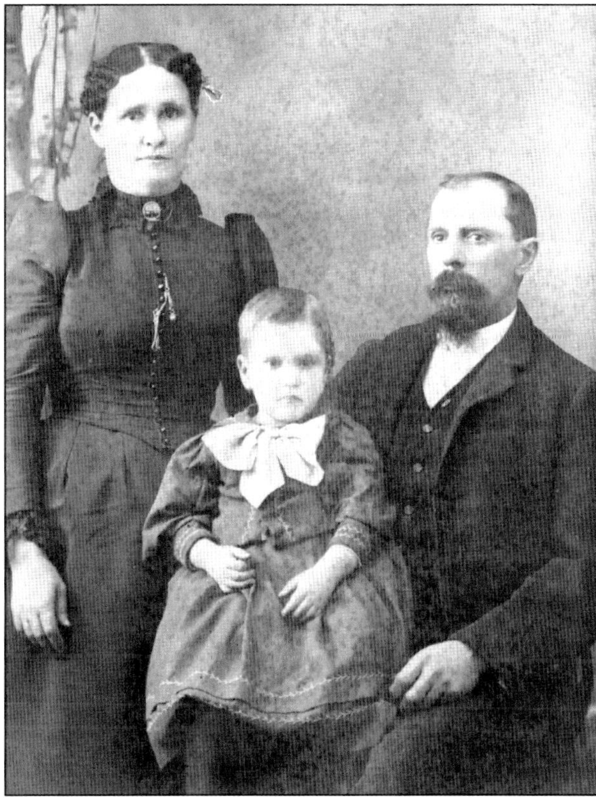

Eight members of the Sayles family pose on the front porch of the Sayles house around 1890. In that year, the home was owned by William and Alvina Sayles Sands.

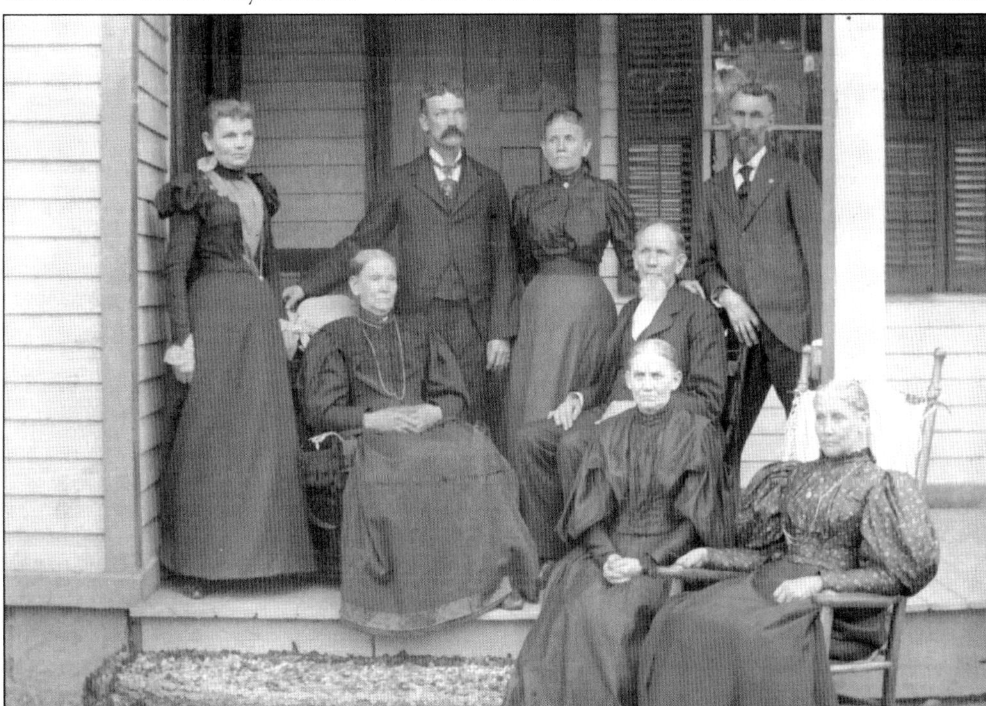

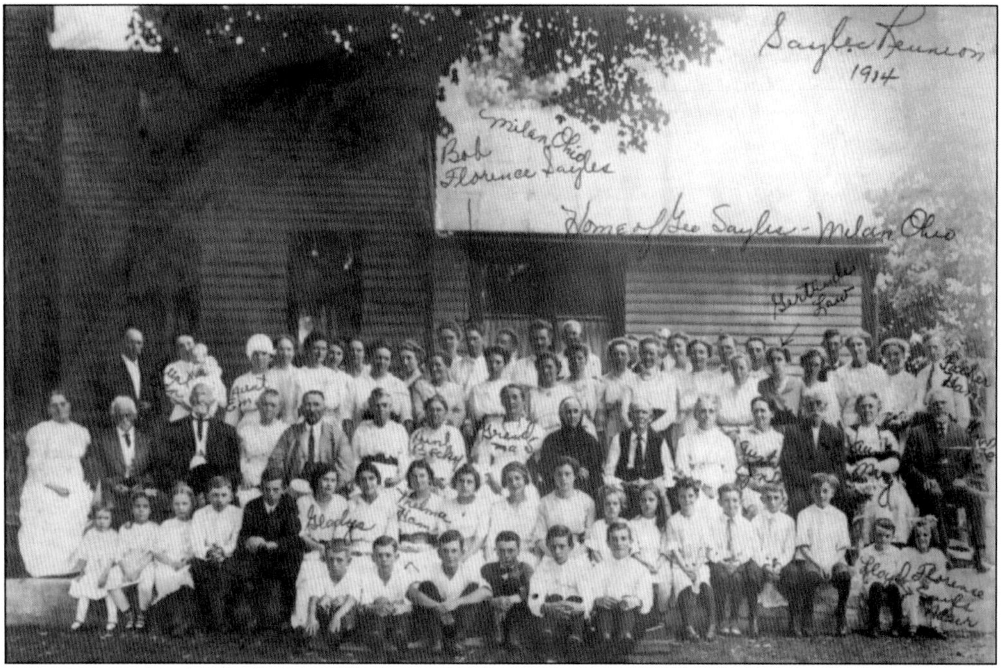

This photograph shows the large Sayles family reunion in Milan in 1914. David Sayles, a motorman with the Sandusky-Milan-Norwalk Division of the Lake Shore Electric, had two sons, Waldo and Ralph Sayles. The boys became avid ham radio enthusiasts, and the Milan Historical Museum hosts an annual radio event each February.

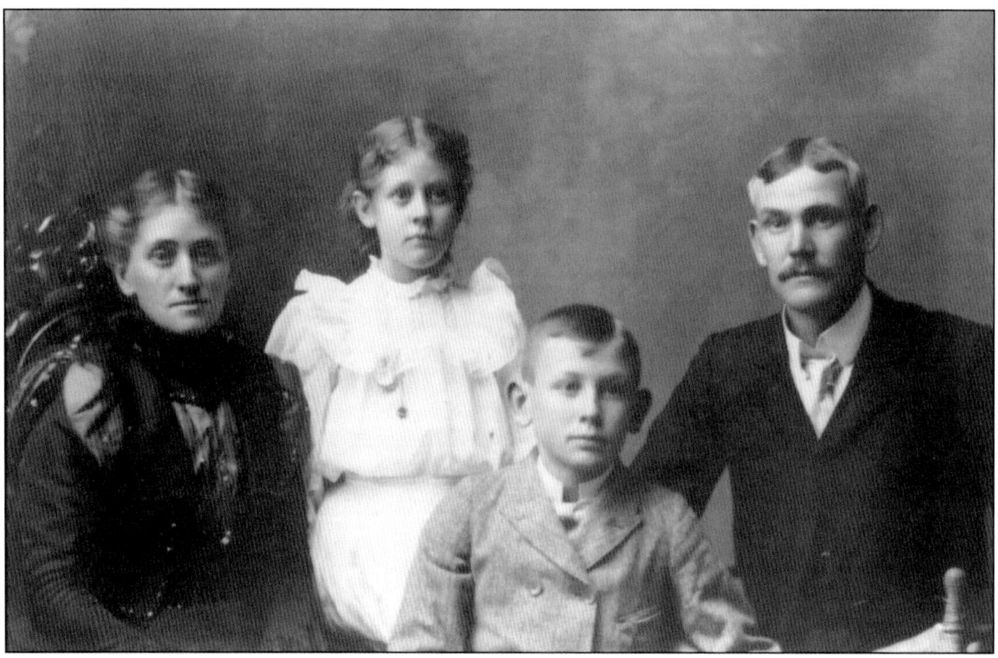

James Sands was the son of William Sands and Alvina Sayles Sands. He is pictured here with his wife, Lavina Jenkins, and children Forrest Evelyn and Roy.

Carrie Hastings was the daughter of Capt. Hugh Hastings and Elizabeth Hastings. She was born in 1869 and died on November 28, 1921.

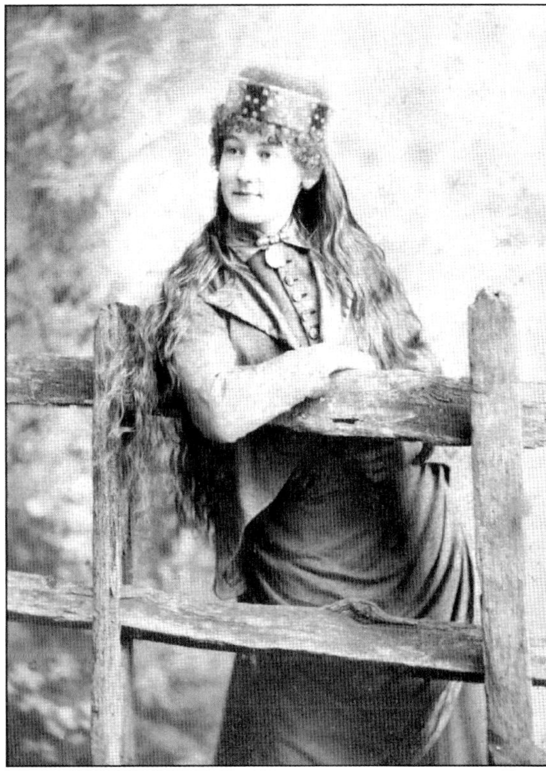

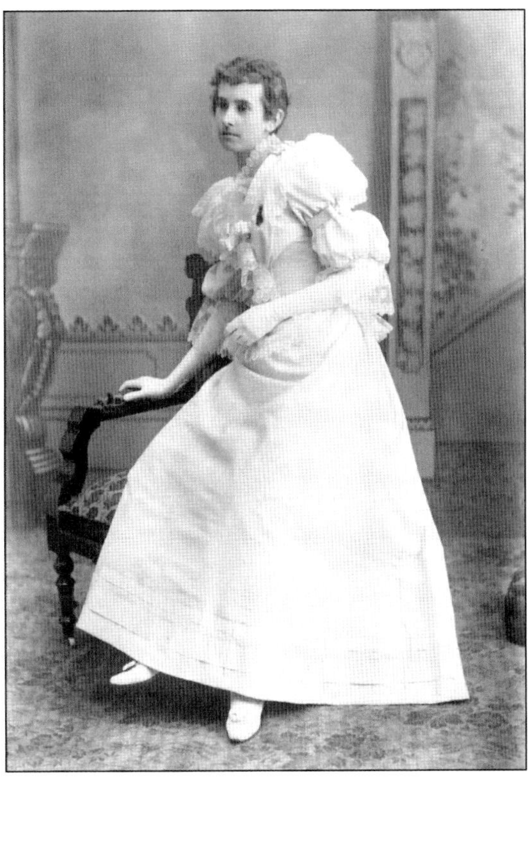

Carrie Belle Eggleston was born in Milan on April 21, 1874, passing at the young age of 36. She graduated from Milan Public School on March 2, 1894, and taught for the next 15 years.

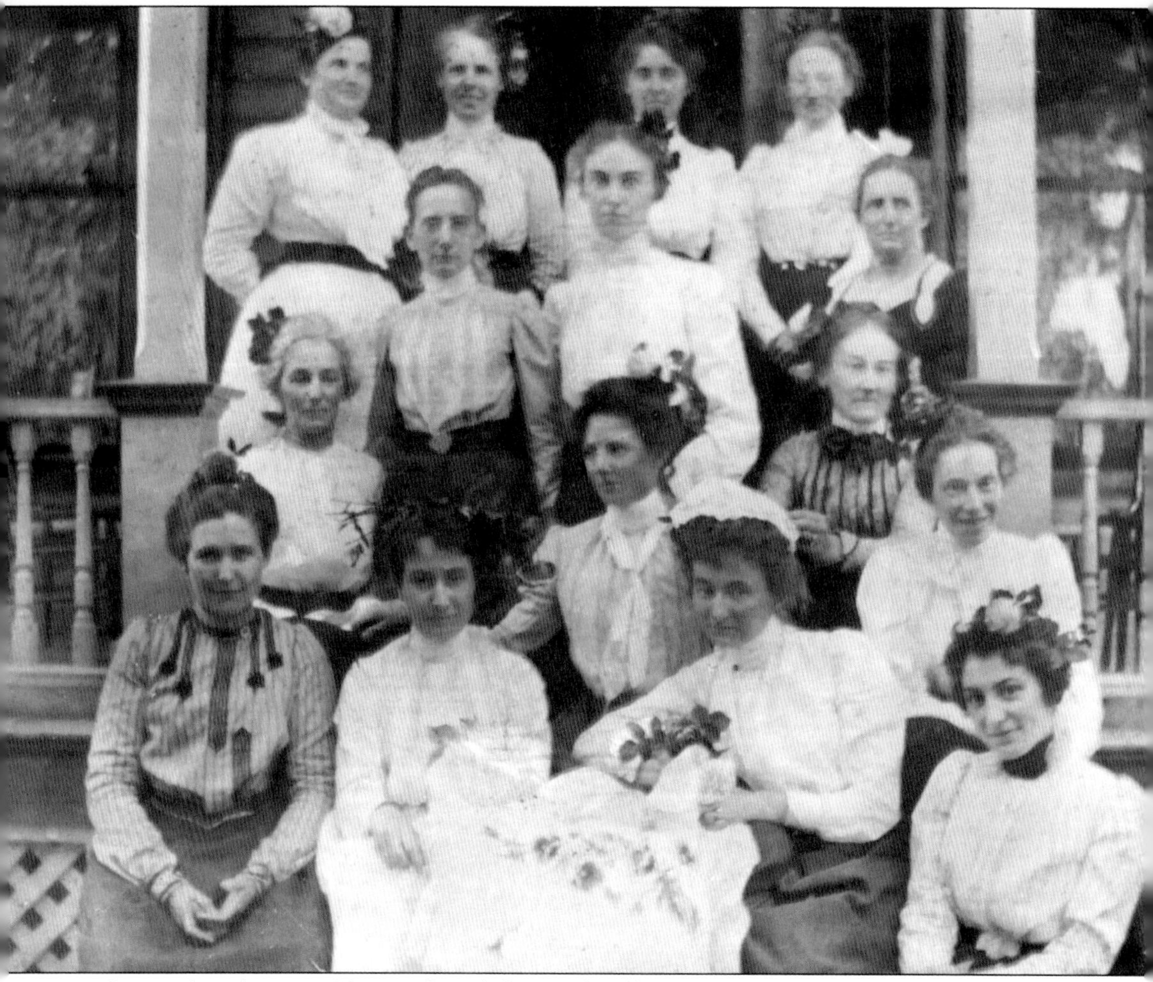

Pictured in August 1901 are, from left to right, (first row) Amanda Bedell, Tate Turner, Fay Coulter, and ? Ripple; (second row) ? Seaman, May Lockwood, Carrie Hastings, and Bell Doane; (third row) Nellie Mixter, Libbie Lockwood, and Mim Mowry; (fourth row) Stella Garnhart, Kate Smith, Verna Williams, and Nellie Kirkpatrick.

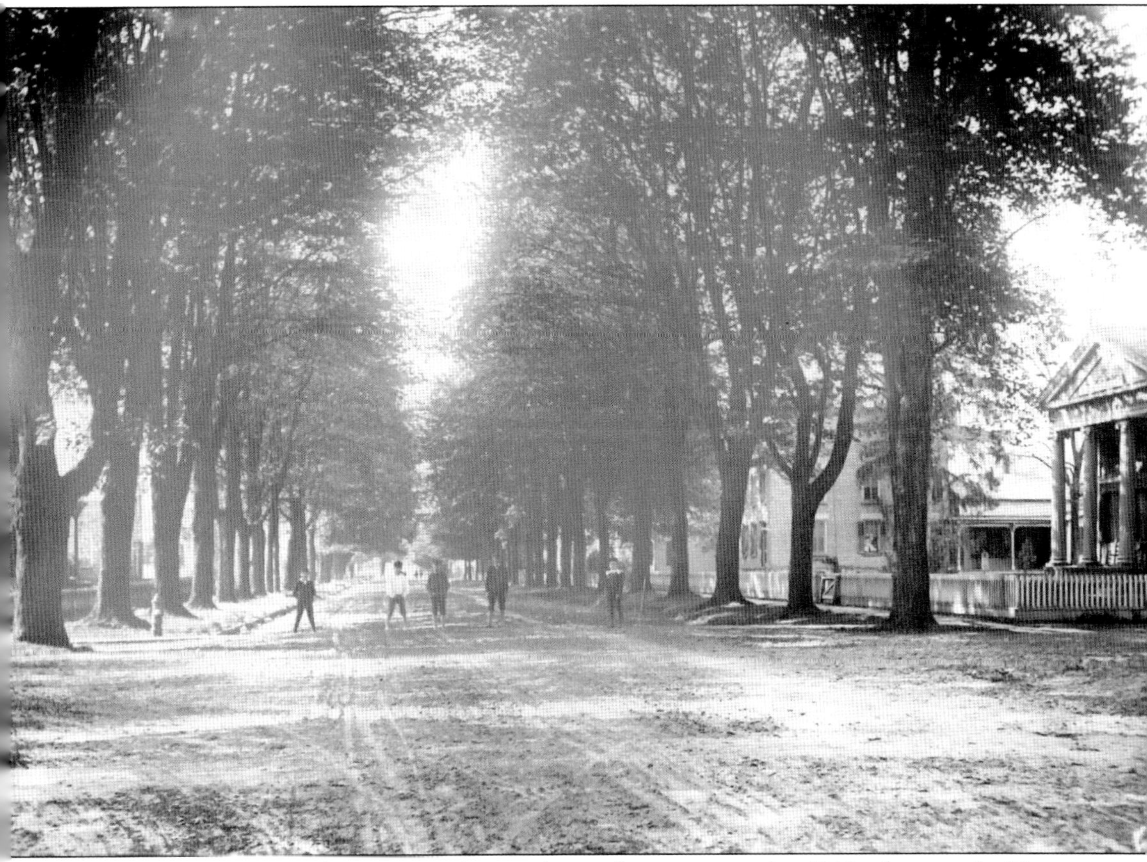

Several boys stand in Milan's Center Street, then a dirt street, in this 1910s photograph. The home built by Zenas King can be seen on the right. King lived in Milan for several years before he conceived and secured a patent in 1858 for an iron bridge. He became the head of the King Bridge Company of Cleveland.

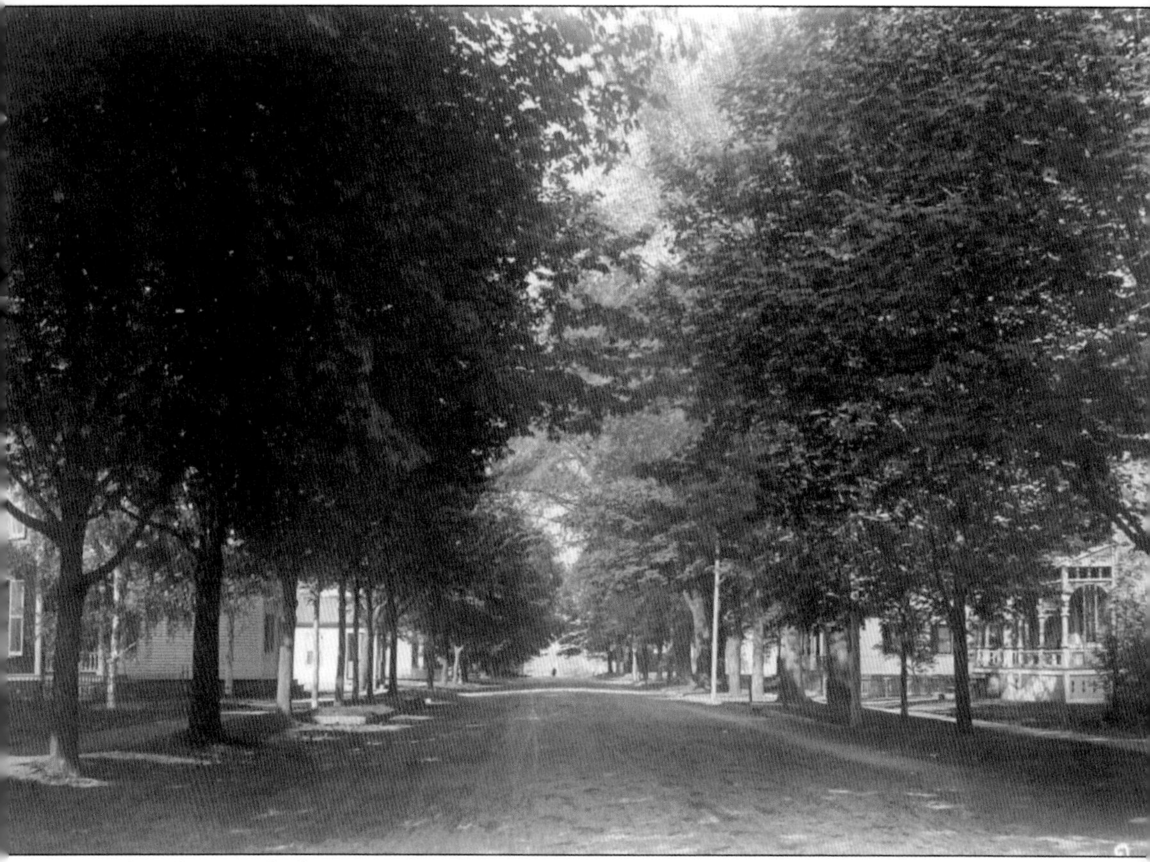

This photograph shows Front Street in Milan. The once-busy streets were quiet and lined with trees. The Nathan Jenkins home, located on the other end of Front Street, was bought by Dr. E.L. Perry. He was born on October 19, 1826, and came to Milan in 1856. He practiced dentistry and was elected mayor of Milan for several terms. He died on September 5, 1910.

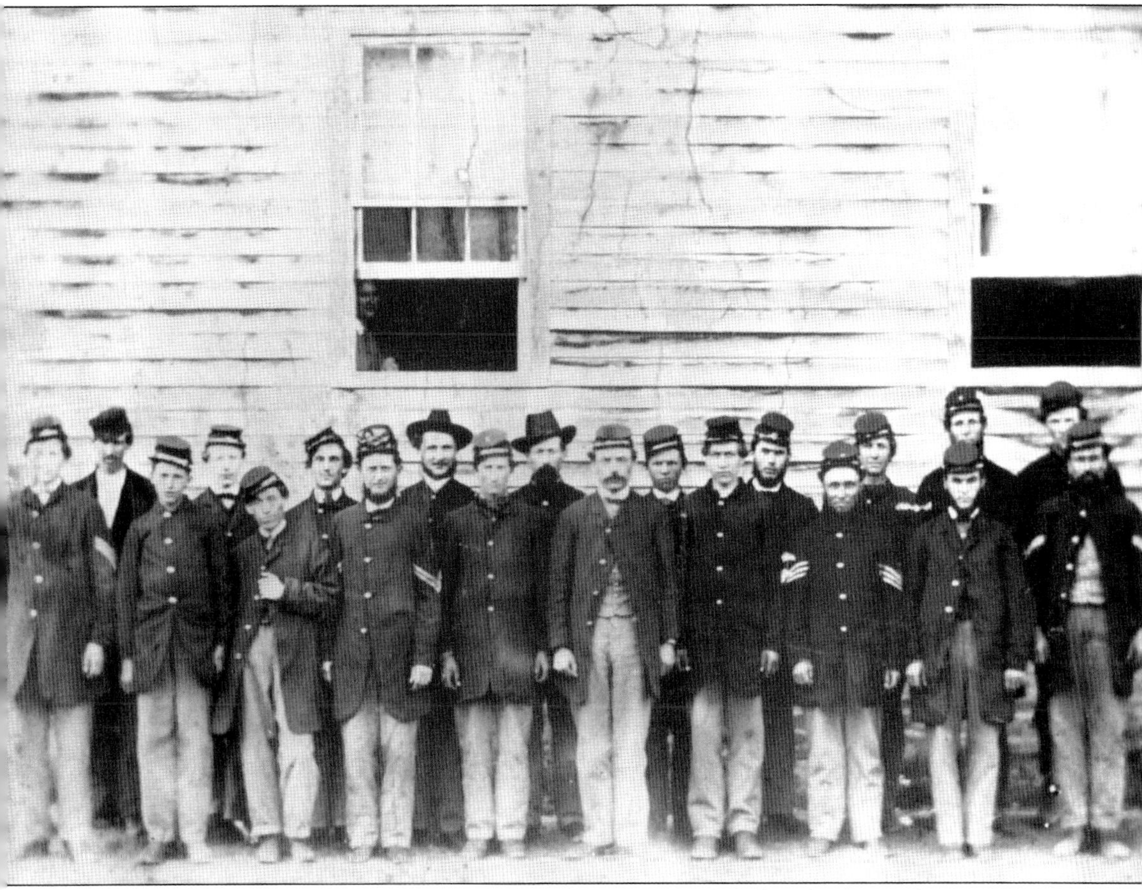

A company of Civil War soldiers in uniform are shown standing beside the Eagle Tavern in the early 1860s. Milan sent 330 men to fight, most in the 55th Regiment of the Ohio Volunteer Infantry, Company C.

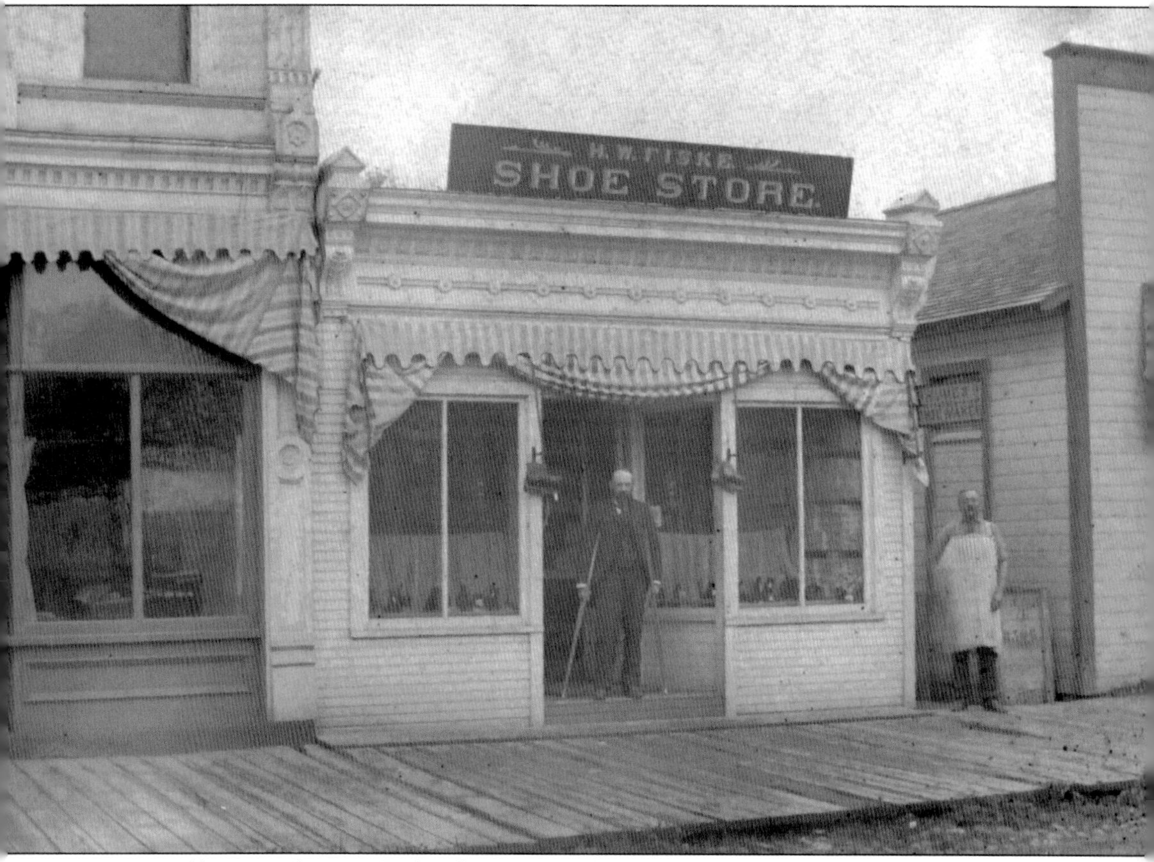

Pictured here are the H.W. Riske Shoe Store and Kent P. Ruggles. Ruggles was the son of Comfort Heber Ruggles, who was born on November 18, 1841. On November 27, 1868, Comfort married Charlotte Harmony Merry. Kent was born June 26, 1880, graduated from Milan High School in 1898, and lived in Cuyahoga Falls with his wife, Bessie James, and son, Arthur James.

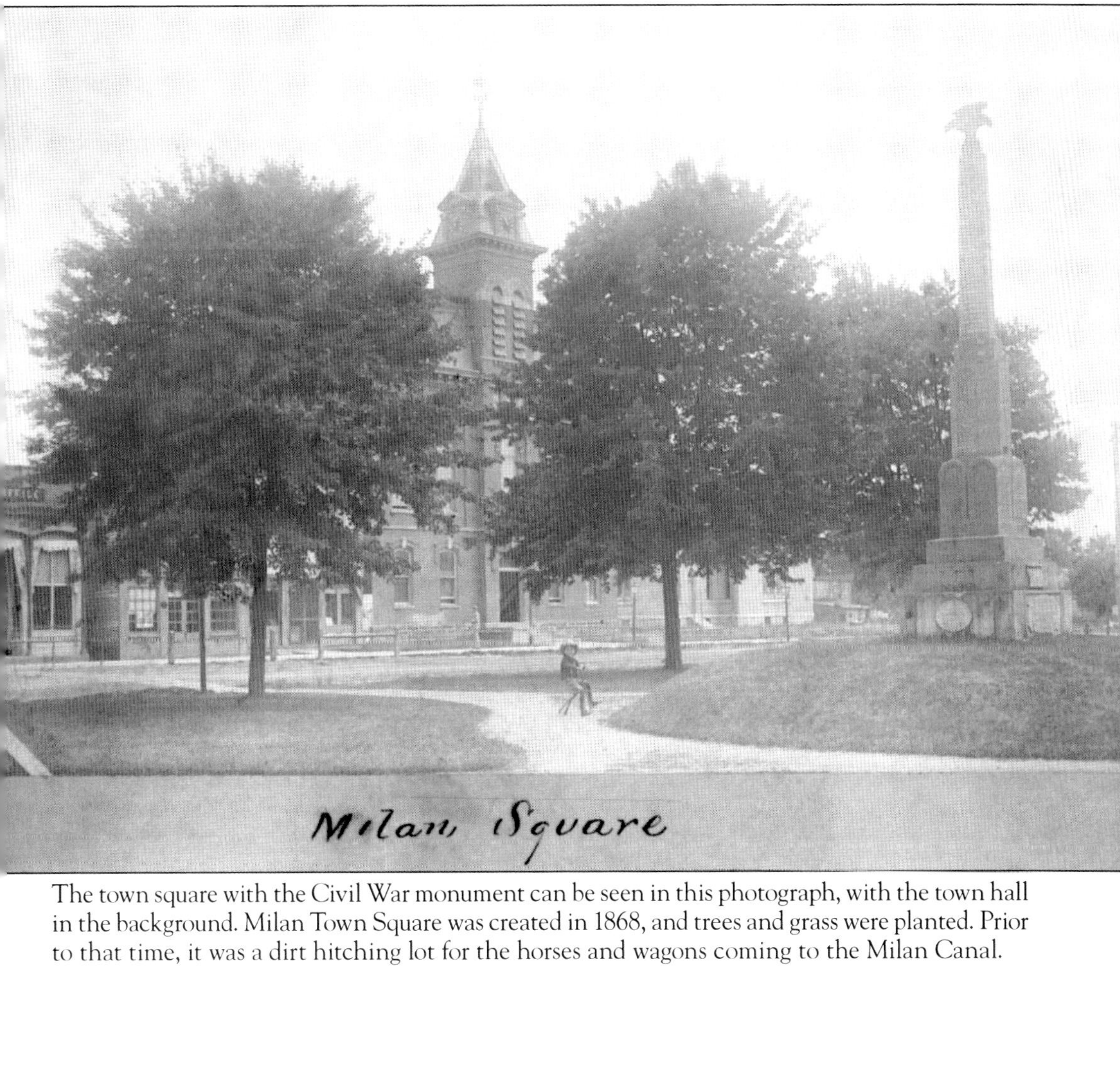

The town square with the Civil War monument can be seen in this photograph, with the town hall in the background. Milan Town Square was created in 1868, and trees and grass were planted. Prior to that time, it was a dirt hitching lot for the horses and wagons coming to the Milan Canal.

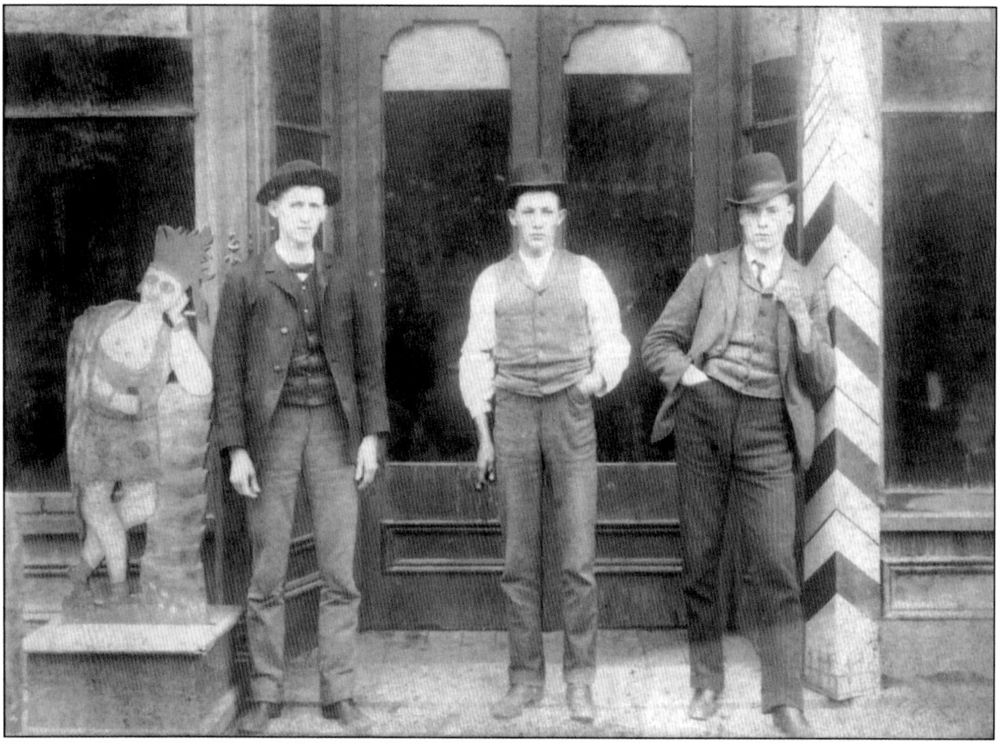

Three men stand in front of a barber shop in Milan. Earl Mann is in the center, with Alfred Walbridge on the right. Alfred and his wife, Lucy, were the parents of George A. Walbridge.

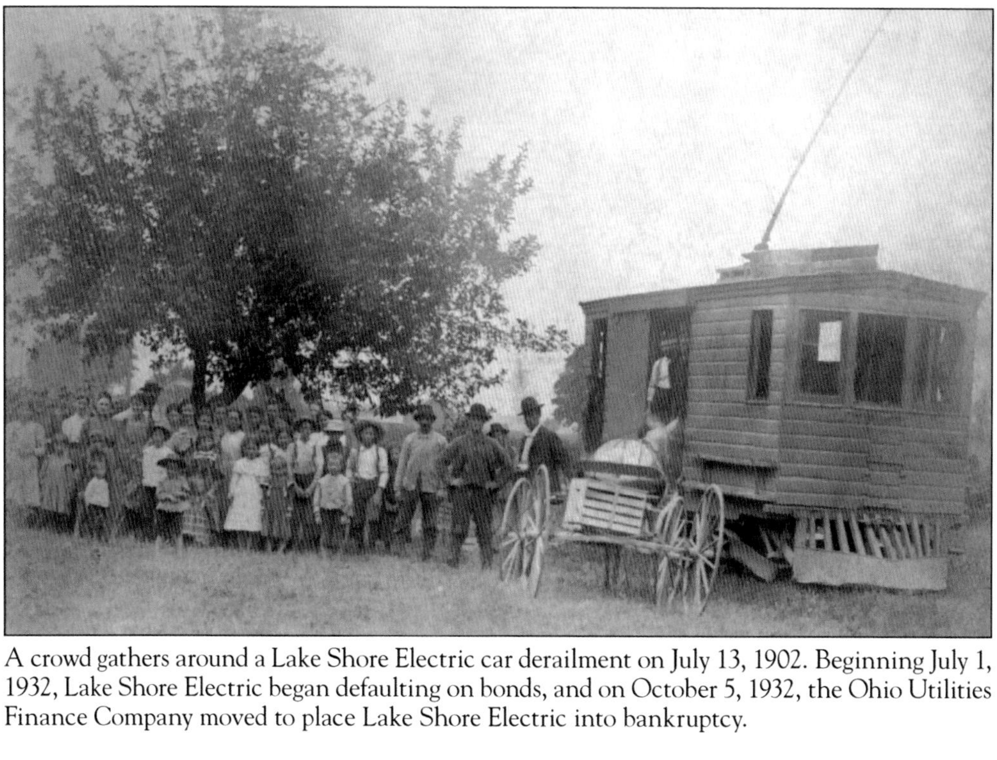

A crowd gathers around a Lake Shore Electric car derailment on July 13, 1902. Beginning July 1, 1932, Lake Shore Electric began defaulting on bonds, and on October 5, 1932, the Ohio Utilities Finance Company moved to place Lake Shore Electric into bankruptcy.

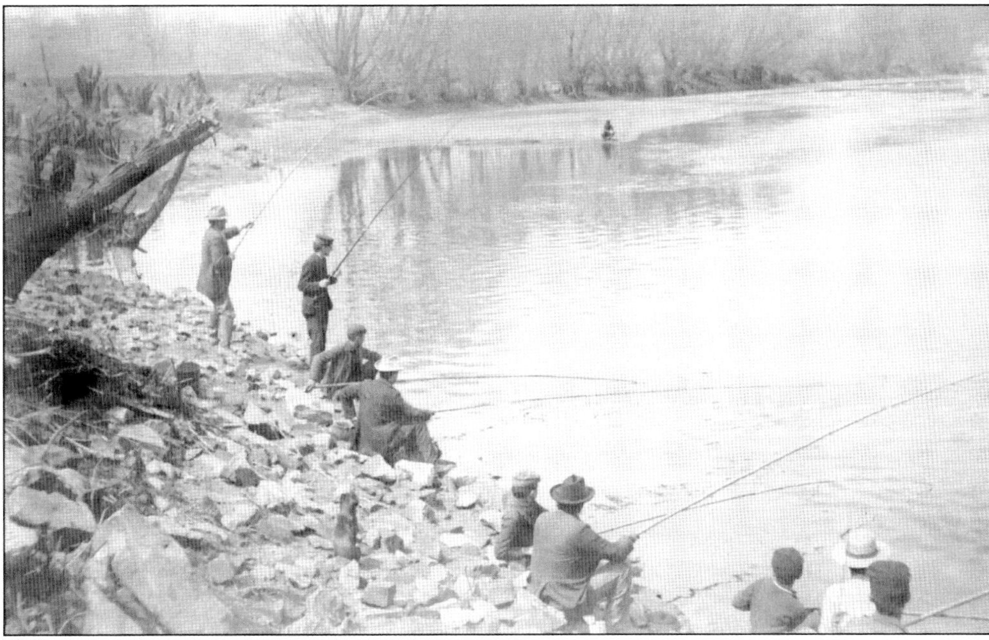

The Huron River presented a peaceful pastime for the men pictured here. Natural formations in the shale known as concretions are scattered along the river banks. These spherical forms vary in size and finding them was another favorite activity.

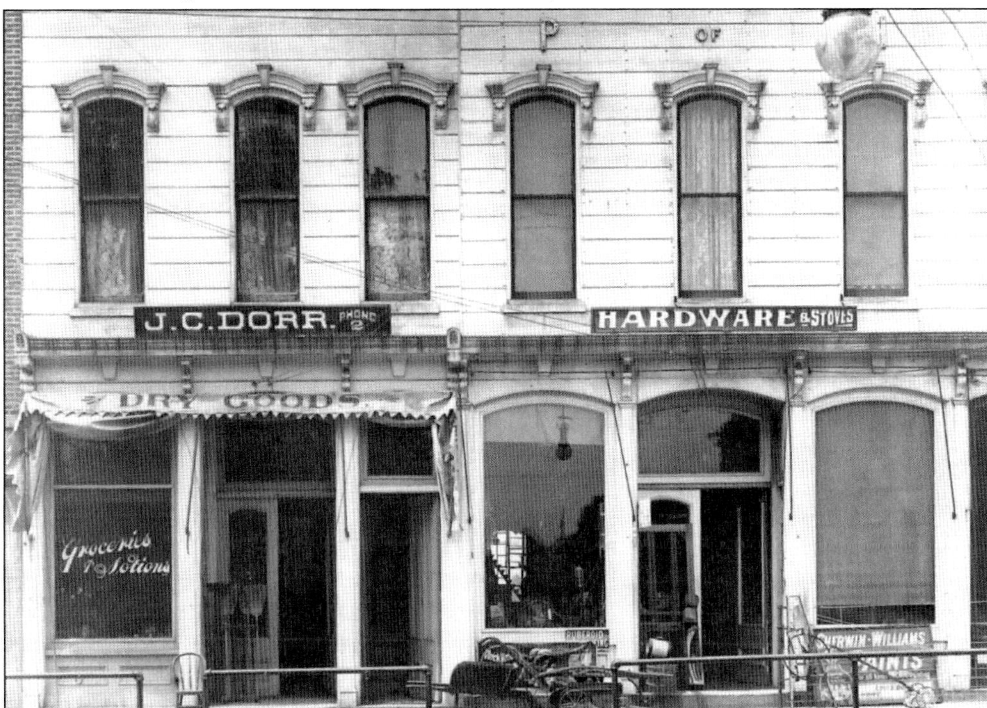

This photograph shows J.C. Dorr Groceries and the Milan Hardware Store on the north side of the square. The second story housed meetings of the local National Grange Order of Patrons of Husbandry, a fraternal organization with a focus on agriculture.

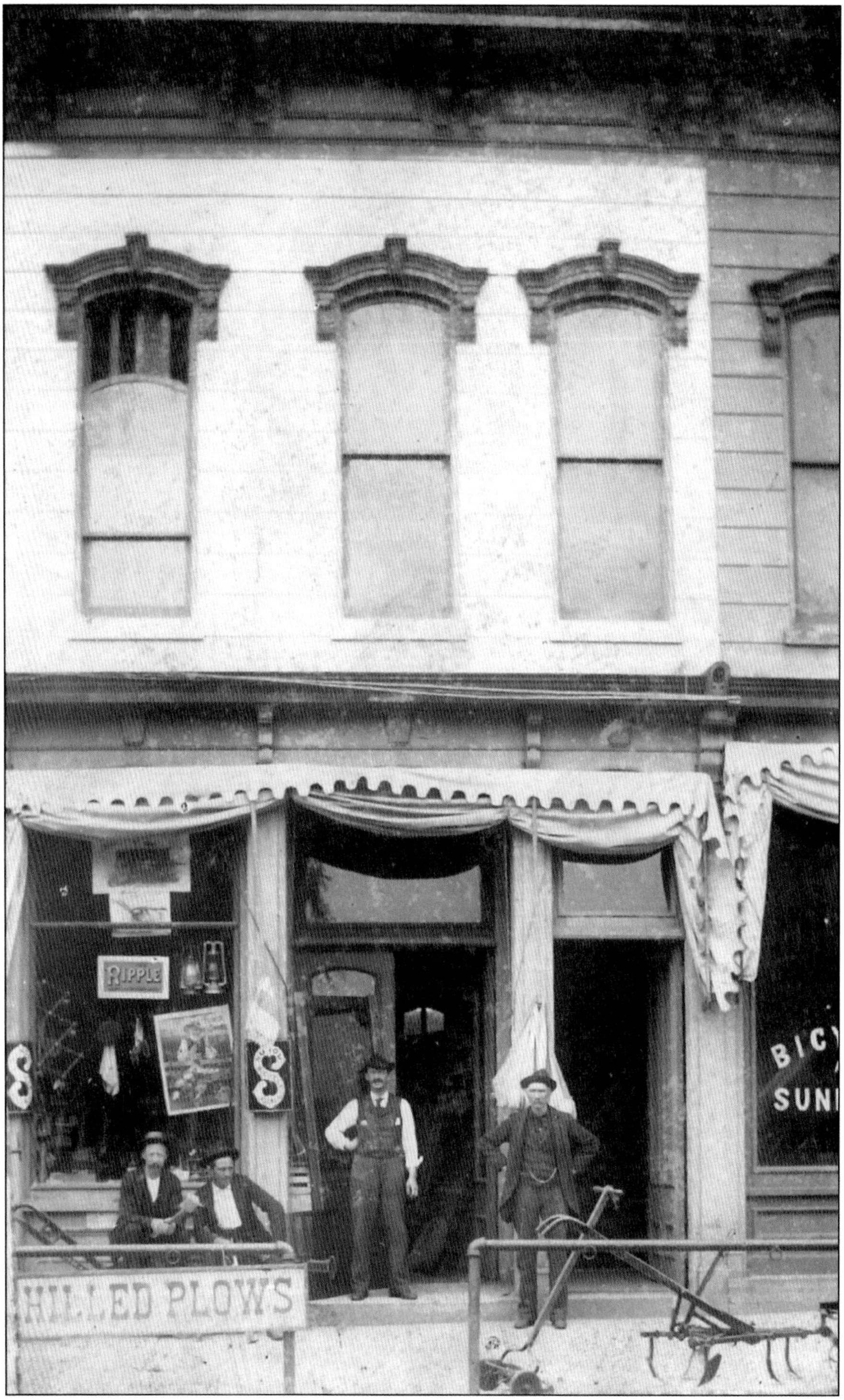

Four gentlemen pose outside the stores on the north side of the square. Located farther east on the north side of the square, the Odd Fellows building was built in 1888 and housed the first chartered bank in Milan.

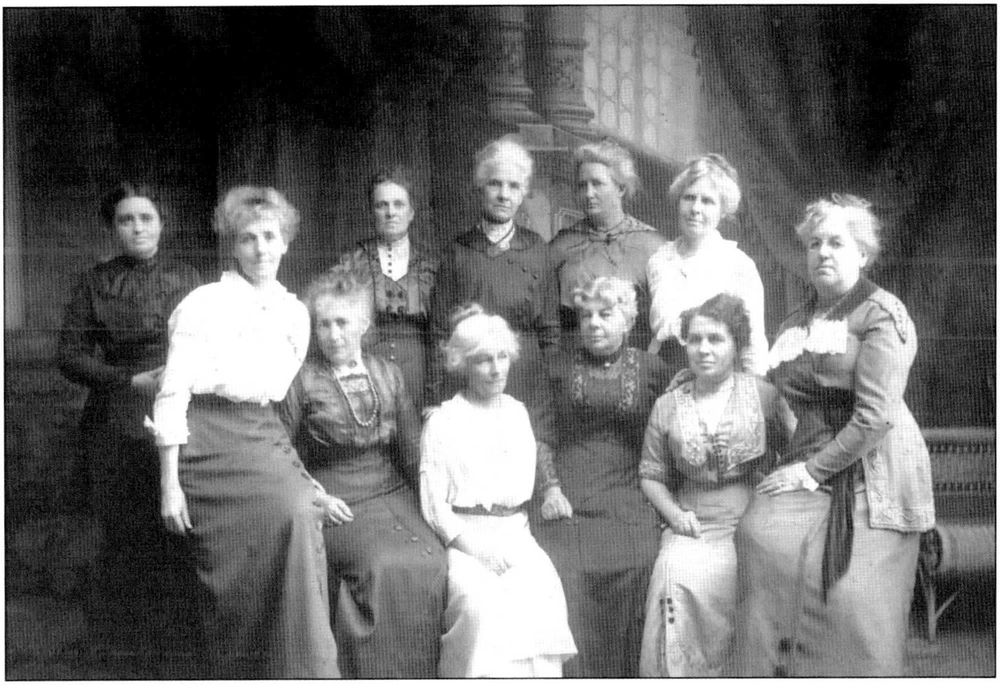

Pictured here are 11 prominent Milan women, including Agnes Root, Ida Mowry, Alice Sisty, and Minnie Mowry. Ida (Wilson) Mowry married A.J. Mowry, and Minnie Mowry was the wife of Frank Mowry.

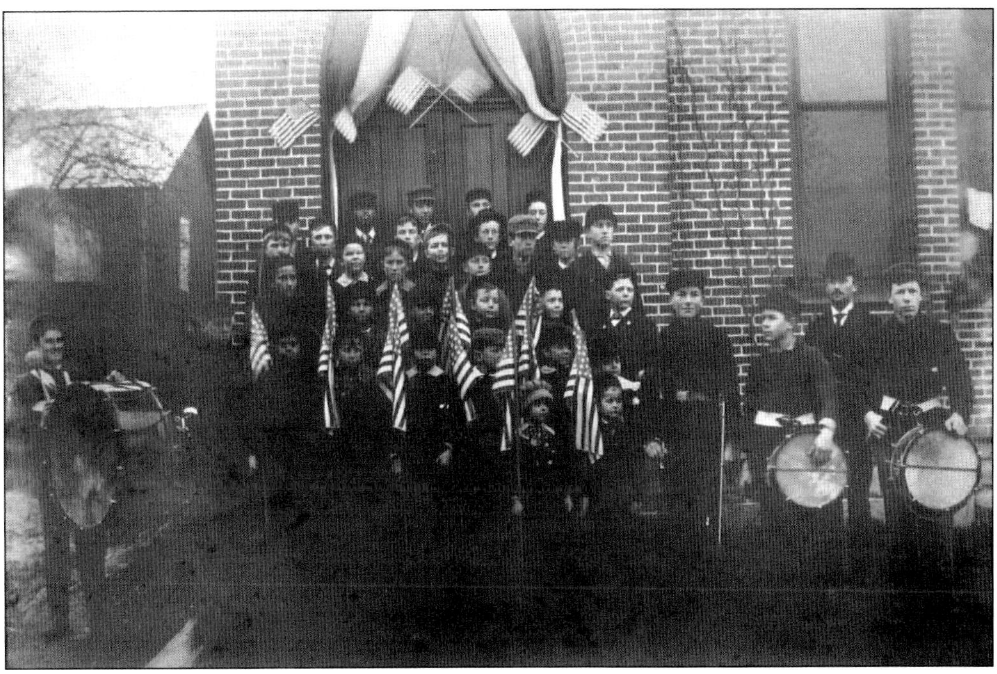

A group known as the Boys Brigade poses on the steps of Lockwood Chapel, holding their flags and drums. James Cannon Lockwood donated the funds to build the Presbyterian chapel, which still bears his name.

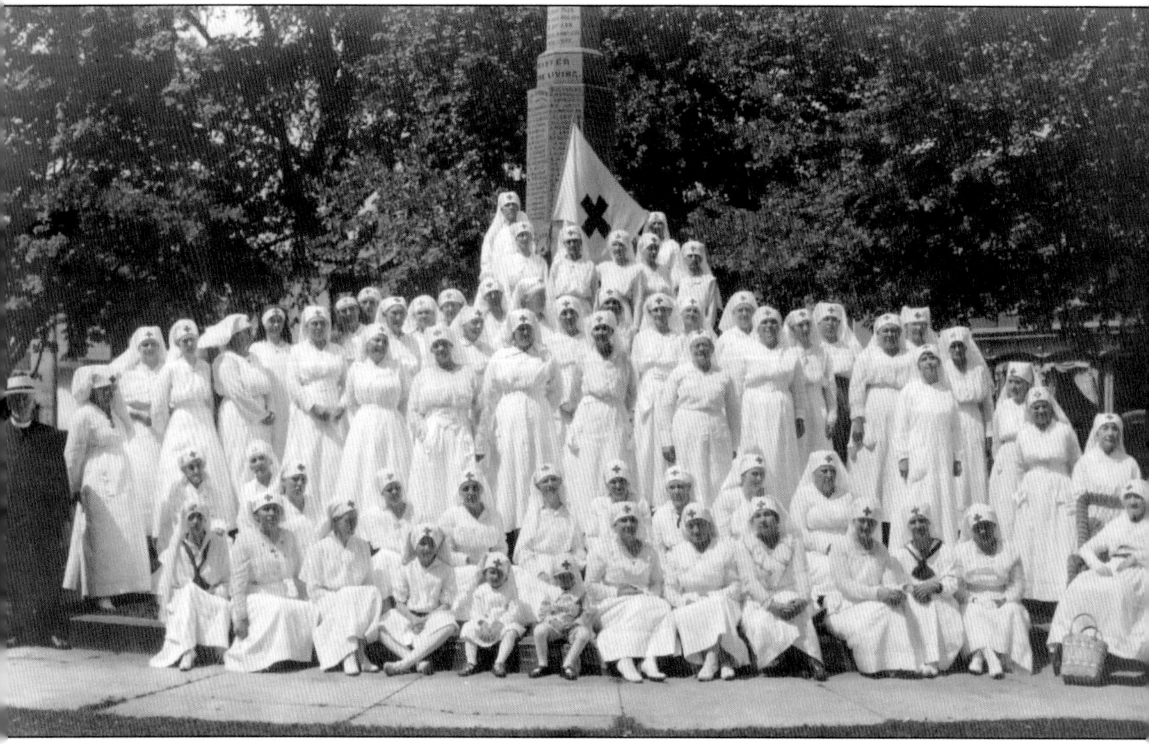

Milan ladies of the Red Cross pose in front of the Civil War monument in 1918.

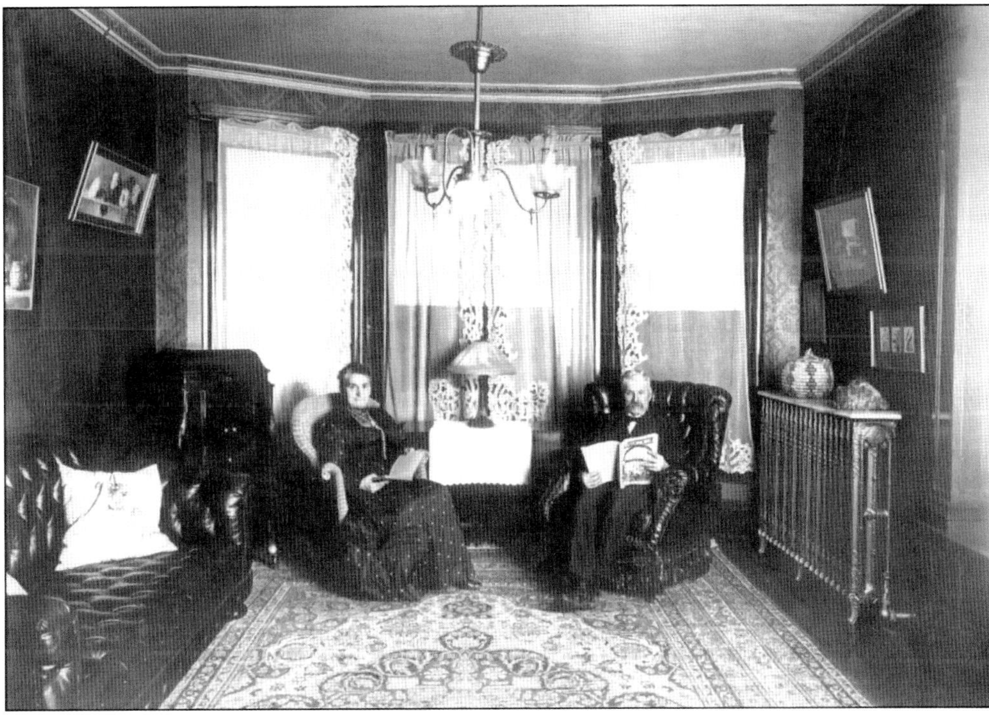

Issac Hoover died on March 4, 1941, having been active in the development of the Milan community for many years. The photograph shows Mr. and Mrs. I.W. Hoover in their home, about 1900.

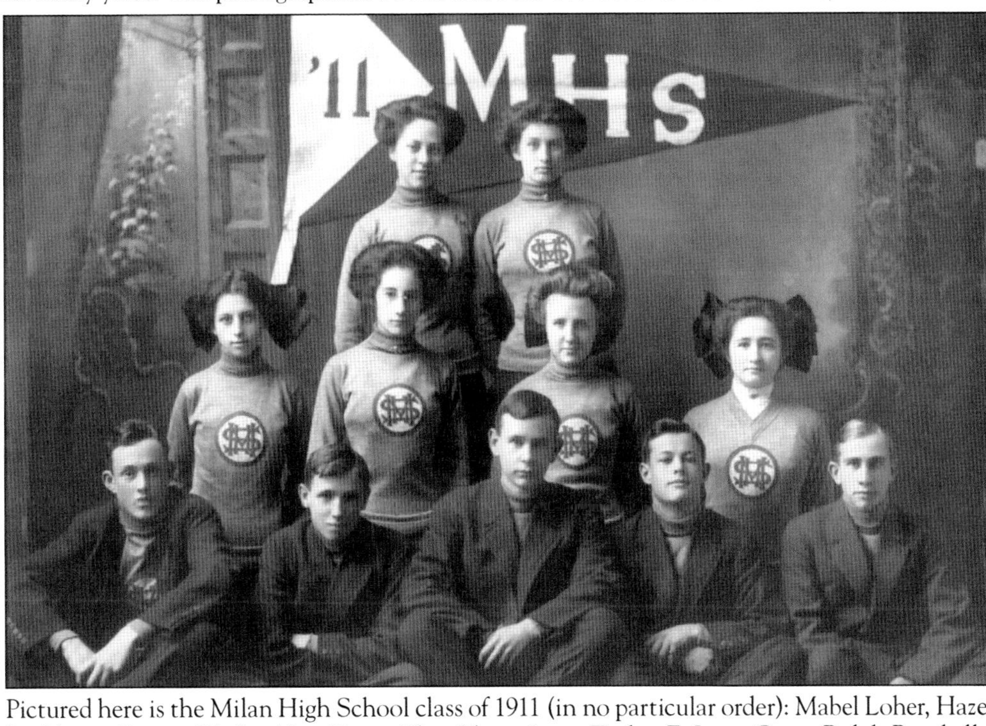

Pictured here is the Milan High School class of 1911 (in no particular order): Mabel Loher, Hazel Rathburn, Rosine Bleile, Alice Kirtz, Olga Olson, Lynn Taylor, E. Leon Gove, Ralph Rosekelly, Fred Mixter, Leland Dimond.

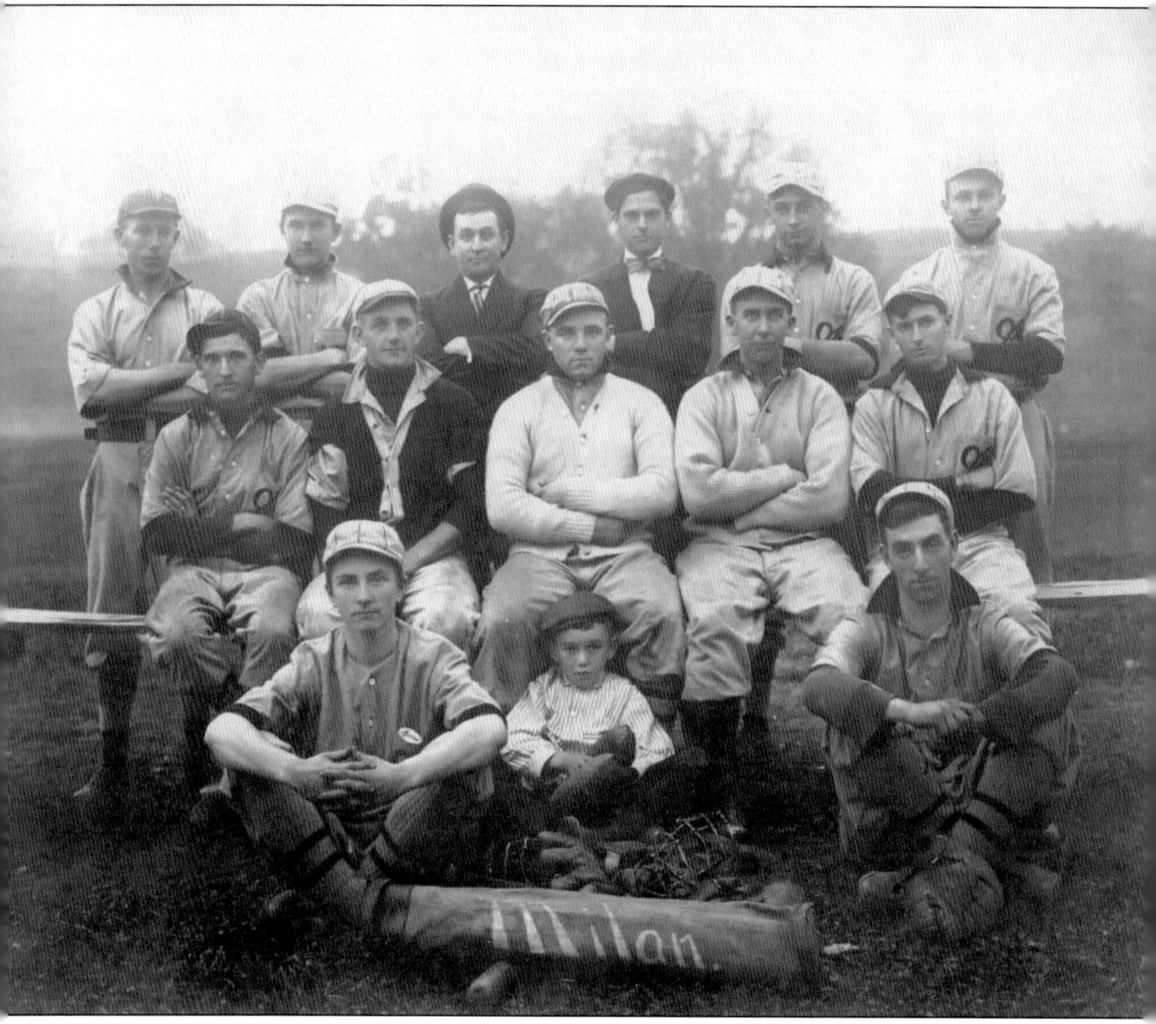

Pictured here from left to right are members of Milan's baseball team: (first row) George Smith, John Riley (mascot), and Van Burrn; (second row) Adam Strunk, "Sticks" Srniff, Oscar Hett, Art Smith, and Bob Sickinger; (third row) ? Broderson, Elmer Smith, Joe Haeuptle, George Britton, Geo Stiert, and Herm Sickinger.

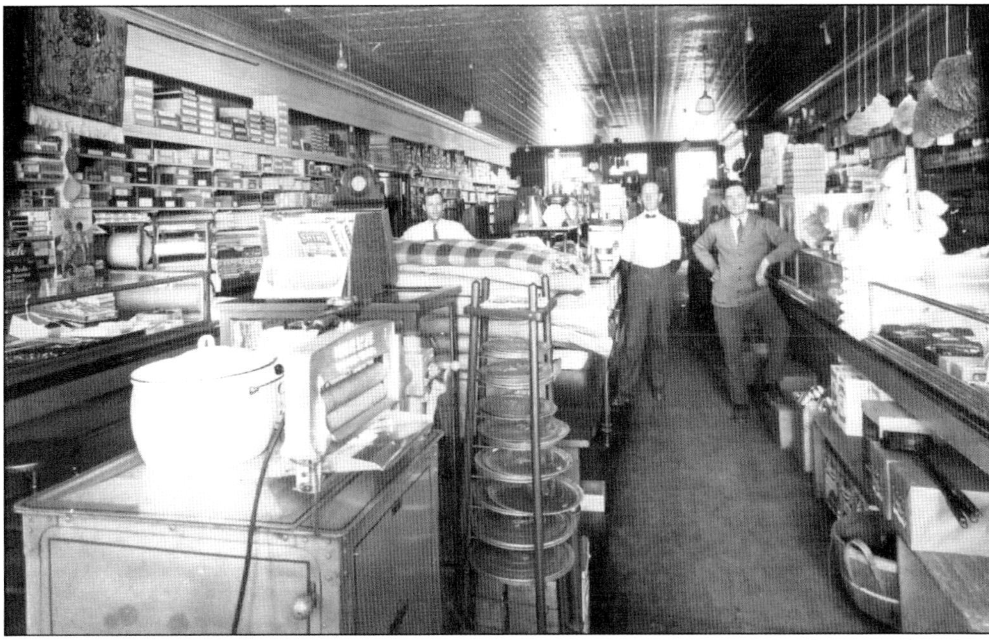

This is an October 27, 1927, interior view of the Lockwood, Smith & Co. general store with Robert Sickinger, Archie Ruggles, and Cliff Sickinger. Clifford Sickinger was born in Milan on March 14, 1895, and graduated from Milan High School and Sandusky Business College. He went into partnership with his brother Robert Sickinger and Archie Ruggles for many years and became the sole owner in 1948.

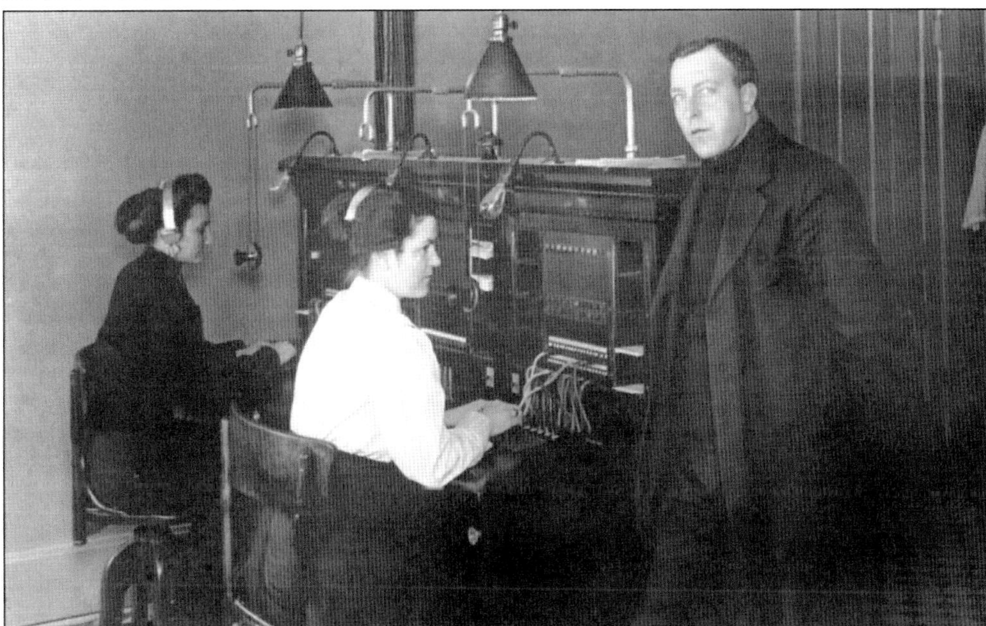

Telephone operators Lena and Mary Emmons are pictured with their manager, Mr. Farley, on February 13, 1911. Lena Mefford Emmons was married to Alden Emmons, an employee at the Hoover-Prout Manufacturing Company. Alden Emmons's father, Ed Emmons, owned the sulky cart shop in Milan with Wayne Stoddard, manufacturing carts from 1888 to 1894.

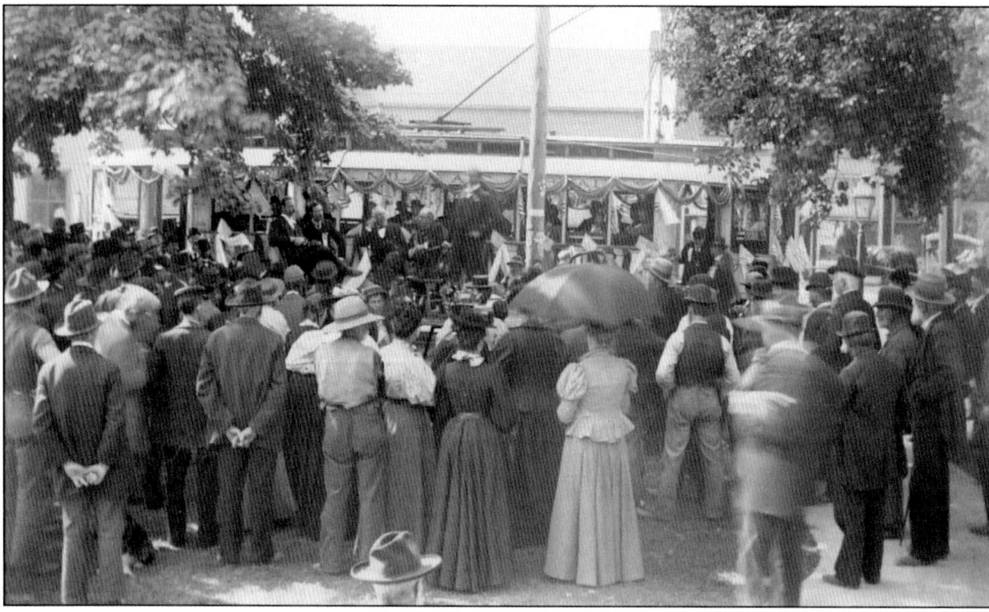

Pictured here is Milan Town Square during the homecoming celebration of 1910. An interurban car can be seen in the background while Mayor Stokes gives a speech. J.W. Stokes moved to Milan in 1860, operating a large business producing the Stokes Automatic Shading Pen and serving several terms as mayor. He died in Spencerport, New York, on July 8, 1909.

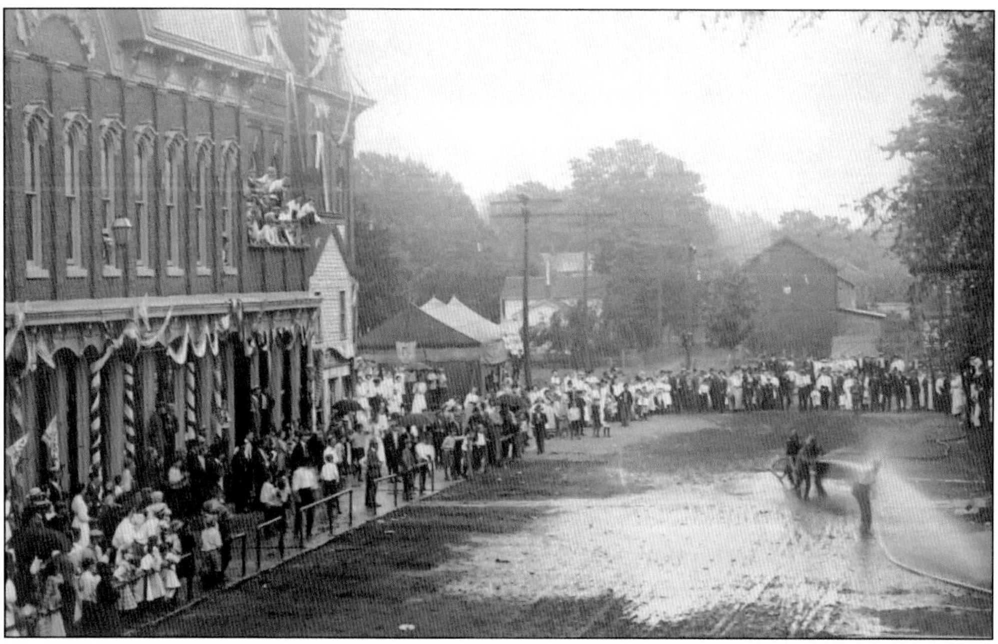

This photograph was taken during the Milan homecoming and normal school reunion in 1910. The water battle on Thursday morning was staged on Park Street in front of the Kelley Block as a part of the official program.

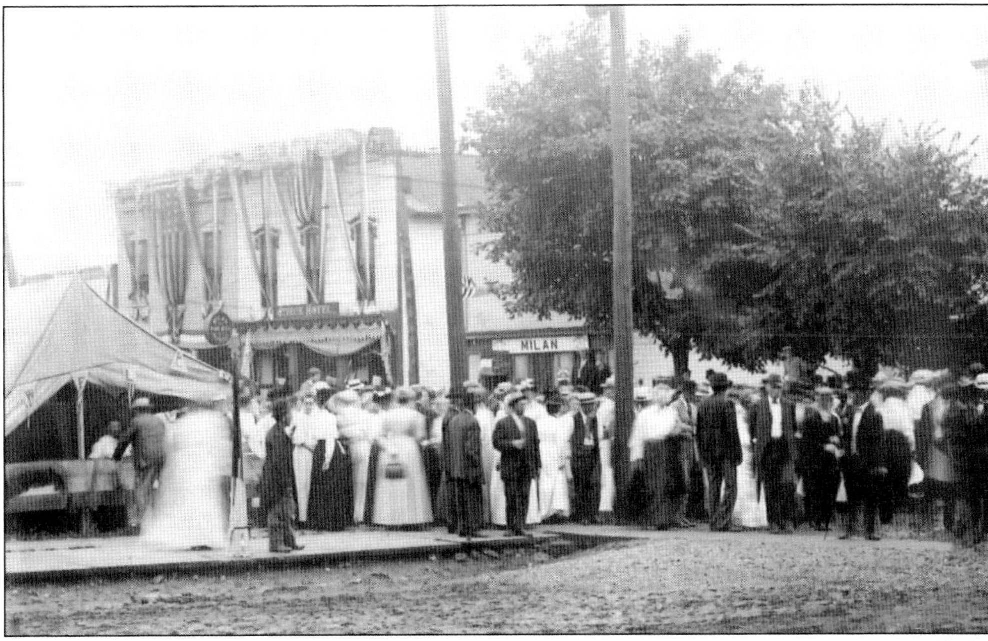

This is a view of the crowds during the Milan homecoming and normal school reunion, with the interurban office and Streck Hotel in the background. Festivities were held August 17 and 18, 1910, to commemorate the razing of the normal school building.

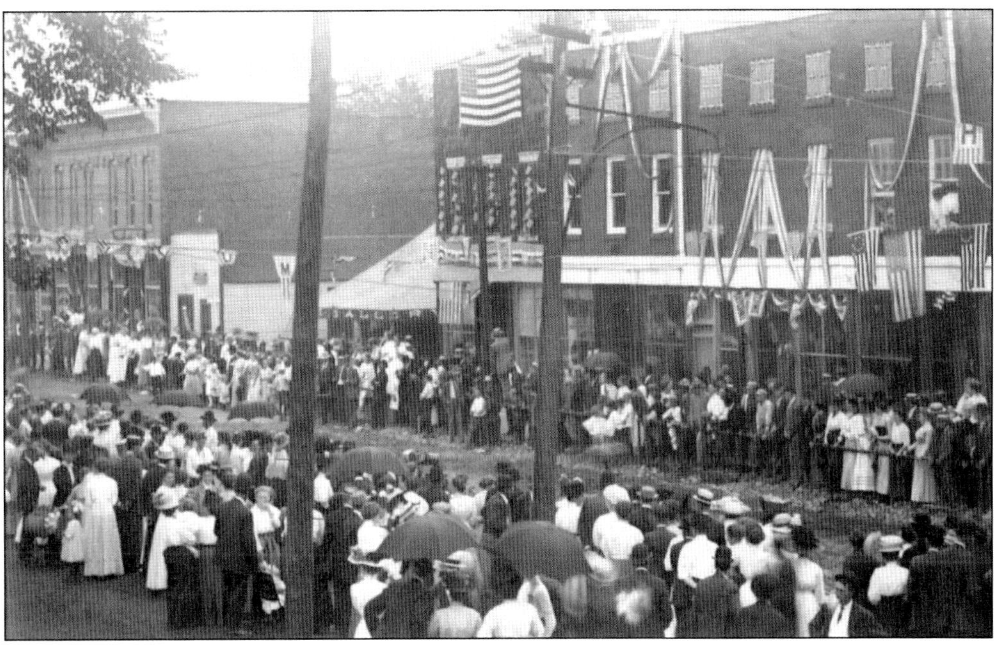

Crowds line the square for the homecoming celebration. Novelist Harold Bell Wright was one of the more famous alumni of Milan's normal school. Wright outsold every other American author at the time and was said to be the first author to sell a million copies of a novel.

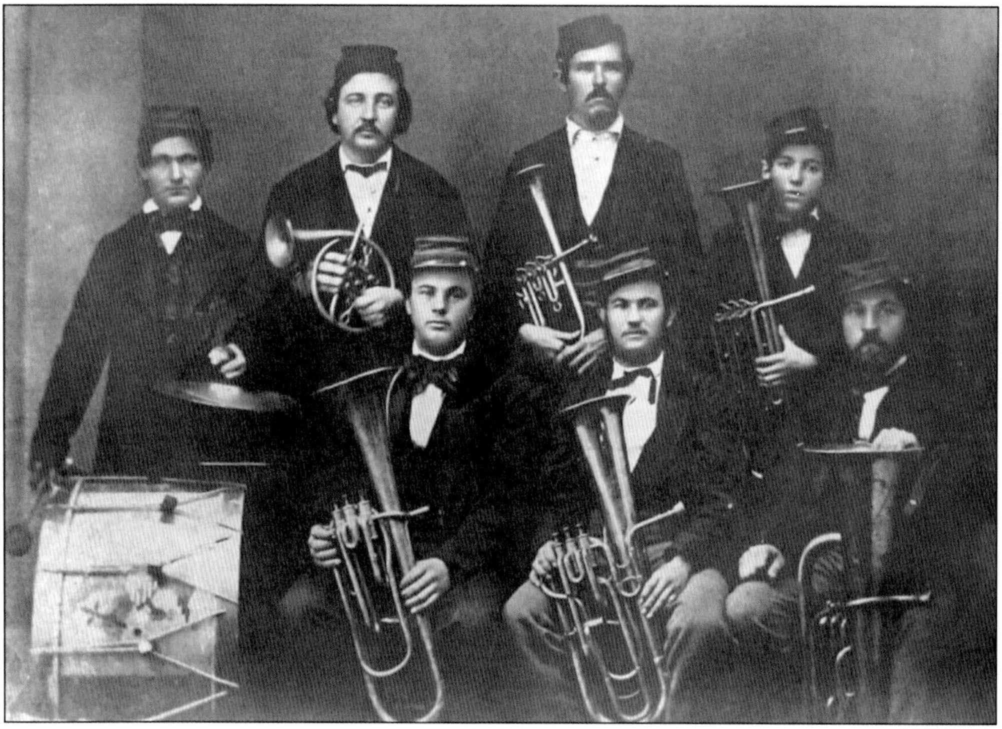

The little German band of Milan included, from left to right, (first row) unidentified, Beckler Collman, and Herman Collman; (second row) Peter Fox, John Beeckley, Anthony Beeckley, and Henry Beeckley. They are pictured around 1866.

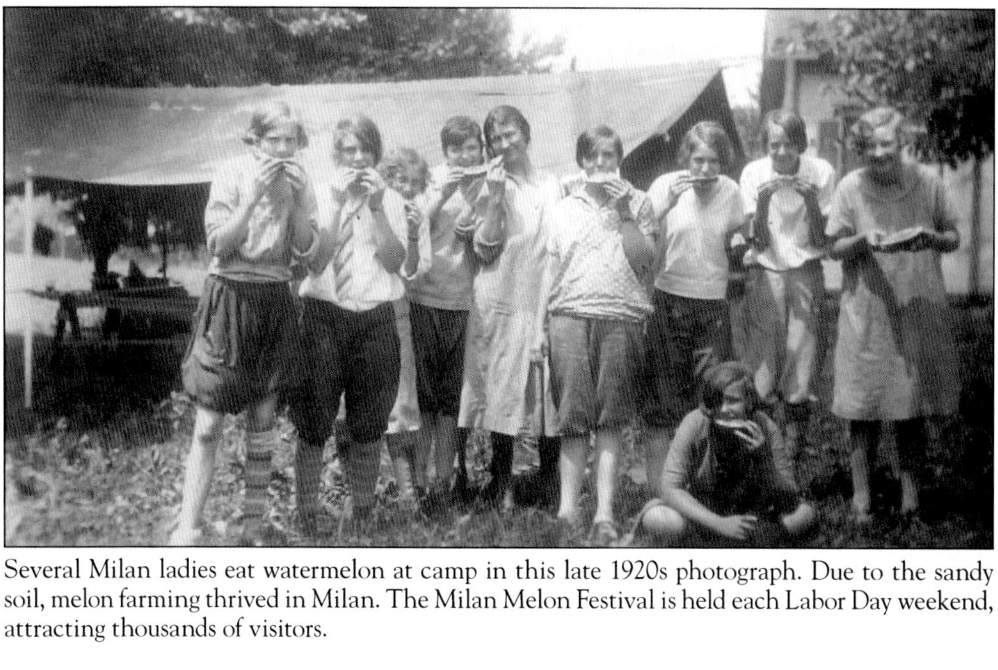

Several Milan ladies eat watermelon at camp in this late 1920s photograph. Due to the sandy soil, melon farming thrived in Milan. The Milan Melon Festival is held each Labor Day weekend, attracting thousands of visitors.

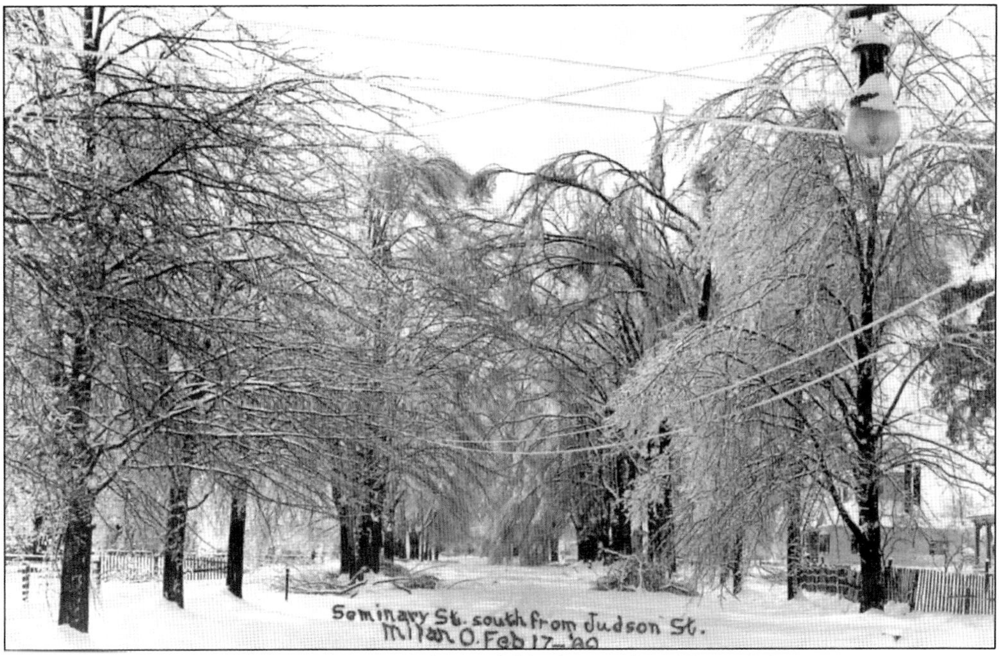

The ice storm of February 17, 1909, gave a beautiful look to Milan. Natural disasters were common subjects to photograph, although the ice caused much damage.

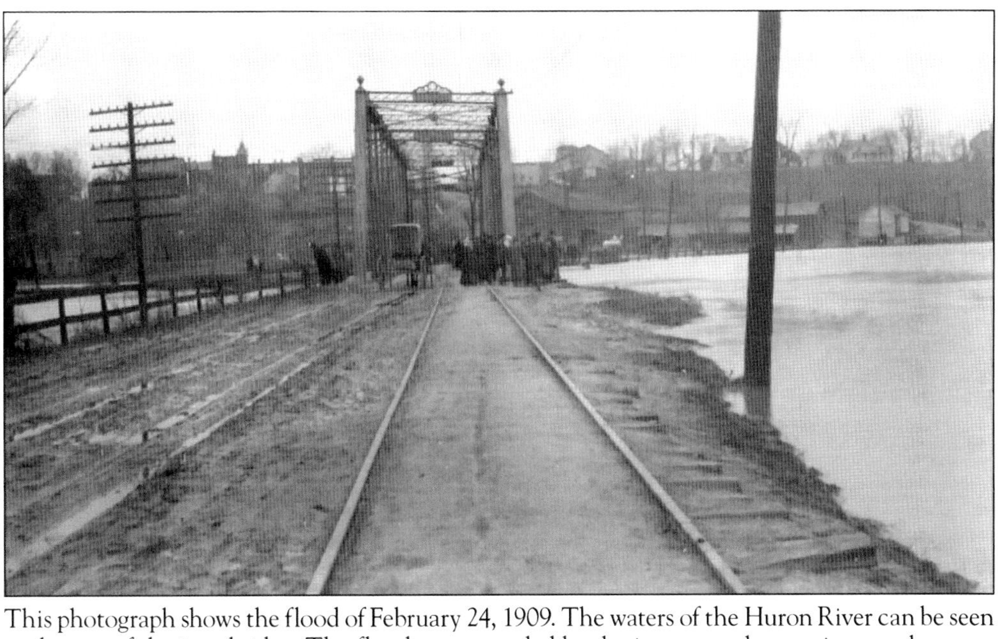
This photograph shows the flood of February 24, 1909. The waters of the Huron River can be seen at the top of the iron bridge. The flood was preceded by the ice storm the previous week.

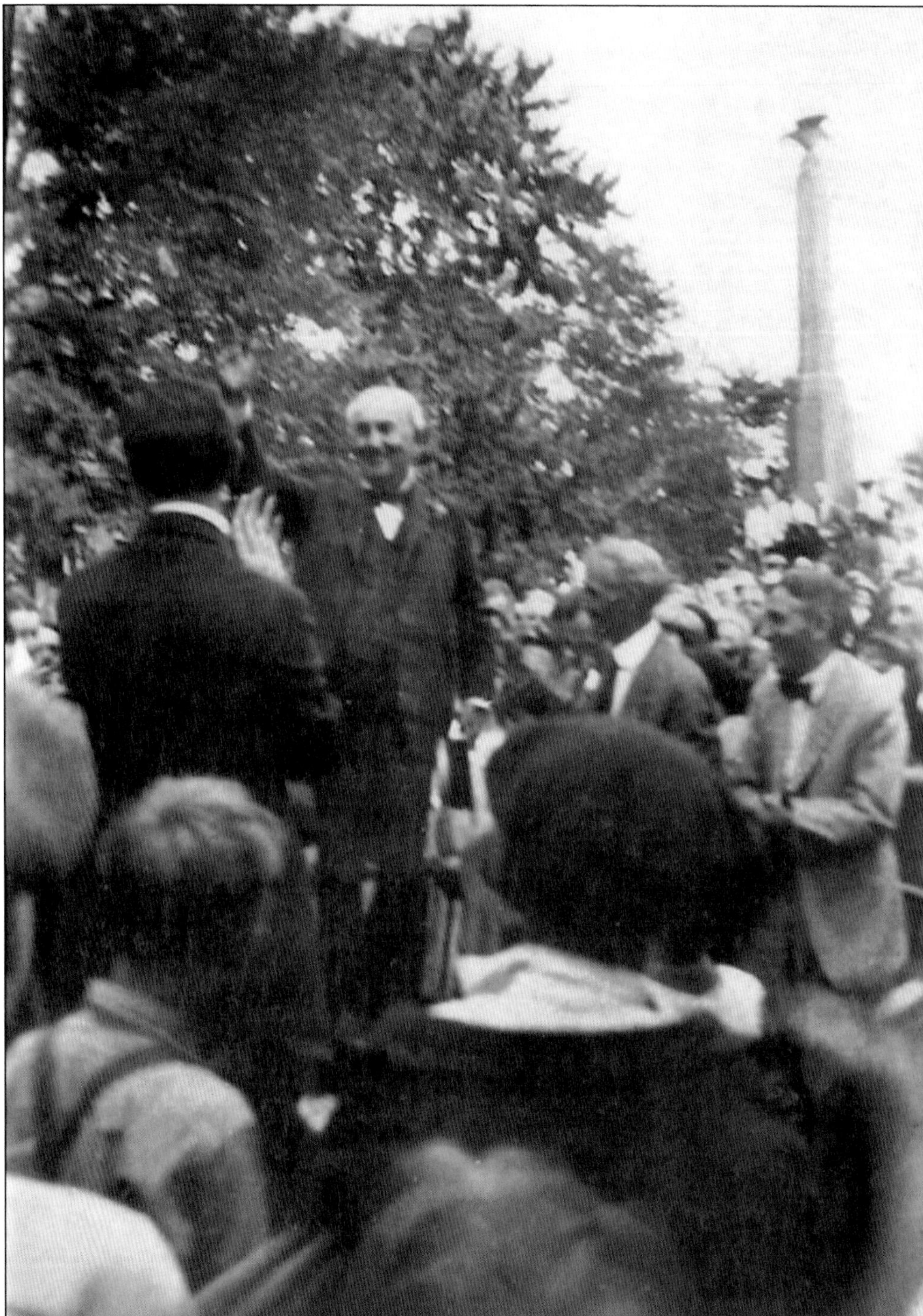

Milan's most famous citizen, Thomas Edison, is pictured on the square during his visit in 1923 with friends Henry Ford and Harvey Firestone. Thomas Alva Edison was born in Milan to Samuel and Nancy (Elliott) Edison. A shingle-maker by trade, Samuel relocated the family to Milan from Canada due to the economic prosperity the Milan Canal offered.

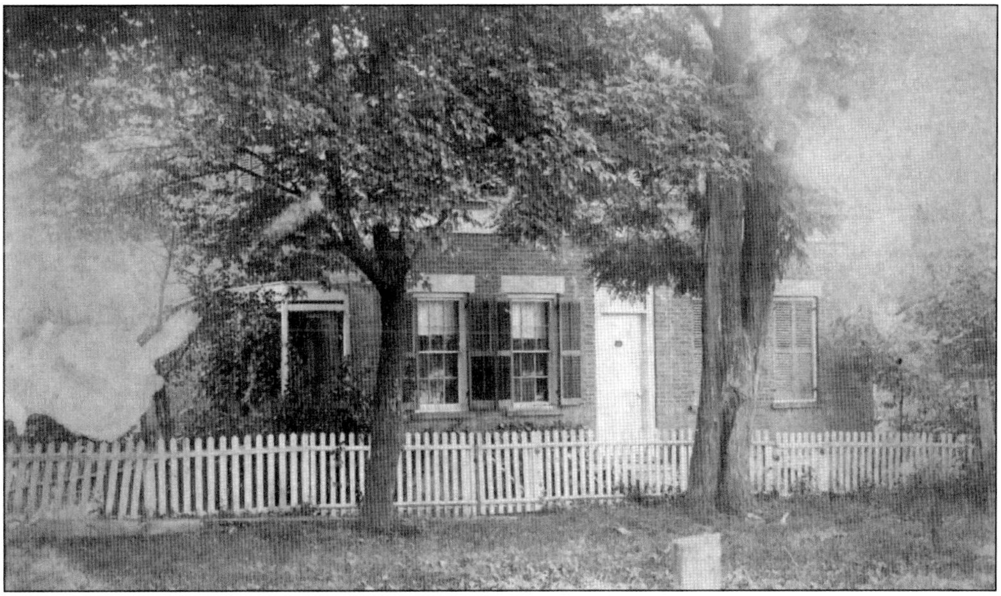

Born on February 11, 1847, Thomas Edison and his family remained in Milan until 1853. Due to the decline of the Milan Canal, the family once again relocated to Port Huron, Michigan. This is one of the earliest photographs of Thomas Edison's birthplace; the home has a picket fence and no front porch.

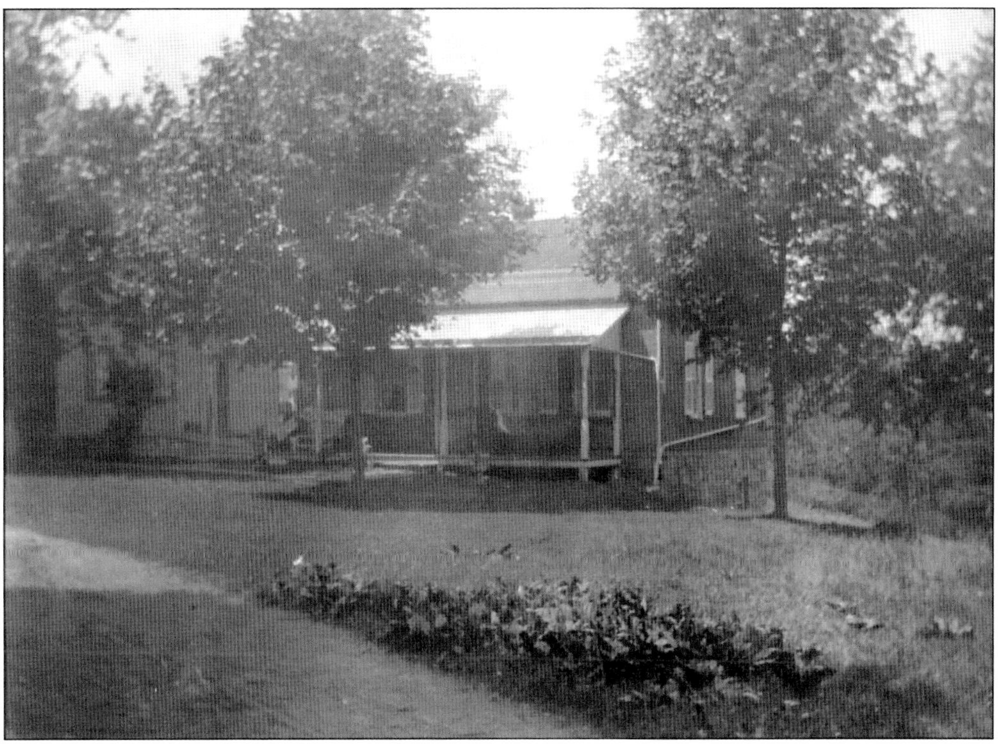

Edison became one of the most prolific inventors and businessmen of all time. His work in electric light, sound recording, and motion pictures forever changed the world. He holds 1,093 patents in his name. This photograph shows the Edison homestead from the east.

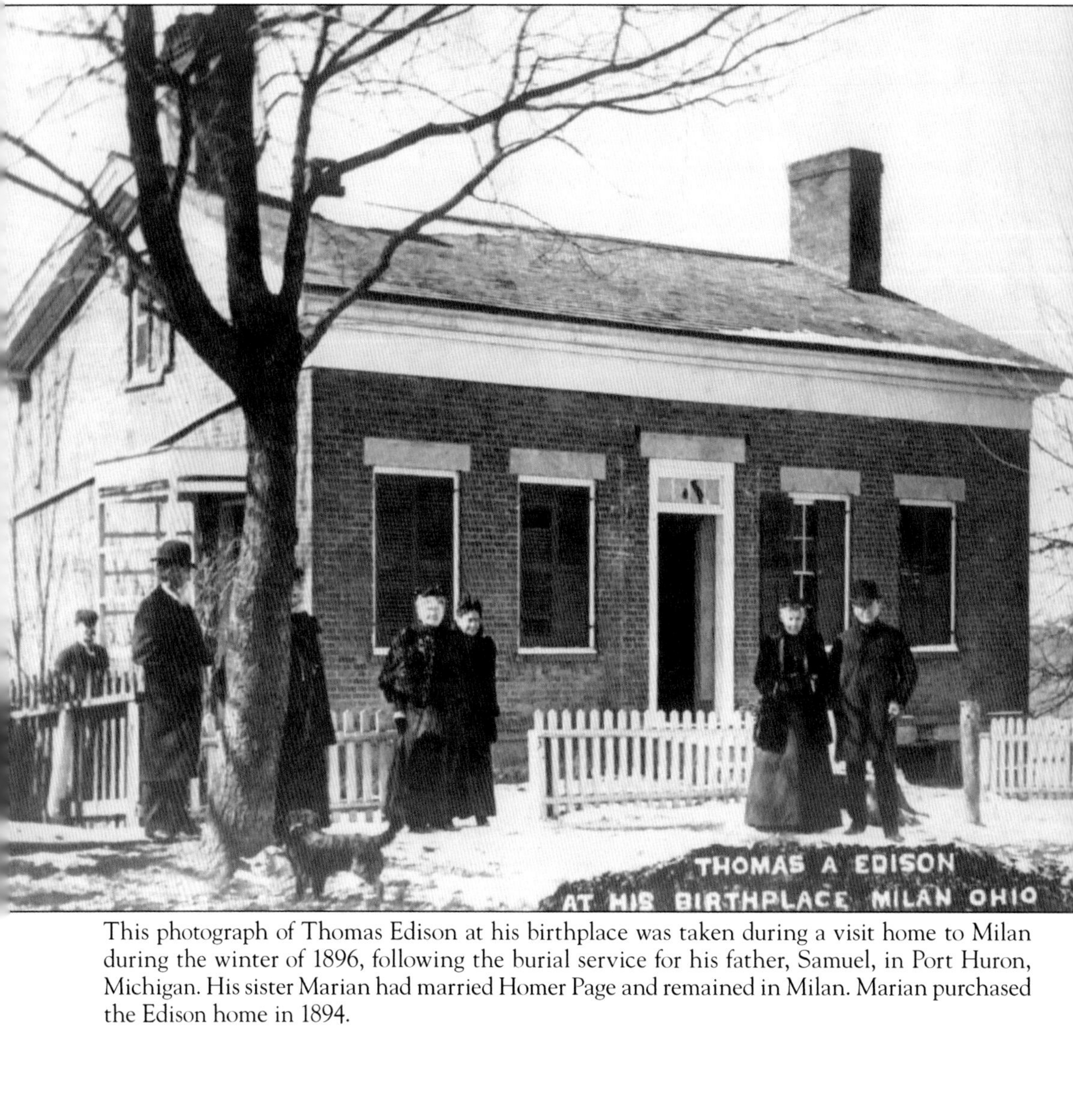

This photograph of Thomas Edison at his birthplace was taken during a visit home to Milan during the winter of 1896, following the burial service for his father, Samuel, in Port Huron, Michigan. His sister Marian had married Homer Page and remained in Milan. Marian purchased the Edison home in 1894.

Thomas Edison is pictured here during a trip to Milan with his cousin Meta Wadsworth. Edison was married on December 25, 1871, to Mary Stilwell. Together they had three children: Marion, Thomas Alva Jr., and William Leslie. Upon Mary's passing, Edison later married Mina Miller on February 24, 1886, in Akron, Ohio. They had three children: Madeleine, Charles, and Theodore.

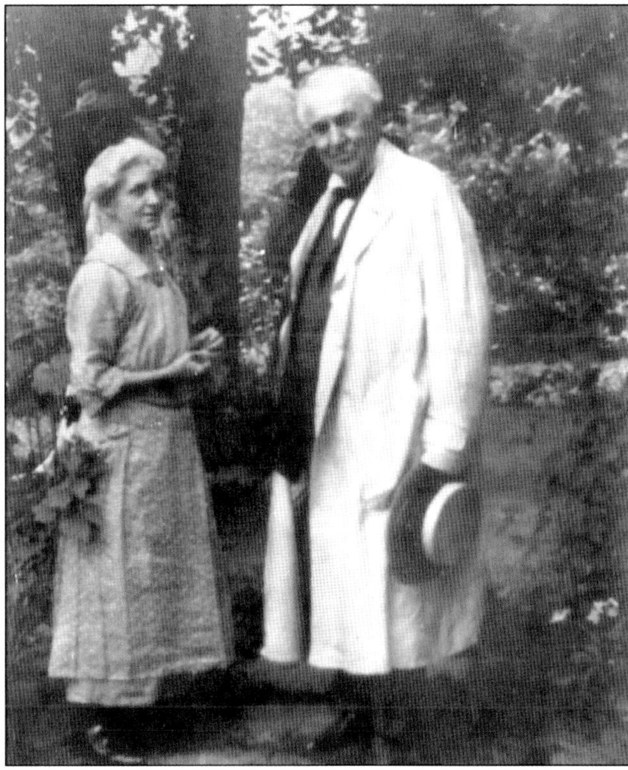

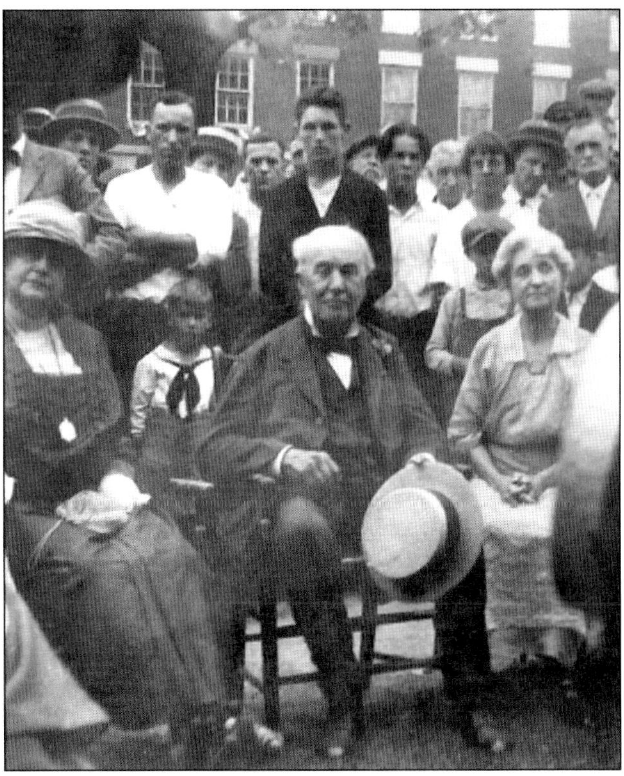

Edison poses with his cousin Meta (right) and wife, Mina Edison, on the square in 1923. During the visit, over 2,000 Milan residents came to the square to welcome Thomas Edison, Harvey Firestone, and Henry Ford. Edison had purchased his birthplace in 1906, and during his visit he found the home to be lacking electric power.

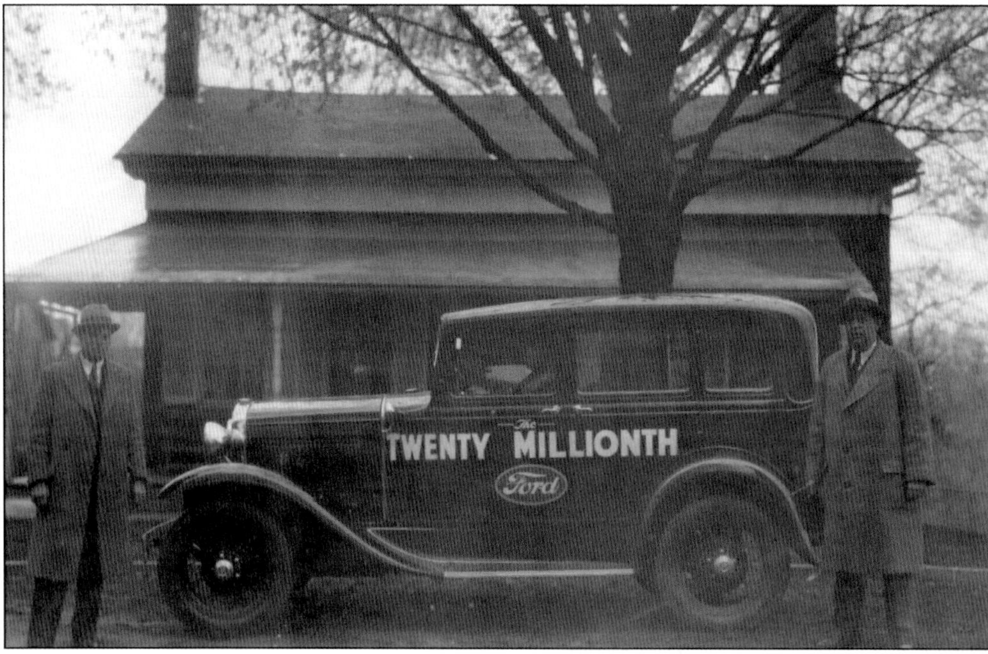

The 20 millionth Ford motorcar is parked in front of the Edison birthplace around 1930. Following the death of Thomas Edison on October 18, 1931, his wife, Mina, and daughter Madeleine began the process of creating a museum at his birthplace in Milan.

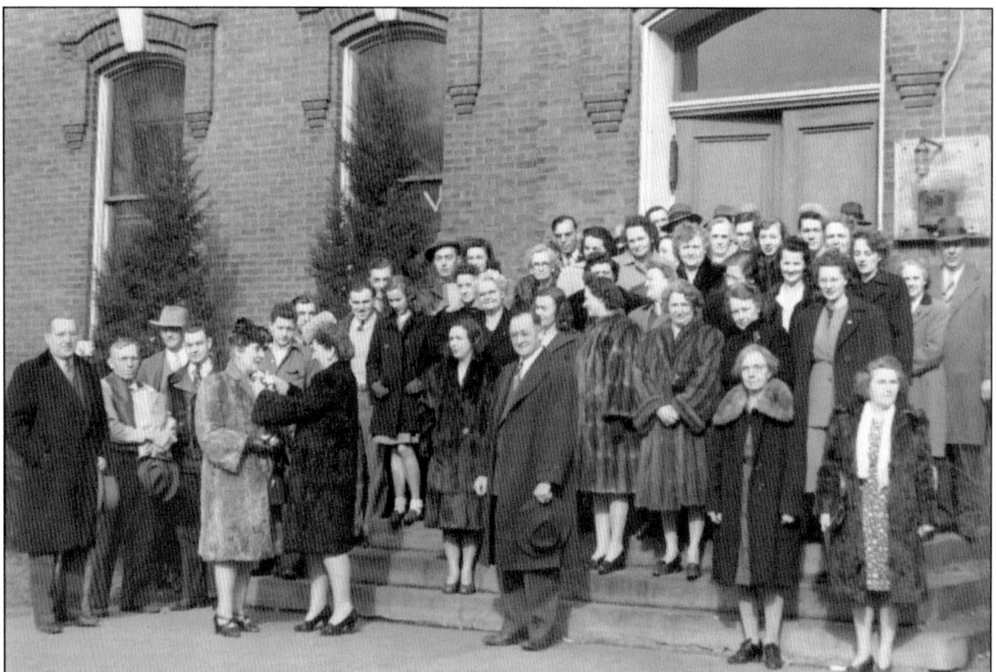

The Edison Centennial Committee gathered on the steps of the Milan Township Hall on February 11, 1947, to celebrate the centennial of Edison's birth. Mrs. Lavey is shown pinning a corsage on Thomas Edison's daughter Madeleine Sloane.

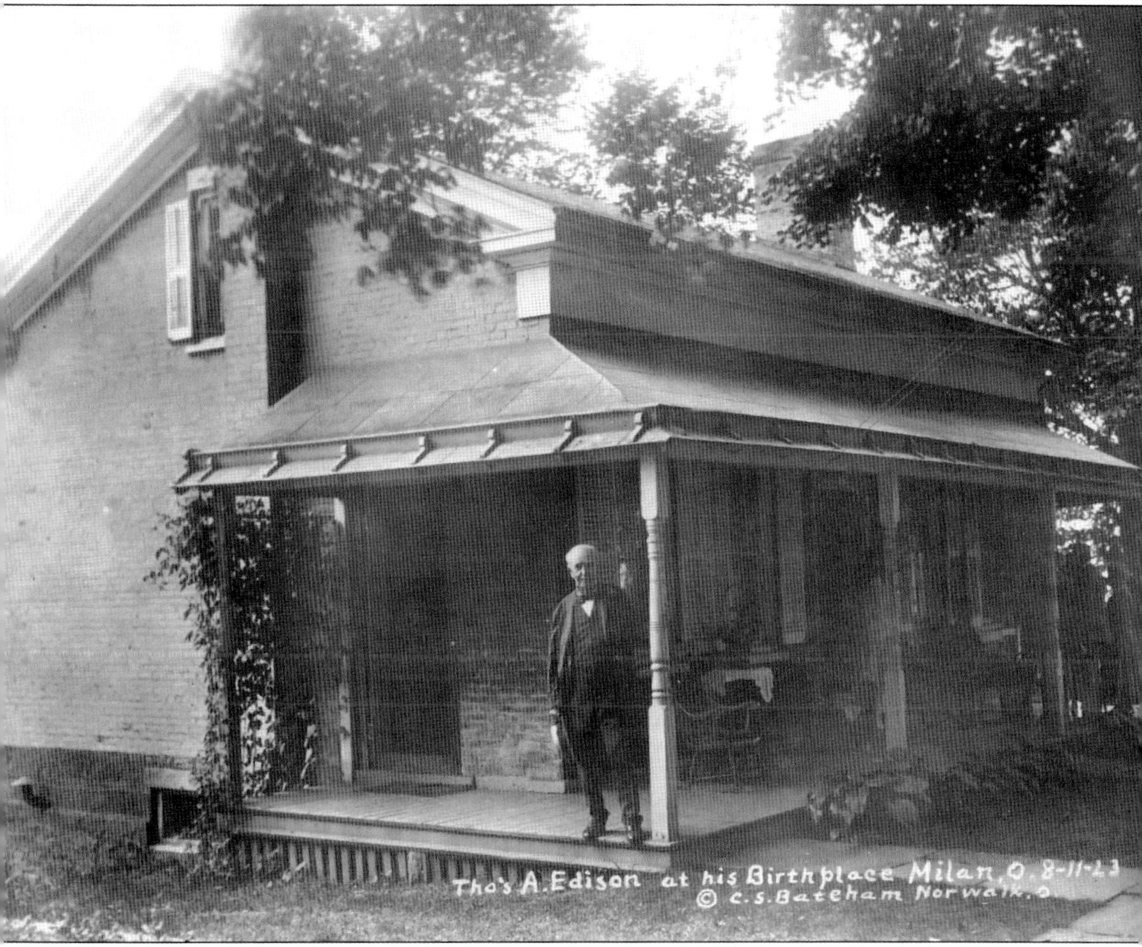

Thomas Edison is seen here standing on the front porch of his birthplace on August 11, 1923. The Thomas Edison Birthplace Museum opened on the centennial of his birth, February 11, 1947.